THE SPIRITUAL
LIVES OF
BEREAVED
PARENTS

THE SERIES IN DEATH, DYING, AND BEREAVEMENT
ROBERT A. NEIMEYER, CONSULTING EDITOR

Davies—*Shadows in the Sun: The Experiences of Sibling Bereavement in Childhood*
Harvey—*Perspectives on Loss: A Sourcebook*
Klass—*The Spiritual Lives of Bereaved Parents*
Leenaars—*Lives and Deaths: Selections from the Works of Edwin S. Shneidman*
Nord—*Multiple AIDS-Related Loss: A Handbook for Understanding and Surviving a Perpetual Fall*
Werth—*Contemporary Perspectives on Rational Suicide*

FORMERLY

THE SERIES IN DEATH EDUCATION, AGING, AND HEALTH CARE
HANNELORE WASS, CONSULTING EDITOR

Bard—*Medical Ethics in Practice*
Benoliel—*Death Education for the Health Professional*
Bertman—*Facing Death: Images, Insights, and Interventions*
Brammer—*How to Cope with Life Transitions: The Challenge of Personal Change*
Cleiren—*Bereavement and Adaptation: A Comparative Study of the Aftermath of Death*
Corless, Pittman-Lindeman—*AIDS: Principles, Practices, and Politics, Abridged Edition*
Corless, Pittman-Lindeman—*AIDS: Principles, Practices, and Politics, Reference Edition*
Curran—*Adolescent Suicidal Behavior*
Davidson—*The Hospice: Development and Administration, Second Edition*
Davidson, Linnolla—*Risk Factors in Youth Suicide*
Degner, Beaton—*Life-Death Decisions in Health Care*
Doka—*AIDS, Fear, and Society: Challenging the Dreaded Disease*
Doty—*Communication and Assertion Skills for Older Persons*
Epting, Neimeyer—*Personal Meanings of Death: Applications of Personal Construct Theory to Clinical Practice*
Haber—*Health Care for an Aging Society: Cost-Conscious Community Care and Self-Care Approaches*
Hughes—*Bereavement and Support: Healing in a Group Environment*
Irish, Lundquist, Nelsen—*Ethnic Variations in Dying, Death, and Grief: Diversity in Universality*
Klass, Silverman, Nickman—*Continuing Bonds: New Understanding of Grief*
Lair—*Counseling the Terminally Ill: Sharing the Journey*
Leenaars, Maltsberger, Neimeyer—*Treatment of Suicidal People*
Leenaars, Wenckstern—*Suicide Prevention in Schools*
Leng—*Psychological Care in Old Age*
Leviton—*Horrendous Death, Health, and Well-Being*
Leviton—*Horrendous Death and Health: Toward Action*
Lindeman, Corby, Downing, Sanborn—*Alzheimer's Day Care: A Basic Guide*
Lund—*Older Bereaved Spouses: Research with Practical Applications*
Neimeyer—*Death Anxiety Handbook: Research, Instrumentation, and Application*
Nord—*Multiple AIDS-Related Loss: A Handbook for Understanding and Surviving a Perpetual Fall*
Papadatou, Papadatos—*Children and Death*
Prunkl, Berry—*Death Week: Exploring the Dying Process*
Ricker, Myers—*Retirement Counseling: A Practical Guide for Action*
Samarel—*Caring for Life and Death*
Sherron, Lumsden—*Introduction to Educational Gerontology. Third Edition*
Stillion—*Death and Sexes: An Examination of Differential Longevity, Attitudes, Behaviors, and Coping Skills*
Stillion, McDowell, May—*Suicide Across the Life Span—Premature Exits*
Vachon—*Occupational Stress in the Care of the Critically Ill, the Dying, and the Bereaved*
Wass, Corr—*Childhood and Death*
Wass, Corr—*Helping Children Cope with Death: Guidelines and Resource. Second Edition*
Wass, Corr, Pacholski, Forfar—*Death Education II: An Annotated Resource Guide*
Wass, Neimeyer—*Dying: Facing the Facts. Third Edition*
Weenolsen—*Transcendence of Loss over the Life Span*
Werth—*Rational Suicide? Implications for Mental Health Professionals*

THE SPIRITUAL LIVES OF BEREAVED PARENTS

Dennis Klass

USA	Publishing Office:	BRUNNER/MAZEL *A member of the Taylor & Francis Group* 325 Chestnut Street Philadelphia, PA 19106 Tel: (215) 625-8900 Fax: (215) 625-2940
	Distribution Center:	BRUNNER/MAZEL *A member of the Taylor & Francis Group* 47 Runway Road, Suite G Levittown, PA 19057-4700 Tel: (215) 269-0400 Fax: (215) 269-0363
UK		BRUNNER/MAZEL 1 Gunpowder Square London EC4A 3DE Tel: 171 583 0490 Fax: 171 583 0581

THE SPIRITUAL LIVES OF BEREAVED PARENTS

1 2 3 4 5 6 7 8 9 0

Printed by Edwards Brothers, Ann Arbor, MI, 1999.
Cover design by Nancy Abbott. Images copyright 1999, PhotoDisc, Inc.

A CIP catalog record for this book is available from the British Library.
∞ The paper in this publication meets the requirements of the ANSI Standard Z39.48-1984 (Permanence of Paper)

Library of Congress Cataloging-in-Publication Data

Klass, Dennis.
    The spiritual lives of bereaved parents / Dennis Klass.
      p. cm.—(Series in death, dying, and bereavement)
    Includes bibliographical references and index.

    1. Parents—Religious life. 2. Bereavement—Religious aspects.
3. Children—Death—Religious aspects. 4. Parents—Counseling of.
I. Title. II. Series
BL625.9.B48K53 1999
291.4'42—dc21
                                                         99-13925
                                                           CIP

ISBN 0-87630-990-2 (case)
ISBN 0-87630-991-0 (paper)
ISSN 1091-5427

CONTENTS

FOREWORD

The mission statement of the series on Death, Dying, and Bereavement, if it were written, might be "to provide authoritative coverage of cutting-edge developments in thanatological theory, research, and practice, with the goal of fostering more informed and compassionate engagement with death, grief, and mortality." The topical range of the series—including serious examination of AIDS, aging, suicide, hospice care, and bereavement—testifies to the many faces of loss in human life and the necessity of understanding both its unique and universal dimensions. Accordingly, different volumes address the specific issues and concerns of particular groups, in different cultural contexts, and at different points in the life span. As a result of this multifaceted and in-depth coverage, the series explores the meanings of death in all its gritty reality, as well as in its transpersonal and transcendent aspects.

Remarkably, Dennis Klass manages to accomplish many of these same ends in the present, compact volume. In a style that is both literate and personal, he sensitively renders the anguish of bereaved parents in their quest to re-establish a world that again makes sense in the wake of unimaginable loss. One measure of his success in doing so is the extent to which readers are drawn into the prose, opening themselves to an encounter with one of the most devastating of life's experiences—the death of one's child. The invitational mood that permits readers to enter—if only vicariously and temporarily—the world of these parents is partly a function of Klass's delicate tacking back and forth between moving parental accounts of their experience and impeccable scholarship. It would be tempting, in the presence of such pain, to seek facile solace in abstract religious or philosophical systems that impose a pre-established order on a disorderly experience. Yet, as both a counselor and a student of comparative religions, Klass consistently avoids this pitfall, and instead takes as his primary task the articulation of the terror and transitions of parental bereavement in terms that are offered by the survivors themselves. Klass's concept of spirituality grows from his broad study of many religious traditions and from his insistence that spirituality can be observed in the lives of ordinary people. In this book, he shows that the task of helping bereaved parents in the spiritual journey that is the resolution of their grief deserves the best personal awareness, intellectual rigor, and clinical skill that we can offer.

The resulting volume is a rich and vivid travelogue of Klass's twenty-year experience as a respectful and interested "fellow traveler," accompanying these mothers and fathers in their forced exploration of a strange and largely uncharted territory.

Because of its sensitivity, subtlety, and sophistication, *The Spiritual Lives of Bereaved Parents* is likely to speak to a variety of readers, including grief professionals, students in death studies, and parents themselves. I hope that each of these readers will approach the book with an open mind and an open heart, and will find in it something elemental and important about the human encounter with loss.

Robert A. Neimeyer, Ph.D.
Series Editor

PREFACE

It always comes up when you are a professor writing a book. "What is your book about?" I'm not very good at small talk and chitchat anyway, so I never now how to field the question when it comes at a dinner party or in the lobby during intermission. "It's about the spiritual lives of parents whose children have died."

Sometimes my answer is deflected. "You are writing a book to help them. How nice. I'm sure they need lots of help." Talking about the weather always seems like a good idea right then.

For most people I meet, the death of their child is both their worst fear and, they hope, a remote personal possibility. "That's the worst thing that could happen to anybody," they say. "I don't think I could handle that. The people you work with must be very strong."

"Well, no. They didn't think they could handle it either, but they didn't have any choice in the matter," I say. "I've been working closely with bereaved parents for twenty years, and I am still amazed that they do it, and lots of them do it really well."

By then people have usually changed the topic, or waved to a friend across the room with whom they really need to talk. But sometimes a person comes a little closer, "You know, I have a friend . . ." or "My brother's child was . . ." or "We lost our oldest ten years ago . . ." or, "That must be a hard road to travel. . . ."

When the editor asked me who the audience for this book would be, I said, "The intelligent reader who is interested in both psychological and religious dynamics of bereavement." It seemed to me that the real answer probably wouldn't pass muster with the marketing department. Here's the real answer: "It's for the people who come closer when I tell them what I'm writing about."

Nobody plans as their career goal to be writing about parents whose children die. When I was a graduate student in the psychology of religion at the University of Chicago, I decided that the meaning of religion in a person's life is more interesting than organized religion. Much that goes on in churches, synagogues, mosques, and temples is about cultural values and maintaining social cohesion. If I were to study the members of Saint Somebody's Episcopal Church, it seemed to me that I would not often see people's lives "where the rubber meets the road."

Then, almost out of the blue, I got an invitation to assist a self-help group for bereaved parents. I had what I wanted as a person, a place I could help. And I had what I wanted as a scholar, a population of people with a guaranteed spiritual crisis. Although they do so unwillingly when a child dies, parents begin a spiritual journey. What they find along the way seems worth sharing with others.

Let me tell you about the book, and then you can decide if you want to spend the next few hours with me. I will try to make the book interesting. I will try to be as clear as I can about some complex psychological and spiritual issues. While I cannot protect you from the pain these parent feel, I will try to balance the pain by showing you that many parents learn to channel their love for the child who died into something very special. In the end, I think that I will show you some ordinary people creating extraordinary spiritual paths. The book is about pain, but it is also about the human transformations inside the pain. By learning about their lives we learn not only about parental bereavement, but also about some modern spiritual possibilities in the face of undeniable and irrevocable loss.

The Plan of the Book

The first chapter is a general orientation to the task of learning about the spirituality of bereaved parents. It tells how I came to study bereaved parents, gives an overview of the concept of spirituality in bereaved parents as I have come to know it, and shares some ways of thinking that have helped me keep listening to bereaved parents and not be overwhelmed or shut down. As part of this orientation, I look at how we can understand a reality that is so unimaginable to us. How can we get inside their lives enough to understand? For researchers and clinicians who are interested in a more technical explanation of how I have tried to understand, there is a concluding chapter on methodology.

The second chapter develops an extended definition of spiritual life. The most significant spiritual development of humankind right now is that all the world's religious traditions are talking to each other and are available as resources in our individual search for meaning. The definition of spirituality, then, must be adequate to encompass the many religious and spiritual traditions of humankind as well as the complexity and depth of the real lived experience of bereaved parents. Within this definition of spirituality, I show that parenting has spiritual qualities that are carried over into parental bereavement. I will explore the spirituality of parenting as it helps us to understand the journey of bereaved parents. Among bereaved parents, the continuing bond they maintain with their deceased child is an important added element to their spiritual lives. The spiritual dynamics of parental bereavement are not unique. If we can understand bereaved parents, we can better understand some other spiritual dynamics. If we understand other spiritual dynamics, we can better understand parental bereavement.

I identify three characteristics of spiritual life that we can explore as a way of describing the resolution these parents find in their grief: first, affiliating with a community that both shares their pain and facilitates the transformations within their bond with their child; second, the sense of connection with transcendent reality; and third, maintaining or revising a worldview. Those three characteristics provide the basis for the next three chapters.

Chapter Three will look at the healing community, specifically at the interactions within the self-help group. I show that grief is not merely a psychological process, it is also an interpersonal process. The resolution of grief happens in community. The complex interactions within the self-help group allow us to see the complexity of the bond with the child, both when the child was alive and now that the child is dead, and to see the significant ways in which the continuing bond with the child is interwoven within the community bond.

In Chapter Four, I look at the parents' evolving sense of connection with transcendent reality, especially as that connection takes the form of a continuing bond with their dead child. Readers will see that, as a sense of transcendent reality develops within the deep pain of their grief, parents find solace. This chapter will explore the experience of solace as a form of spiritual connection that is under-appreciated in the contemporary world.

In Chapter Five, I explore the ways in which the parents maintain or change their worldviews, their theologies or philosophies of life, in the light of their child's death and of the changes that have taken place in their own lives. For many North Americans, the first question of belief they ask about bereaved parents' worldviews is, "Do you still believe in God?" We will learn that the question cannot be reduced to simple terms of belief or nonbelief. Parents test the worldview they brought to their child's death. Some worldviews can be maintained with little change, other worldviews can be modified in ways that make the parents' new reality make sense, and some worldviews must be abandoned and new ones constructed in their place. We will see that finding an order in the world after the death of a child is a task dependent on both finding a continuing bond with the child and on finding a community in which the death and the bond with the child can be real.

In Chapter Six I turn from describing the spiritual lives of bereaved parents to exploring how professionals can help parents along their way. People with many kinds of professional education can find ways of helping, so the chapter explores the common ground that professionals share as they try to help. Since we can never find common ground separate from the particulars of individual practice, I rely on my own experience as a professional advising a self-help group and maintaining a counseling practice.

The book concludes with a chapter that explains the research method on which it is based. I left this material out of the main body of the book because I think the question, "What do we know and how do we know it?" is of compelling interest to only a few scholars. I must admit that I am among those for whom the question is interesting, so I hope the chapter supports the book in contributing to better work in the difficult-to-research field of parental grief.

The People in the Book

The book's setting is, for the most part, an extended study within my role as professional advisor to the local chapter of a self-help group of bereaved parents. When the chapter formed, it was affiliated with the Compassionate Friends, a national organization of bereaved parents. In 1995 and 1996, a series of policy and personal issues on the national board of the Compassionate Friends resulted in a group of former national board members leaving Compassionate Friends and forming a new national organization, Bereaved Parents of the USA. The local chapter on which the book is based dropped their membership in Compassionate Friends and affiliated with Bereaved Parents. Leaders of both national groups are now working toward reconciliation, though it is not clear now if one or two national organizations will remain. I have used Bereaved Parents as the name for the self-help group throughout the book, partly because the local chapter has now adopted the name, and partly because the new name is more descriptive. Where there are references to literature or materials from the Compassionate Friends, I have tried to note it in the text. In those parts of the book that were first published as scholarly articles that cited the earlier name, I have changed the group name to Bereaved Parents.

All the parents in this book are real. They are people who have allowed me to listen and to interact with them as they come to terms with the death of their children. Some of the quotations from parents are taken from what they have written, some are from transcripts of interviews, and some are from notes I made as soon as I could after the meeting, conversation or therapy session. I have tried to keep the individual sense of parents' remarks, but I have made grammatical changes or inserted a few words to make the context clearer. I have changed the names in all but a few cases in which people asked that their real name or the child's real name be used. If I tell the story in extended detail, I have changed it in some important ways in order to disguise the identity of both parent and child, but the core of the story remains as I heard it.

1

CHAPTER

The Aftermath of Spiritual Storms

Walking along the Cape Cod shore one day, Henry David Thoreau saw a sloop from Chatham dragging for the anchors of ships that had foundered in storms.

> She had her boats out at the work while she shuffled about on various tacks, and when, anything was found, drew up to hoist it on board. It is a singular employment, at which men are regularly hired and paid for their industry, to hunt to-day in pleasant weather for anchors which have been lost,—the sunken faith and hope of mariners, to which they trusted in vain.

As Thoreau watched, he thought about the aftermath of human spiritual storms.

> If the roadsteads of the spiritual ocean could be thus dragged, what rusty flukes of hope deceived and parted chain-cables of faith might again be windlassed aboard! enough to sink the finder's craft, or stock new navies to the end of time. The bottom of the sea is strewn with anchors, some deeper and some shallower, and alternately covered and uncovered by the sand.

Thoreau, however, rejected such work:

> But that is not treasure for us which another man has lost; rather it is for us to seek what no other man has found or can find,—not be Chatham men, dragging for anchors. (Thoreau, 1951, pp. 160–161)

The task before us in this book might seem like a job for Chatham men. The death of a child brings a storm in the individual and in the family that tests the surest spiritual anchor. Some hold, some don't. Some are dragged until they find better purchase. Unlike ships that break free in the storm, good only to be salvaged for their cargo and hardware, the parents in this book are condemned to continue living. Many of the people whose lives are reported in this book wished they could die, and most have, at some point, thought it would have been better if they had died rather than their child. But they go on living. When someone says, as if in admiration, "I don't know how you do it," bereaved parents often answer, "I don't have a choice."

Thoreau, of course, saw that the purpose of his life was to find a new transcendental way of being-in-the-world. Bereaved parents, like Thoreau, are seeking new meaning. I remembered the passage about the Chatham men after a mother whose teenage daughter died in a car accident spoke to my class on death and dying. To describe how her life had changed since her daughter's death, she read a passage from *Walden* that her daughter had copied and tucked into a school notebook and that the mother found after the girl died.

> I went to the woods because I wished to live deliberately, to front only the essential facts of life, and see if I could not learn what it had to teach, and not when I came to die discover that I had not lived. . . . I wanted to live deep, and suck out all the marrow of life, to live so sturdily . . . as to put to rout all that was not life (1960, p. 66).

Her adolescent daughter had left behind a key for the mother to resolve her grief. If she was to make sense of her daughter's death, and thus of her own life, she would have to rearrange her values—to be and act in a new way. The mother could hold her dead daughter close by living the life her daughter had vowed to live.

Perhaps it was good that the girl's idealism shielded her from a part of the passage in *Walden* that she did not copy. Thoreau wanted

> to drive life into a corner, to reduce it to its lowest terms, and if it proved to be mean, why then to get the whole and genuine meanness of it, and publish its meanness to the world; or if it were sublime to know it by experience (1960, p.66).

The mother has learned that life can be mean in a way that her daughter perhaps knew only in the last few seconds of consciousness. The mother publishes to the world the meanness she finds in her daughter's death. If the mother finds in her resolution of grief that life is also sublime, as I hope her daughter knew in those last seconds, the sublimity is firmly grounded in life's meanness. The spiritual life of bereaved parents does not deny suffering, it recognizes, honors, and understands it. They do not "get over it." As Paul Tillich taught us, *new being* and *the courage to be* emerge when we embrace, not deny, nonbeing (Tillich, 1951, 1957, 1963).

We will see in this book people who now live more deliberately and deeply, who do not take life for granted, and whose life is more fully lived. Life has driven *them* into a corner and reduced them to its lowest terms. Their new life is achieved only after deeply knowing life's meanness and knowing pain that seems never to end. When, after their long journey, we meet parents living their rebuilt lives, we know they, as Thoreau suggested, have sought and found for themselves, "what no other man has found or can find." No one else could find it because it is deeply personal and intensely connected with the one-of-a-kind bond each parent has with their child. Like Thoreau, we will treasure that.

☐ Spiritual Anchors

This book, then, is about spiritual life in the aftermath of personal devastation. It is about how average, normal people go about reconstructing their lives when one of the foundations they thought they could trust has shifted. It is about how people reconnect with their world and with each other after a child, one of a parent's primary attachments in the world, has been lost. It is about how people find meaning in their lives after one of their centers of meaning has been removed. In short, it is about losing, finding, or relocating spiritual anchors after the death of a child.

We will think about spirituality from the point of view of comparative religious studies. For most of human history, spirituality has been contained within particular cultural frameworks. That is, the spiritual experiences of individuals were almost completely molded and intertwined with the symbols, myths, beliefs, and rituals of their tribe or nation. If someone spoke of spiritual realities, it was about a deeper form of the accepted religion. The spiritual person was the monk or nun who gave up the common life to pursue a profounder version. Spiritual exercises were those prescribed within the tradition: prayer, fasting, meditation, pilgrimage, celibacy, vision, or whatever. Those who followed the spiritual path had a place within the community. They might be healers, or say prayers on others' behalf. They were supported by the ruling class who built and maintained the monasteries or retreat centers.

The decades leading up to the new millennium have seen a breakdown in the boundaries between religious traditions much as they have seen a breakdown in the boundaries between the economies of the world. We now trade spiritual techniques and insights in a single world market just as we trade goods, labor, and securities across international boundaries. In Japan, while a Buddhist priest drove me through terrifying Tokyo traffic, Bobby McFerrin sang "Don't worry. Be happy" from the car's CD player, and the Buddhist priest sang along. Spirituality has been separated from its cultural roots. At the same time, individuals have been separated from the certainties their grandparents knew. Death, even the death of a child, has its place in traditional societies. But children's deaths do not seem to make sense in the consumer culture of the international marketplace. Parents are on their own as they try to anchor their lives.

This book shows that parents do figure it out, do find ways of connecting to transcendent reality, do make a community for themselves where none exists for them in the larger society. They do anchor their lives. The spiritual realities that we see in the resolution of parental bereavement are universal. They transcend any particular religious belief, myth, symbol, or ritual. As I describe the parents' journeys, therefore, I will do so using terms that can apply to many of the world's religious traditions.

A good way to begin thinking about spiritual life, either our own or that of someone else, is to look at those moments when we feel most deeply connected to our world, when we feel least isolated inside our usual ego boundaries. We feel a part of something larger than ourselves, and the rest of the world makes sense.

One part of the connection is a direct interaction with the most elemental reality in the world. We can call it God, so long as we remember along with St. Anselm, that God is a being greater than can be conceived. We are in touch with the Mystery, not a mystery that needs to be solved, but a Mystery in which we feel at home. When Catholics go to the communion rail, the bread that they eat is the body of God become human that now becomes part of the communicant's body. When Taoists cast the I Ching to discern the proper behavior for the present moment, they are aligning themselves with the flow of yin and yang as it is now. As pilgrim Muslims enter the holy city they cry out, "I am here, Oh God. What is thy command?" In their meditation, Zen Buddhists turn off the "monkey mind" of everyday thinking and find instead the Void, the emptiness that is true reality. God is, Muslims say, as close as our jugular veins. Relax, say the Hindus, Brahman is already apparent in the multiplicity of the illusory world. Let go, say the Christians, grace has already been given.

We anchor ourselves as we trust the Mystery because the reality we know in the Mystery provides strength and meaning in our world. In

Brown's Chapel in Selma, Alabama during the Freedom Movement, people who were turning the world up-side-down by simply asserting their rights as human beings in the face segregationalist violence sang "Before I'll be a slave, I'll be buried in my grave, and go home to my Lord and be free." The alcoholic trusts in the "Higher Power" when human power is ineffective in recovering from addiction.

Within our connection with the Mystery, we know, however vaguely, that the world makes sense, that our world is meaningful, that what we do has larger purpose. The opposite is nonsense, nonmeaning. People marching out of Brown's Chapel might face police dogs, beatings, or fire hoses, but they could do it because what they were doing made sense. They sang, "We are not afraid, for we shall overcome *today*." The simple act of walking down the sidewalk was transformed into a claim to human dignity. The alcoholic with the shakes, staring at the bottle, knows what it would mean to take the drink and what it would mean not to.

When a child is born, the parent gains a new connection to God. No matter how scientifically we might now understand human reproduction, the baby feels like a new creation. Once there was one, then in the sexual union there were two, and at the birth there are three. The world makes sense in a new way. As a father or as a mother, I am now responsible for nurturing and guiding this new life. My job may not mean much, but at least it puts food on the table for the kids. The world may be going to hell in a hand basket, but, if we are to clean up the environment and try to build a more peaceful global community, we do it for future generations, for our children.

But what happens when the Mystery we trusted fails us? When the world is no longer an orderly place, when our spiritual anchor looks as if it might not hold, or worse, when we feel the snap and know we are adrift and out of control? That is the story I have to tell.

Part of the story that has not been told often is that a significant portion of a bereaved parent's spiritual life revolves around developing and learning to live with a continuing bond with a dead child. The bond with the dead child is, for most of the parents in this book, a new way in which they experience transcendent reality, a new way to experience God. We will see many parents who experience their child's presence as a spiritual force that guides their lives. The sense of the child's presence, as we will see, can be gained by many means and be incorporated into the individual life and into the parents' communities in a wide variety of ways. We will see that for most of the bereaved parents in this book, the child functions in their lives as saints, angels, and boddhisattvas function in several religious traditions, as intermediaries between the sacred and profane worlds, between the land of the immortals and the land of the living. Thus, we will see that, just as the birth of their child gave the parents new spiritual connections, in the resolution of their grief, parents find those spiritual connections extended.

The fact that we find growth and new spirituality in the resolution of parents' grief does not make the death a good thing. Those of us who are not bereaved parents do not want to know how bad it really is. We find ways of telling ourselves that they can take it because they are strong, or that some compensating factor (they can have other children, or their child is fine in heaven) makes the death okay. Well, it doesn't. I have met many parents who have used their pain as an occasion to grow to be better people, who have seen their families and marriages mature in ways they could not have predicted. But when I have asked them, all have said that they would trade all the growth and all the gains if only they could have their child back. The spiritual connections and spiritual life parents find after the death of a child includes the deep pain of knowing that the child is dead and the abiding realization that dead means a long time gone.

☐ Book's Setting

What I report about bereaved parents in this book comes from two settings, one far more important than the other. I have learned most of what I know from my association with a self-help group of bereaved parents. I have confirmed what I learned there and have understood some individual lives at greater depth in my psychological counseling practice that has always included a number of bereaved parents. Throughout the description I rely on the interactions within the self-help group to provide the conceptual framework, and I use case material from my practice to set what I have learned into a wider frame of parents' personal and family histories. A more detailed discussion of how I have used what I learned in these settings is found in Chapter Seven, which is devoted to methodological issues.

I have been fortunate that beginning in 1979, a local chapter of the Bereaved Parents, a self-help group, has allowed me to be part of their process. Chapter Seven is a scholarly description of my research, but the process has been a very human one, so it seems to me that telling the personal story first is a truer introduction. It began rather simply. Margaret Gerner, whose six-year-old son Arthur had been killed nine years earlier, said that she intended to start a St. Louis chapter. She asked me if I would like to help. I said yes, probably for a lot of reasons to which I had not given much thought. I did not know it then, but it turned out to have been a decision that has opened many paths. So I began a relationship with the group. They assigned me the title "professional advisor." The role has evolved over time as the group has developed wisdom and a body of practical knowledge passed from one generation of members and leaders to the next, and as the group has expanded by adding meetings in different parts of the metropolitan area. Early on, my focus was largely learning with the parents how to be part of a self-help group of bereaved parents. Later, my role was to assist in developing a governance structure of a large multimeeting chapter. For five years, I attended one or two meetings a month and met often with the leaders. Now, I am an exofficio member of the Advisory Committee, a group made up of parents whose grief is reasonably well resolved, and most of whom are former meeting facilitators. One of the Advisory Committee members and I lead a bimonthly or quarterly Meeting Effectiveness Workshop for the meeting facilitators and the core members of each of the meetings. My role in the group remains a valuable part of my self-identity. I feel good being part of something good.

Nine parents attended the first meeting on a very cold December night. They knew nothing about each other except that each had had a child who died and that they were in deep pain. So we went around the room and everyone told their story, which turned out to be not just the story of their grief, but also the story of their child. They wanted to say their child's name. They wanted the others to know who their child had been. They wanted to show pictures of their child. They wanted to tell about how their family and friends often could not understand. Then some people raised practical problems with which they were having trouble. "What have you done with your child's things?" "Christmas is coming, and I don't know how to make it through without him." And others shared what they had done. By the end of the evening, they had bonded in a special way. I knew then that the bond was complex, but it took me several years to get inside the complexity enough to put it into words.

I felt like an outsider. I still feel like an outsider, though with time, I have been accepted enough so that I feel like an adopted member of the family. Maybe I have just been around so long that I am "old shoe." As I reflect back, the moment they let me in, or maybe it was the moment I let them in, was a night they shared pictures of their children. Photographs were passed around—a boy in his scout uniform on his way to camp, a baby in the family's baptismal dress. Stories were told about the child, about the occasion when the picture was taken, and about how the picture captured an aspect of the child that was special. At the end of the meeting, as happened in those early days, I was asked to say a few words to sum up the meeting. I usually used the minute or so to pull back and reflect on the group processes or to find a theme which I had seen in the discussion. But I had no words that could explain a group of people sitting around for an hour and a half with obvious enjoyment looking at pictures of each other's dead children. So I just said what I felt, "Well, now we know there are a lot of good-looking kids in heaven." I now know that, by getting acquainted with the children and sharing the joy the children brought, I could also share the pain. In other words, as I got in touch with their children, I got in touch with the parents, and they felt I could be trusted. It would take me a long time to put words to the profundity of that bond. Maybe in some ways this book represents my hope that I can now explain what was happening that night.

The first meetings were overwhelming. More people came each month and each brought their pain. Each person struggled with inner conflicts that seemed to defy resolution. It would have been easy for me to fall into helplessness because I knew I had nothing to give them that would take the pain away. I often wanted to say the magic word, but never knew what word that might be. Still, the group grew and we soon had 25 people, then almost 50. We started a second meeting in another part of the city, and we kept growing. Now we have five meetings in different parts of the metropolitan area. Not everyone came back for another meeting, but many returned month after month. They were finding something there. During the third meeting, after a pause in the discussion, one woman looked at another and said, "You know, something you said last month really helped me." She then went on to say how. I needed that. If I could not help them, at least I could trust that they could help each other.

The pain was overwhelming and, I learned to understand, would never go away. Parental bereavement is a permanent condition. A reporter in my university's newspaper once wrote that a "former graduate" would speak the next week. I wanted to attend the lecture because I had never seen a "former graduate" before and I thought I should see such a thing. Had the school taken back the diploma? There are former wives, former husbands, former employers and employees, former neighbors, and even former lives. But I have never heard anyone refer to their former parent, and bereaved parents do not say that they have a former child. The pain does not go away because the bond with the child does not go away. That does not mean it remains as sharp and constant as it feels the first few years. As time went on, I saw that parts of the pain can be transformed within the healing. The pain and the bond with their child remained with them, and within their pain and bond their lives took on new meanings, not in spite of their sorrow, but within it. Psychiatrist Oliver Sachs says, "Nearly all my patients, so it seems to me, whatever their problems, reach out to life—not only despite their conditions, but often because of them, and even with their aid" (1995, p. xviii).

After it was clear that this group process worked, it was still overwhelming, but in a more positive way. The death of a child is awful and the processes in which parents resolve their grief are awesome. I felt the same in Glacier Bay, Alaska, near the place John Muir had come to, to figure out how the Yosemite Valley had been formed. Landscape is being created there as glaciers advance and retreat over a place where one tectonic plate slides beneath another. It was, Muir knew as he looked at the place, fire and ice and time. The rock is created in volcanic eruptions and from the sediment of ancient sea floors. The glacier carves valleys in the solid rock. And after the glacier melts, the land springs up, rising several feet in the next century, because the ice's weight had compressed the land and, when released of the load, the land seems to breath deeply, spread its shoulders, and come erect. And then come the lichen and moss, and then the bushes, and then the trees. The realities in parental bereavement are the primal forces—fire, ice, and time—forming the human landscape: they are birth and death, love and destruction, bonding and losing, individual solitude and community membership, devastation in grief and triumph in remaking a life. Sometimes it still takes my breath away.

For the parents in this book, the resolution of grief after the death of a child is a spiritual journey, not just a psychological process. The parents' anchors in life—their sense of connection with transcendent reality, the myths and symbols by which they make sense of their world, and the community in which their lives are embedded—must be rearranged to include the fact that a child, their child, has died. I have taken it as my task to describe their spiritual journey, to say as best I can what they have found along the way about themselves, about grief, and about life.

Most books on spiritual life are about the author's spirituality, or what the author thinks the reader should believe or do to improve the reader's spiritual life, or about a person, usually long dead, whose life can be a spiritual exemplar for others. This book is about my life only to the extent my life has become interwoven with those I try to describe. I do not presume to say how the spiritual life should be lived, nor do I think I have any universal truth about the cosmos which can guide us all. But I think I can say how these people have lived their spiritual lives in the face of the potential absurdity and meaninglessness of their children's deaths. The parents in this book would, I am sure, not be comfortable being held up as exemplary lives. I hope I present them as human as they feel themselves to be. They say at the beginning that they are just making it one day, or even one hour at a time, and experienced members tell new members, "You never get over it." Their children have died, as any of our children could. They are like us except that fate has found them in a special and terrible way. If we who are not bereaved parents can begin to understand their journey, we might learn to be more helpful to them along their way. In Chapter Six, I will speak more directly about how we can help, but if we are to help, we must first learn by walking with them. Helping the healing begins with recognizing the pain. As we walk with them, we might discover that bereaved parents can also help us. We might be less afraid to face our own journeys after we have learned how they have found their way on the road that seems so much harder than our own.

For me, the joy is that the parents in this book are a seemingly random sample of the community. They are just ordinary people, but their children have died. There are few predisposing factors to having a child die. It happens in functional and dysfunctional families, in rich neighborhoods and in poor, to individuals whose lives have heretofore been easy and to individuals whose lives are already heavily burdened. And all in their own way find new anchors. They rebuild their lives with care and kindness. Their lives seem to me to be, like the birth of a child or of Yosemite Valley, another miracle of creation. I have found hope in knowing those who are constructing new anchors in their lives. "All life is suffering," says Buddhism's first noble truth. All of us suffer, though not as bereaved parents do. If they can do it in their grief at the death of their child, so can we in whatever pains we find in our own lives.

Perhaps all who set out on a spiritual quest do so of necessity. Surely a theme echoing through the spiritual literature of all religions is that the spiritual journey begins with a call that must be answered. But the journey of bereaved parents, while grounded in their inner reality, is occasioned by an undeniable objective truth that, though it could happen to any of us, it has happened to them. Only other bereaved parents can really know the pain, and so know the meaning of the journey. The rest of us can merely try to understand as best we can. This book is an effort to get inside their lives enough to observe and, perhaps, to learn to help the healing.

There is a way this book can be misused. Every description can become a prescription, and every spiritual revelation can become a stifling orthodoxy. This book describes one path that the spiritual journey through grief may take, the path offered within Bereaved Parents. It seemed to me that it was like the path taken by many bereaved parents who came for counseling. The population I have observed is self-selected and may not be representative of bereaved parents in general. It is true that a great deal of what I have observed is supported by research on bereaved parents, but many studies of bereaved parents have found their subjects in self-help groups because it is the one place bereaved parents gather and identify themselves. Clearly there are other paths through the valley of the shadow of death. Some of those other paths are used within the families of those who attend Bereaved Parents. When one parent attends and reports that his or her spouse does not like to come to the meetings or when some family members quickly seek counseling while other family members come reluctantly or not at all, the nonattending spouse or reluctant family members may be using different dynamics by which to reach resolution. It would be a shame if the dynamics of the resolution of parental grief that I have described were to be made part of the *musts* and *shoulds* of any grief intervention program that claims to provide help based on what we have seen with these parents in these settings. The spirit blows where it will and we may appreciate and participate in its works even as we know we cannot control it.

☐ Some Thoughts for the Reader

This book is short. I think it should be because coming into close contact with bereaved parents is very difficult for those whose children have not died. I do not want to overwhelm readers. I have tried to write in a style that both opens the reader to the parent's lives and allows the reader to keep enough distance that they can hear the story to its end. When I talk to outsiders who have attended a Bereaved Parents meeting, they often tell me that after a while they just shut down because they could no longer deal with what they were hearing. I think a long book would put off readers before they begin, and would run more of a risk that readers will find themselves shut down or will set the book aside and find reasons for not picking it up again. The best advice I can give readers who are not bereaved parents is what I have had to learn in order to stay so close all these years.

First, yes, it does really hurt as bad as they say.

Second, there is nothing we can do to make it better. We are as helpless as the parents to change the world back to the way it was before the child died. When we accept our own powerlessness, however, it turns out that we can help. When we accept their painful reality, then we can help by not saying stupid things that only make the parent feel more estranged. Comments that seem so insensitive to bereaved parents come from our own discomfort. More importantly, when we accept that the pain is irreparable, then we are ready, if we want to, to be there in the pain with the parent. We can be part of the healing community by sharing in the pain, by allowing ourselves to grieve over the dead child, by remembering the child and allowing the child to be part of our lives as the child remains part of the parent's life. In other words, we live in a paradox. When we realize there is nothing we can do to take away the parents' pain, then we can do something to be part of their healing.

Third, we can trust the parents, and we can trust a community that opens itself to resolution and change. The human organism is resilient. We have been coming to terms with the death of our children since we began as a species. The resolution of parental bereavement seems hard wired into our psyche and into our community. It takes time, but in a nurturant environment, parents do grow toward a positive resolution of their grief. We can trust that. One of the early comforts newly bereaved parents find in the self-help group is that they see others who were like themselves only a year or so earlier. "I liked that I saw people laughing," said one parent. "I didn't think I would ever be able to do that again, and then I thought maybe I would." It helps those of us who are not bereaved parents to look ahead, not just to look at our own fears for our children, not just to look at the devastation of the first year or so after a child dies. We can be there better for parents who are newly bereaved after we have gotten to know some parents four or five years after the death, parents who have not "gotten over it," but who have grown in the ways I hope the book describes.

If we who are not bereaved parents let ourselves realize the pain, accept that we are powerless to take away the pain, and trust the resilient capacity of individuals and healthy communities, we can be awed by the pain, and we can also be awed by the healing. In Chapter Six I will speak directly to professionals who are not bereaved parents. I hope professionals will read the descriptive chapters rather closely because the chapter written for them will simply draw out the implications for professional practice. If, however, the description seems too thick, professionals might want to read their chapter first and then look through the earlier chapters to find parts that seem relevant to them.

I hope bereaved parents who read this book will hear in it the voice of a friend. I believe what other bereaved parents have told me: that no one can really understand but other bereaved parents. I have tried to listen and to say what I have heard. I have tried to put the spiritual journey after a child dies into a wider context. It seems to me that the road parents travel after the death of a child is like the spiritual road other people travel, both in their grief and in the other suffering life brings. I think bereaved parents have some lessons for the wider society and I hope this book will be a vehicle by which those lessons can be transmitted. I hope the book helps bereaved parents put their experience in some perspective. If reading the book allows bereaved parents vicariously to be members of the healing community from which the book grew, it might be helpful, but the book grew from rich, intense, and very human interactions. I hope the book helps, but bereaved parents will probably benefit more from finding or creating a place where they can have those interactions face to face.

A special word is in order for readers who are bereaved parents new in their grief, or who have put off working toward some kind of resolution. The first message of the book is that you are not alone. It may feel as if you are crazy, but you are not. You are a bereaved parent. A lot of bereaved parents feel crazy a lot of the time, especially if they live in a community that does not acknowledge how bad and how long it hurts, or if they live in a community that wants to forget their child. The second message of the book is that you will never get over your grief, but the pain will not stay the same. Your life will never be as it was before, but it will not stay as it is now. "This is what it is all about," says one bereaved mother in the book. "It is one person stepping back into the darkness to help the next one through." If, in the darkness of your early grief, this book can be the means by which some people can step back in and help you through, that is probably as much as you can expect from this book. I hope the book does that for you. If the book gives you an inkling of the spiritual path available in a well-run self-help group, you might want to try a meeting near you. Maybe in a few years you can come back and read the book again to get a little perspective on where you have been.

☐ Conclusion

I hope that by both looking at the shared experience of bereaved parents and looking at the complex history and experience of individuals I can adequately describe their journey. I hope that through these lives we can see ways by which we can help them along their way. The success of the attempt is, of course, not an objective question, but is intersubjective. If bereaved parents find their lives adequately reflected here, then I have been successful. I have tried to open myself to the lives of these parents. It is often painful, but in the end very rewarding because it shows the possibilities of the human spirit. I hope the book helps readers who are not bereaved parents to open themselves to the pain as well as to the triumph, and that by seeing a spiritual life that includes the deepest kind of human suffering, they will see one of the further possibilities of the human spirit.

We are not Chatham men dragging for anchors. We are the witnesses of survivors taking their bearings after the storm, assessing the damage to their stores, repairing their boats, putting down new moorings, charting the shoreline, and making forays inland to survey the resources available in this strange land. If we learn something of how they do it, perhaps we can learn something of what they have found.

The Spiritual Aspects of Parents' Grief

It is difficult to define "spiritual," because the word often refers to experiences and realities that are beyond words. But we know when a moment is sacred, when a relationship has meaning beyond the present, and when our actions have moral consequences beyond their immediate effect. Even if our spiritual life is beyond words, it remains in our awareness. In this first part of the chapter, I will try to outline a definition of spirituality taken from many of the world's spiritual traditions. In the second part of the chapter, I will define spirituality more particularly as we understand it in the journey parents make after the death of their child. In the final part of the chapter, I will discuss a unique aspect of spirituality among bereaved parents, their continuing bond with their deceased children. I will show how that continuing bond is an expression of spiritual dynamics found in most of the world's religious traditions.

As we define, we need to be careful that we do not confuse *knowing about* with knowing. A definition is not the reality it defines because to define is to talk about. We may be able, for example, to define love, but that is not the same as knowing what it is to love or to be loved. We may be able to define a cow, but the definition does not help us get the cow to come into the milking stall. A farmer, on the other hand, can *know* cows very well without any abstract definitions. Some Eastern spiritual traditions say that ideas and definitions are like fingers pointing to the moon. The finger is a good guide, but once we have seen the moon we should stop focusing on the finger. The spiritual life is known in its living. Parents whose lives I have followed know. I hope that this chapter can be like the finger pointing to the lives on which I report. If it helps us see the realities in those lives more clearly, that is enough.

Some readers may find this chapter rather abstract, especially if they have limited background in the world's spiritual traditions or limited exposure to scholarship in comparative religions. I will try to make some hard concepts accessible by giving examples from our everyday life and by giving some quotes from the traditions that say things as clearly as possible. If the concepts seem difficult, I hope you will pause and try to understand, because, as we try to understand their lives, parents whose children have died deserve the very best scholarship available.

If you do get bogged down in this chapter, stop reading it and go on to the next chapter that moves closer to the parents' lives. Then, having read the chapter on community, the chapter on solace, and the chapter on worldview, you might want to come back to this chapter and see if these themes from the world's spiritual traditions seem clearer after you have seen them played out in the lives of bereaved parents.

☐ The Nature of the Spiritual

It has become common in the last decade to differentiate *spiritual* from *religious*. In a pluralistic and individualistic world, the distinction probably represents a protest against the particularity of most religions and a longing for a more universal set of myths and symbols. The distinction also represents the modern split between personal experience and social forms. In modernity, the spiritual is mostly known in transitory present moments, while religion, rooted in the past, endures in social structures which take on a life of their own. But religion and spirituality cannot be fully separated in the individual's experience or in the study of spirituality. For one thing, the reality known in spiritual moments is usually perceived using symbols handed down through religious traditions even though the individual may not be conscious of the history of the symbols. For another, the reality known in spiritual moments is maintained over time by symbols, rituals, and affiliations which have a religious character.

> Religious belief systems have the job of giving voice to the seemingly ineffable hints provided by various religious experiences, so that religion can emerge out of the isolation of its interiority and become a full and important component of the public sphere (Barnard, 1997, p. 96).

Spirituality and religion are in a constant interchange. Alone each becomes sterile. When religious forms are taken too literally, they can become rigid and thus suffocate the spirit. But spiritual experiences without religious ideas, myths, or rituals tend to evaporate. One ancient sage put it this way:

> If the practitioners discard their various practices and seek to dwell only in that without form, they will not succeed. On the other hand, neither will they succeed if they cling to their practices, seeking to dwell in that which has form (*The Commentary on the Dainichi-kyō*, quoted in Yamasaki, 1988, p. 109).

Is Spirit Something or Somewhere?

The concept of *spirit*, like the concept of *mind*, raises the simple question: Is it real? We can ask if a spirit is a thing like other things, just as we can ask if an idea is a thing like other things. We commonly think in spatial terms about spirituality. So, for example, if we say the spirit is eternal, many people think of eternity as a pile of hours or days. When the pile gets so high it cannot be counted, then it is eternity. The concept of eternity as a pile takes the form of words when people make a stack of *evers*, as in "forever and ever and ever." More often we think of the spirit as like a place with geographic reality. In Western medieval thought, for example, human reason could arrive at limited ideas about God (*Natural Theology*), but only God could supply the fuller understanding (*Revealed Theology*). For generations teachers at the chalkboard diagramed a triangle with a line half way up. Above the line was Revealed Theology and below was Natural Theology. The spatially-represented theological division was also the popular division of the spiritual and the mundane; the spirit was up, humans were down. When somebody died, the spirit went up, the body stayed down. God was up in heaven, the devil down in hell. Our good impulses came from head and heart in the upper part of our body, and bad impulses came from further down. So, whether it was in the doctrine of revelation, in answers to what happens to us after we die, or in adolescent struggles with sexuality, spirituality had a concrete character in that it could be located.

The idea that the spirit is a thing like other things or a place like other places is a simple concept that is easy to teach because it fits the young child's concrete, operational cognitive level. In one of his earliest studies, Jean Piaget (1965) looked at how moral judgement develops as the child grows up. He found an interesting paradox. Young children do not know the rules, but what they know about the rules is that the rules are outside themselves and have absolute authority. Young children think rules and punishment for infractions of the rules have objective reality and are outside themselves. He called it *heteronomy* (1965, pp. 84–108, 197). Even the rules of the game of marbles for these children have sacred authority. Young children think the rules of the game were given at the creation of the world, or at least by writ of the town council. These young children do not actually know the rules. They play the game in a seemingly random fashion and cannot explain the rules in any coherent way. The rules in the family also come from on high. Bad is what adults say is bad. Arbitrary punishment for infractions of the rules is accepted. Like God's commandments, what adults say is right because they said it.

Older children, on the other hand, have internalized the rules. Piaget called it *autonomy*. Rules no longer feel objective to older children because they see the game rules as a product of the mutual consent of the players. Older children know the rules and can follow the rules as they play the game. The rules are internal, like the conscience, inside the self and available for inner dialogue and reciprocal interactions. Moral and religious ideas are often a product of early indoctrination, so many people retain heteronomy in their spiritual life long after they have abandoned it in other relationships. If people remain in the concrete operational level in their spiritual life, then, whatever the spiritual is to them, it remains "out there," that is, outside the self. The first answer, then, to the question, "Is Spirit Something or Somewhere?" is, at the concrete operational level, Yes.

Piaget notes that adult authority in a child's life supports heteronomy. He would have understood the sweatshirt that says, "Because I'm the Mom, That's Why." It may very well be that religious authority, like adult authority, supports heteronomy. It may be that the more spirituality is connected to political power or to religious dogmatism, the more likely the spiritual is to be regarded as outside the self and having concrete reality.

Higher developmental levels leave concrete operations behind and accept "as axiomatic that truth is more multidimensional and organically interdependent than most theories or accounts of truth can grasp" (Fowler, 1981, p. 186). At these higher levels, a person's own experience, not external authority is the test of any religious teaching. In the Western traditions, even God is not "out there" for more highly developed religious consciousness. Martin Buber said, when the external reality known in I-it relationships gives way to the intersubjective reality of the I-Thou, then God is known. *Thou* is the old English familiar pronoun, like the German *Du*, used in intimate family or friendship bonds. God is not separate from other I-Thou relationships, but (in a translation which uses *You* instead of *Thou* for Buber's German *Du*): "Extended, the lines of relationships intersect in the eternal You. Every single You is a glimpse of that. Through every single You the basic word addresses the eternal You" (1970, p. 123). Teachers in the Eastern traditions arrive at similar conclusions, that there is no spiritual "out there" apart from living in the everyday world. In Mahayana Buddhism, for example, the world of suffering and spiritual liberation are interconnected and co-dependent. An ancient sage wrote:

> There is nothing whatsoever which differentiates the existence-in-flux (*samsara*) from nirvana (*liberation*);
>
> And there is nothing whatsoever which differentiates nirvana from existence-in-flux (Nāgārjuna, quoted in LaFleur, 1988, pp. 24–25).

In the twelfth century series of pictures by Master Kukuan on *Taming the Ox*, the ox represents the Buddha nature that is found in enlightenment. In the last picture, after the process is complete, the person goes to the marketplace. The discovery is that enlightened life is not different from everyday life, but is a transformation of the mundane. Eternal life is in the present. The poem for the last picture reads:

> I use no magic to extend my life;
> Now, before me, the dead trees become alive.

The commentary on the picture and poem reads:

> The beauty of my garden is invisible. . . . I go to the market place with my wine bottle and return home with my staff. I visit the wine shop and the market, and everyone I look upon becomes enlightened (Reps, 1961, p. 154).

When a young man seeking enlightenment entered a Zen monastery, he went to Master Joshu and asked for instructions. Joshu said, "Have you had your breakfast?" "Yes, I have," replied the monk. "Then," said Joshu, "wash your bowls." By which he seems to mean begin seeking enlightenment in the present task. And, it is said, the young monk had an insight (Shibayama, 1974, p. 69).

The point seems to be that, at the more mature levels of spiritual sensitivity, the answer to our question, "Is Spirit Something or Somewhere?" is, No. The spiritual is not a separate realm, an "out there," or an "up there." So, it seems, as we try to understand the spiritual lives of bereaved parents, we will just have to wash our bowls. Bereaved parents do not escape from their grief into a purer place called the spiritual, rather the spiritual emerges in the day to day coming to terms with the death of their child. Their spirituality is not a refuge from their grief, but a part of their lives that develops as they grow in their grief. Like the bereaved parents, we who try to get inside their lives must get inside each life as its history unfolds. As we try to understand spirituality, we find nothing that is merely psychological or only group dynamics. The spiritual is within the everyday life if we would just see it. We use psychological and sociological constructs to understand spirituality because spirituality is not a realm separated from psychology, sociology, or even politics. Spirituality is embedded in every aspect of human life. The world seen by the color blind is the same world as seen by the color sighted; the difference is in the seer not the seen. As we stop looking at bereaved parents with our I-it selves and let them become real to us with our I-Thou selves, we can see the spiritual realities with which they wrestle and the spiritual resolutions they sometimes find. And in those moments we might even understand as Master Kukuan did, that everyone we look at becomes enlightened.

The Contemporary Spiritual Landscape

As the twenty-first century begins, humankind's spiritual/religious landscape has changed. Satellite communications and air travel are quickly erasing geographic distances and cultural barriers. When the twentieth century began, religious traditions were for the most part separated from each other by geographic distance and cultural barriers. The European colonial empires justified their power by claiming to bring what they believed to be their superior Christian religion to those they labeled ignorant heathens. The World Parliament of Religions, held in 1893 as part of the Columbian Exposition in Chicago, was the first attempt in several centuries to bring the world's many religious/spiritual traditions into dialogue as equals. The Parliament set the tone for the next century. As European colonial empires collapsed after World War II, and as technological breakthroughs in travel and telecommunications changed geographic scale, religious traditions found themselves interacting as equals on a planet that seemed much smaller. I once heard Margaret Mead say that the most important religious symbol of the twentieth century was the photograph of Earth as seen from our Moon. It was, she said, the first time we could see ourselves as one. I remembered Mead's comment when I was a guest at a teaching temple of the Shingon sect of Japanese Buddhism. The teacher who was my host told me that the week before he had chanted at the Bob Dylan concert in Nara in front of the world's largest wooden temple. The world Mead noted is one world in which all religions are interacting with each other and in which all religions are coming to terms with the changes technology has brought. The work of scholars throughout the century has yielded excellent translations of the important texts from around the world. Our grandparents were, for the most part, born into one religion. Our children are born into a world in which all religions have a voice.

☐ A Definition of Spiritual

Our definition of spiritual must be useful in two ways: First, it must be applicable to all the world's religious/spiritual traditions. Second, it must allow us to understand better the complexities of people living their everyday inner and interpersonal lives. Using these criteria, three characteristics would be implied if we are to understand experience as spiritual: (1) Encounter or merger with transcendent reality; (2) Finding a worldview, that is, a higher intelligence, purpose, or order that gives meaning; and (3) Belonging to a community in which transcendent reality and worldview are validated. We will look briefly at each characteristic in this chapter and then in the next three chapters explore them in detail as they play out in parents' lives. The thread that holds the characteristics together is what Paul Tillich (1952 and 1951, 1957, 1963) called ultimate concern. That is, what makes an event, experience, object, or idea spiritual is that it seems to be vitally important to us. Although the spiritual may come with more than a tinge of irony, and occasionally with a rush of sparkling humor, for bereaved parents, it is deadly serious. The spiritual engages us at the existential core of our being, or as Tillich says, at the ground of our being. A reality, a meaning, or a membership seems spiritual when "it is a matter of infinite passion and interest, making us its object whenever we try to make it our object" (Tillich, 1951, p. 11). Like Buber's eternal Thou, the spiritual speaks to us, addresses us, knows us personally. As bereaved parents encounter transcendent reality, know the meaning of their children's deaths, and of their lives, and know the community in which they feel most at home, they also know themselves as they feel they really are. They know for moments how the universe functions and they know their place and power in the universe.

Encounter or Merger with Transcendent Reality

The first characteristic of the spiritual is that, as an ultimate concern, we encounter or merge with that which we know to be beyond space and time, beyond the immediate biological and social reality. William James said:

> It is as if there were in the human consciousness *a sense of reality, a feeling of objective presence, a perception* of what we may call *"something there,"* more deep and more general than any of the special and particular "senses" by which the current psychology supposes existent realities to be originally revealed (1958, p. 61).

We are often beyond the limits of prose as we try to understand what it means to encounter or merge with that which had been the not-self or other. In most religious traditions, it is the extreme (or supreme) of such moments which are cherished. In Sufi Islam it is *Identity*, the goal of the mystical quest, when I and God are one.

> Though from my gaze profound
> Deep awe hath hid Thy Face,
> In wondrous and ecstatic Grace
> I feel Thee touch my inmost ground (al-Junayd of Baghdad, quoted in Armstrong, 1993, p. 228).

When al-Ghazzali, Islam's great medieval teacher, incorporated Sufi insights into his philosophy, the question ceased being "Does God exist?" That would make God an object among other objects. Rather, he said, the question should be, "Can God be found?" His answer was that God could be found in direct intuitive experience which is beyond rational or metaphysical understanding. In Buber's Judaism, as we noted earlier, it is in the *I-Thou* relationship that God is known as another person is known. We do not *know about* God; we *know* God as we know our children or our spouse. In Bhakti Hinduism it is *Dar'san*, in which the devotee looks into the eyes of the god and, more importantly, the god looks back into the eyes of the devotee. As a symbol that reality is in the relationship, not in the idol, at the end of many Hindu festivals, the statue is put into a river or lake where it dissolves.

It seems to people who are spiritually attuned that what they know in these moments is not something they can understand, but rather something that creates understanding. In many religious traditions we find the paradoxical teaching that humans cannot understand transcendent reality, but rather, transcendent reality allows humans to understand. St. Anselm said, "I do not seek to understand that I may believe, but I believe in order to understand. For this also I believe, that unless I believed, I should not understand" (St. Anselm, 1968, p. 7). The Kena Upanishad puts it this way:

What cannot be spoken with words, but that whereby words are spoken: Know that alone to be Brahman, the Spirit; and not what people
here adore.

What cannot be thought with the mind, but that whereby the mind can
think: Know that alone to be Brahman, the Spirit; and not what people
here adore (The Upanishads, 1965, p. 51).

If such high mystical insights seem to be too esoteric, most people
can recall moments when they have felt a loss of ego boundaries, that
is, when the normal sense of what is *me* and what is *not-me*, dissolve.
In those moments, the individual leaves behind the usual sense of
separation, and instead feels at one with another, with the divine, or
with the environment. In such moments, the distinction between inner and outer reality blurs. Some people in love, for example, say
their beloved is inside of them, that they and their beloved are one, or
that they are not complete without their beloved. Religious traditions
often use love as an analogy to spiritual experience. Soldiers sometimes feel so integrated with their country, comrades, or cause that
they willingly give up their individual lives. Athletes describe moments when they lose their separateness and become one with the
team, or with the ball. The art form that is almost universally associated with spirituality is music. Most people have at some point experienced the blurring of inner and outer reality when the physical sen-
sory experience of the music becomes the truth in our soul (see Batson,
Schoenrade, and Ventis, 1993, pp. 148–51).

In these moments when we encounter or merge with transcendent
reality, we remain in our life's circumstances. We do not go somewhere else, or become someone different. We are who we are when
we encounter the divine. Because we retain our unique life circumstances, the experience has different meaning depending on our life
circumstances. The spiritual moment has a different meaning for an
alcoholic hitting bottom, for an adolescent seeking a vocation, for an
octogenarian on a deathbed, for the minister searching for next Sunday's sermon. Surely, to parents whose children have died, the encounter with transcendent reality has a different meaning than it has
for others. The moment may transform the individual, but the individual's
circumstance remains the same. The young monk's breakfast bowl
was still dirty. The immortal and unchangeable reality that bereaved
parents know beyond space and time does not change the awful truth
that their children were all too mortal and that the parents lives have
changed for the worse. Whatever else these moments bring into human life, when we look at this characteristic of the spiritual in bereaved parents, we will find that transcendent reality brings solace, or
consolation, in the face of irreparable loss.

Adopting a Worldview

The second characteristic of the spiritual is that we become aware of a higher intelligence, purpose, or order which we do not control, but in which we can participate, and which provides the pattern to which we can conform our lives. As James said:

> Were one asked to characterize the life of religion in the broadest and most general terms possible, one might say that it consists of the belief that there is an unseen order, and that our supreme good lies in harmoniously adjusting ourselves thereto (1958, p. 58).

Ideas and teachings become existentially real and bring order to our inner world. We experience the "multifaceted relationship or connection between human and metaphysical systems" (Prest and Keller, 1993, p. 138). When we participate in or conform to the higher intelligence, purpose, or order, we live more authentically, more meaningfully. Such meaningful living has both a cognitive and a moral aspect: our thinking is set straight, and our actions toward others are right and true.

In the study of comparative religions, the order people find in their world is called a worldview (Smart, 1996). A worldview can be defined as a set of beliefs, myths, rituals, affiliations, altered states of consciousness, and ethical standards, often unarticulated, by which individuals and communities answer two questions: How does the universe function? and What station or power does the individual or community hold within the universe? Worldviews function like a map of both visible and invisible reality on which individuals locate external and internal events. From them individuals discover or choose religious, political, or ideological affiliations, and upon them individuals base moral judgments and actions. Worldviews are not held as abstractions, but rather as a collection of symbols, myths, beliefs, personal experiences, altered states of consciousness, and ritual behaviors that can have varying degrees of internal coherence or intellectual consistency. Because a worldview can be codified in precept and example, it is the focus of religious teaching: *Dharma* in Hinduism, Doctrine in Christianity, *Tao* in Chinese religion.

The easiest worldviews to identify are those which have been worked out in religious traditions over time, though the actual worldviews used by individuals and communities are considerably less coherent. We study well-developed worldviews when we learn about different religions. When we learn about the world's religions, we find what appears to be an incredible variety of worldviews. At the surface, they often seem to have little in common with each other. Salvation in the

Christian tradition, for example, seems very different from liberation in the Hindu tradition. We find a great many words and images, yet it does not seem possible to arrange them by their content or to find a systematic theology that puts all the pieces together like a big jigsaw puzzle. Near the end of his long and distinguished career studying both ancient and modern religions, Erwin Ramsdell Goodenough said that the common element within the diversity is not of one design nor is it a universal core of archetypical themes. Rather, he said, the common element is in our shared humanity, in "the insecurity and universal anxiety which various peoples and individuals all experience, along with the equally universal craving for explanation and control" (1986, p. 18).

As we listen to bereaved parents struggling to find a worldview adequate to their circumstances, their insecurity and anxiety and their craving for explanation and control are very much in evidence. Their questions are not metaphysical, but personal. Is there any order in the world? If so, how did the child or the parent violate this order to deserve the child's death? The meanings of daily tasks are called into question because the meaning of parenthood is in providing for the child. The perception of the self is changed. People who thought they were strong now find that they do not have the strength to make it through a day, and those who thought they were weak surprise themselves with their power to survive and to help others. The death of a child makes the questions of how does the universe function and what station or power does the individual or community hold within the universe existential and immediate.

These first two characteristics of the spiritual, the experience with transcendent reality and worldview, are in constant interplay. Turner (1969, pp. 94–97) finds both elements in religious rituals. His term for encounter and merger with transcendent reality is *liminality*.[1] In liminal situations, the usual individual and social boundaries are not in effect. People from different racial groups and social classes, for example, can find a unity in prayer that escapes them in the world of politics and economics. Turner's term for order is *communatas*. He says that in communatas individual and social boundaries are discovered, altered, or maintained. In religious ritual, he finds an alternation between these two ways of being. So we may come out of our experience with transcendent reality with a new or changed understanding of the underlying order in our world. We can, of course, also come out

---

[1]From the Latin *limen*, which means door, threshold, or wall. Thus the word signifies both the limits of human existence and also openings between the world of living humans and other worlds.

of our experience with transcendent reality believing more strongly as we did before, though that is less common among bereaved parents for whom the world has fallen apart. We can think of the liminality/communatas relationship, Turner says, as the relationship between *ecstasy,* which literally means standing outside the self, and *ideology,* in which the world and self are defined. Maslow (1964, pp. 91–96) finds a similar interplay in the relationship between peak experience and self-actualization. The peak experience is of nonordinary realities; within the peak experience a person discovers Being values which are guidelines to living a more integrated and authentic life.

Belongingness in a Community

The third characteristic of the spiritual is that we feel ourselves to belong to a community in which we are bonded to others at our essential human core. Our spiritual life is within our community membership (Durkheim, 1915, 1951). The root of the word "religion" means "to bind." In the study of comparative religions, the binding is usually considered to be the social bond, because it is the shared vision of the underlying order of the visible world and the shared vision of the realities in other worlds that binds a society together. Every religious tradition stresses membership in a community that transcends ordinary human boundaries: *Sanga* in Buddhism, the *congregation* in Protestant Christianity, the *Ummah* in Islam. At every outbreak of spiritual fervor, communities spring up. Christian and Buddhist mystics form monasteries; converts at Protestant revivals form themselves into churches. True spirituality creates communities. As a few alcoholics began to find sobriety within a 12-step spiritual program under the leadership of Bill W., they found that they wanted to be with each other, so the meetings began. "They knew that they had a host of new friends; it seemed they had known these strangers always. They had seen miracles, and one was to come to them" (Alcoholics Anonymous, 1976, p. 161).

Community is the most difficult and paradoxical aspect of spirituality, because religious communities function as the keepers and transmitters of the symbols by which spiritual reality is perceived and expressed. But too often those same religious institutions turn spirit into letter. The rules of the underlying order of the universe can be discovered and embraced in joyful freedom, but the rules can also be enforced externally in ways that crush the individual spirit. The awe and wonder we feel when we encounter the reality of the unseen can be turned into fear and foreboding. The guidance we find in a worldview can be shaped in a way that it is put in the service of political leaders and religious authorities. The spiritual sense of community becomes intertwined with our sense of tribal or ethnic identity, and inside the tribe or ethnic community, it becomes intertwined with power/hierarchy interactions. Thus, the same religious symbols that underpin our sublime mystical moments also justify racial, ethnic, and nationalist aspirations. Within every tribe or nation religious symbols legitimate the political and economic power of the standing order (see Roberts, 1992).

Still, our spiritual life cannot be lived alone. If we feel at one with the divine and in touch with the basic order of the universe, but the experience does not bring us into communion with at least some of our fellow human beings, we have the symptoms, says James Hillman (1986, pp. 46–56), of paranoia. We are living in a pseudo community, that is, a community of people who are only in our imagination. Without community, the spiritual life is Buber's *I* without the *Thou*. As H. Richard Niebuhr said,

> Every view of the universal from the finite standpoint of the individual . . . is subject to the test of experience on the part of companions who look from the same standpoint in the same direction as well as to the test of consistency with the principles and concepts that have grown out of past experience in the same community (1962, pp. 20–21).

The community is so central to the spiritual journey of bereaved parents in this book that we will begin our description of their journey by looking at the transformation of their lives within the self-help process. The self-help group is a temporary community for the members. Parents only stay in Bereaved Parents for a few years, and then, unless they decide to stay and help, they move on with their lives and integrate the ways they have changed into their larger community memberships. Perhaps a more fluid and free community can form in the existentially transforming moment than can form in longer lasting social contexts. Perhaps the authentic community we see in Bereaved Parents is like the authenticity we see at the beginnings of religions. Perhaps, if the groups were to move from charisma and human interactions to institutionalization and authority, we would see dry doctrine rather than spiritual transformation. Fortunately, I got acquainted with Bereaved Parents when the group was new. I saw that the pain the parents feel could not be accepted in many of the social networks to which parents belong, so they began their own. The community we will see is neither paranoid or authoritarian. It is a vital community that thrives because it delivers healing to people who turn to them in deep pain.

Three Characteristics of Spirituality in Religious Traditions

The three characteristics of spiritual experience that we have found, then, are: first, a sense of encounter or merger with that which is beyond the self; second, an adoption of a worldview, that is, a higher intelligence, purpose or order to which we can conform our life; and third, a sense of bonding with others within a community. We can see this triune definition of the spiritual life in many religious traditions. Buddhism has the three refuges: the Buddha, the Dharma, and the Sanga. Christianity affirms the trinity of God the father who is unknowable in Himself, God the son, who is in human form, and God the holy spirit, who is the giver of understanding and the undergirder of the church. In Islam, Allah is the God who can be found but cannot be understood by human intelligence, the Prophet Mohammed was given the revelation to which humans should conform their lives, and the Ummah is the community of all those who submit to Allah. In Chinese religion, which is an amalgam of Taoism and Confucianism, Heaven or Ti is the unnameable reality; Tao is the ordering principle in nature and Li is the ordering principle by which humans can find harmony within society. In each of these traditions, the sense of the transcendent, finding purpose, and membership in community are all necessary elements of the spiritual life.

In the resolution of parental grief, we find experience which has the spiritual characteristics we discussed in the first part of this chapter. First, the parent finds, renews, or modifies the bond to that which transcends immediate biological and social reality. This spiritual connection provides solace, or comfort, in a world which is forever diminished. Second, the parent discovers or modifies a worldview which answers the questions of how the world functions and what is the parent's place and power in the world. In the face of the absurdity which the child's death might signify, the parent's worldview allows life to be meaningful and authentic in a world that still seems to have an underlying order. Third, finding solace and affirming a worldview are done within an affiliation to a community in which the parent feels identified and accepted.

☐ The Nature of the Spiritual in Parental Grief

The definition of spiritual as we have discussed so far in this chapter could be applied to the spiritual aspects of any human situation. It is the finger we can point at the moon for everyone. As we try to understand the spiritual issues in parental bereavement, we can focus more narrowly. We can examine the spiritual aspects of being a parent, because the grief that comes after a child dies is grounded in the bond between the parent and the living child. In the next section we will look at the special qualities of parental grief and then at some spiritual aspects in parenting that continue over into parental grief.

Irreparable Loss

Contemporary Western culture, built around winners, purchasable satisfaction, and happy endings, provides few myths or symbols with which to come to terms with the death of a child. Twentieth century myths and symbols protect us from the reality of death. The modern ritual presents cosmetically restored corpses with lifelike shape and color. The funeral, which for most of human history was to ensure safe passage of the dead to the next world is now for the living, to help them recognize their loss and thus begin life without their bond to the deceased person.

> In an era dominated by symbols of entertainment and pleasure, where individuals are neither trained nor equipped to cope with death or grief, the expectation that one copes with one's own grief personally and privately is deeply problematic and places an unrealistic expectation on [those who are] grieving (Moller, 1996, p. 134).

When a child dies, the parent experiences an irreparable loss, because the child is an extension of the parent's self (Benedek, 1959, 1975). Parental bereavement is a permanent condition. Bereaved parents do adjust in the sense that they learn to invest themselves in other tasks and other relationships. Still, somewhere inside themselves, they report, there is a sense of loss that cannot be healed. When Freud's daughter died he wrote,

> Since I am profoundly irreligious there is no one I can accuse, and I know there is nowhere to which any complaint could be addressed. "The unvarying circle of a soldier's duties" and the "sweet habit of existence" will see to it that things go on as before. Quite deep down I can trace the feeling of a deep narcissistic hurt that is not to be healed (in Jones, 1957, p. 20).

One of the psychological tasks of parenting in modernity is to separate the child from the self so the child can be experienced as a separate being (Elson, 1984). Such separation is, however, seldom complete. Parents feel pride in their children's successes, and a child's failure feels to parents like their own failure. When a child dies, a part of the self is cut off. Many parents find the metaphor of amputation useful. In a meeting a father said, "It is like I lost my right arm, but I'm learning to live as a one-armed man." Like amputation, parental bereavement is a permanent condition. The hopes, dreams, and expectations incarnate in the child are now gone. A parent who seems to have had experience with amputees wrote in a newsletter article:

> For the amputee, the raw bleeding stump heals and the physical pain does go away. But he lives with the pain in his heart knowing his limb will not grow back. He has to learn to live without it. He rebuilds his life around his loss. We bereaved parents must do the same.

In a newsletter, a young mother says that she feels as though she is presenting a facade to the rest of the world and only at her child's graveside can she express the self she knows inside. She carefully guards her bond with the child from others, and as she writes, she thinks, "It will never heal . . . I will only wrap it differently with time."

Bereaved parents do find resolution to their grief in the sense that they learn to live in their new world. They "re-solve" the matters of how to be themselves in a family and community in a way that makes life meaningful. They learn to grow in those parts of themselves which did not die with the child. One mother wrote, "Being a bereaved parent will always be a part of our lives—it just won't be the most important or only part." They learn to invest other parts of themselves in other tasks and other relationships. But somewhere inside themselves, they report, there is a sense of loss that remains. A bereaved father wrote in a newsletter:

> If grief is resolved, why do we still feel a sense of loss on anniversaries and holidays and even when we least expect it? Why do we feel a lump in the throat even six years after the loss? It is because healing does not mean forgetting and because moving on with life does not mean that we don't take a part of our lost love with us.

One of the parts of the self that many parents lose when their child dies is the sense that they are linked to the spiritual world. A woman who had two babies die said:

> There's lots of people who go around thinking if they are good then bad things can't happen to them. I just tell them, "It has to happen to somebody." I don't pray in church anymore. I go because you are supposed to. How can I tell the children to go to church if I don't? But I don't pray. I just do my grocery list. I think I used to pray and feel close to God. But not anymore. I don't feel anything there.

She does not find the presence of God in her solitude as she once did. But her living children should go to church, for that is a rule. And if she is to enforce the rule, she, too, must follow it. God still reigns supreme in her superego and in her family system, because there is still a need to maintain external order in the world. But for now, the God, who was a living reality before her children died, is dead in her soul.

As scholars have come to understand grief better in the last decade they have begun developing models of grief which account for the continuing bond between the deceased and the survivor (see Klass, Silverman, and Nickman, 1996). Still, any concept of deep and abiding pain at the heart of the human condition has been abandoned by modern social science. Because contemporary culture does not easily include the idea of irreparable loss, it is very difficult for contemporary bereaved parents to use the spiritual frameworks in which humans have cast their grief for most of human history. Over the course of the twentieth century, grief has changed from being regarded as a core part of the human condition, and has been reconceptualized as a psychological process which is painful, but which, when the work is done, restores the survivor to *status quo ante.*

"Rather than focusing on essential religious truths and experiences," say Simonds and Rothman in their study on popular literature written for grieving people over the last 150 years, books or articles in the middle and late twentieth century, "report on scientific or pseudo-scientific research about grief, legitimating and validating the grief itself" (1992, p. 158). This psychological view of grief, they say, reduces the bereaved parents' experience to "stages or temporary feelings. Thus anger, and to a lesser extent, guilt, are dealt with not in substantive ways but only as transient feeling states—to be experienced and then surpassed" (p. 161).

> Conceptualizing the grieving process as if the emotions could be sorted and as if time guaranteed the safe and easy passage from one stage to another, marginalizes and trivializes the people who experience it (p. 163).

The myths or symbols of winners, purchasable satisfaction, and happy endings that so dominate contemporary culture do not speak to the irreparable loss experienced by the woman who does her grocery list in church, nor do the psychological theories of stages and feelings. If we are to understand the spiritual lives of bereaved parents adequately, we will do so within the context of pain and suffering that cannot be fixed.

Parenting as a Spiritual Bond

Bereaved parents cannot escape the religious and spiritual realities in death, because the child is one of the bonds parents have with sacred reality. There is something in the adult's bond with the child and the child's bond with the parent that is akin to the bond we feel with the larger invisible realities. Indeed, when we think about how humankind has tried to describe the spiritual life, we find parenting as the most common symbol for connection between humans and their gods.

From the earliest cultural artifacts to the present, we find evidence that the parent-child bond is likened to the bond between humans and gods. We do not know much about the spiritual life of humans before about fifty thousand years ago, but we know that in Europe and the Middle East, from very early times statues and carvings of women with large stomachs, hips, and breasts were common. These were the Great Mother. She was the earth, related somehow to the crescent shaped cow horn and to the moon. About ten thousand years ago, the development of agriculture allowed permanent cities to be built. Lands could be captured and held by armies. Society was organized by male hierarchies because some men could specialize in the warrior role. The power passed to the male gods, but the parent-child symbol remained. The mother goddesses were repressed, and male father gods, incarnate in warrior kings, took the world stage. In Egypt the sun god was Ra. The earthly ruler was Pharaoh, literally, the son of Ra. More recently, about two thousand years ago, Jesus, who was called the "Son of God," taught a prayer to his followers that begins, "Our Father who art in heaven." On another part of the planet, Master Kung, known in the West (where all wise men had Latin names) as Confucius, taught that the benevolence of the father and the pious obedience of the son were the best ethics on which to base a government that could protect civilization against chaos. In some places the goddess remains. In a Kali temple in India where I had been taken to perform some rituals, I was staring at a painting of a decapitated male body from which fountains of blood shot up, when my hostess came behind me and said softly, "Kali is like your mother. Her anger can be strong, but when she is angry at you, it is because she loves you."

A common explanation in the middle of the twentieth century for the connection between spirituality and parenting was psychoanalytic theory that says all spirituality is grounded in the desire to regress to primary infantile narcissism, that is, to the sense of unity with the world that the infant feels at the mother's breast (Freud, 1961, pp. 19–20). For psychoanalytic theory, our spiritual life is a continuation of the basic trust we first experienced in the undifferentiated bond with our mother (Erikson, 1963, pp. 250–251; for a good contemporary discussion of the psychoanalytic theory of spirituality see Pals, 1996, pp. 54–87). Psychoanalytic theory, however, is difficult to apply to parental bereavement because it assumes that in our spiritual life we always play the part of the child, never the parent. In Bereaved Parents, the child has died and the parent's caregiving instincts are left without an appropriate object. Spirituality need not be reduced to a regression into the parent's own infantile bond with the mother. Humans understood spirituality in a fuller way when they began using parenting as a symbol for sacred reality. It feels different to be a parent than to be a child. Parents report that when a child dies the grief is different than when a parent dies. We would probably, therefore, do better to look beyond psychoanalytic theory as we try to understand the spirituality inherent in parenting.

Central to the spiritual reality of parental grief is the loss of one of the parent's hopes for immortality. Parents feel the bond with the child as a connection that transcends death. When we are confronted with the undeniable fact that each of us will die, one of the ways we can be certain to live on is in our children. Parents hope their children will live out the parent's best self, that the child will fulfill their dreams, and in doing so, will carry on the parent's life after the parent has died. When a child is born, the father and mother take their place in the genealogical succession. In some cultures genealogical immortality is the most important kind of life after death. So child rearing and ancestor veneration go hand in hand. For prophets of the Old Testament, the barren woman was the symbol of the nation bereft of its God. Lineage and pedigree are less important in modernity, where marriage has become primarily an emotional bond with a self-chosen mate. Today, as divorcing parents make new couplings that meet their individual economic and intimacy needs, the parent-child bond often seems like the only relationship that endures.

In every culture, parenting is linked with central spiritual truths. At the birth of a child, the bond between human beings and sacred reality is renewed. Every tradition has rituals in which the birth of a child is connected with transcendent reality. The first words whispered into a Muslim child's ear are the *Shadah*, "There is no God but God." Those should also be the last words a person hears before they die. In the *bris*, a Jewish boy child is circumcised, the sign, given to Abraham nearly 4,000 years ago, of the covenant between God and Israel. Christians baptize or dedicate their child as a sign of God's grace. In agricultural religions, the fertility of the land and human fertility participated in the same sacred reality. Among the complex rituals at childbirth in central India, for example, the new mother blesses the family water supply by placing her hands on the family water pots. Her symbolic extension of fertility stresses the creative powers of the female, the *Shakti*, the consort or female aspect of the gods. The new mother places the ritual offerings into the well, draws some water in the household water pots, and carries it home. This becomes a symbolic extension of the fertility of the new mother to the rest of the village (Jacobson, 1980).

From the parents' point of view, then, the bond with their child symbolizes their larger bond with transcendent reality in many ways. When a child dies, the parent loses that sacred connection, thus one of the spiritual tasks faced by bereaved parents is either to reestablish or to create a new connection. We will see how parents accomplish that task in our discussion of the continuing bonds parents have with their dead children.

Parenting and Higher Spiritual Development

Parenting is an expression of the higher spiritual development of human evolution. With rare pathological exceptions, we parent with the best part of ourselves because higher levels of spirituality are built into our genetic inheritance. If we think of human evolution, it is easy to see that the sacred quality of the bond between parent and child is grounded in the fact that parenting is the key to the survival of our species. The oldest human footprints discovered so far are of an adult holding a child's hand as they walked across wet ash from a volcano erupting nearby. The three and a half million year old footprints were found by Mary Leaky in Laetoli in Tanzania. The people who made the footprints were a somewhat different kind of human than we. They were *australopitecines*, perhaps an ancestor of ours, or perhaps a branch of our family tree with no survivors. They probably had not learned to control fire, and they disappear from the fossil record before they could invent atomic bombs or cigarettes, but they walked upright and they took care of their kids.

In his study of the evolution of human instinctual life, Paul Gilbert says that the major challenge to human social life is the interplay between individualistic, power seeking instincts that developed early in vertebrate evolution and cooperative behavior, including parenting's care-eliciting and caregiving, which evolved later.

> Love, after all, is not a mystical something that someone is lucky enough to buy, inherit, or is God given. It is a creation of the most phylogenetically advanced possibilities of humankind which is actualized in relationships (1992, p. 196).

When we talk about instincts, we are talking about worldview and the meaning people make of their lives, because instincts are not simply the basis for action, they are also the basis of perception. In the computer metaphor, instincts act in real time. That is, a situation is perceived in terms of the instinctual system under which a person is operating. A person largely governed by the drive to dominance is conscious of other people in terms of strengths and weaknesses, and assumes that other people are using the same standard of evaluation. A person governed by cooperation and caregiving is more aware of cues given by other people that suggest the others wish to join in community or that the others are willing to care or be taken care of. Our worldview forms our way of being-in-the-world. Thus, when we think about the instincts on which parenting is based, we are talking about the basic worldview questions: How does the world function and what is my place and power in the world?

Competition, both for natural resources and for access to mates, that evolved earlier is primarily individualistic behavior directed toward power and dominance. Cooperative behaviors do not replace competitive instincts, but are added to them. So, the cooperation must still compromise and integrate with the earlier competitive instincts. All human cultures have developed rules of justice that appeal to religious authority in order to ensure that cooperation remains possible. When either individuals or social systems are under stress, competitive instincts may very well override cooperation and care-eliciting or care-giving. Still, parenting remains among the strongest elements of our cooperative heritage. We find, in stressful times, that parents put competitive instincts in the service of caring for the child. Individual and social systems must be under extreme stress before parents abandon their children in order to care only for their own individual needs. Parenting, then, is on the more highly evolved side of the struggle between competition and cooperation.

Emotions and thoughts are different in spirituality grounded on domination and competition than in spirituality grounded in cooperation and caregiving. When dominance is won, the feeling of elation is strong. This elation is for some people a spiritual feeling that they have conquered in the name of their god or that their god has given them the victory. The new dominant male, the conquering hero, is often regarded as god-like, whether it be in the executive boardroom or on the athletic field. The problem with spiritual feelings and thoughts based in competition is that the feelings and thoughts are hard to sustain. Dominance must be constantly defended and so is maintained uneasily by constantly evaluating threats and defending against attack or criticism and against the self-evaluation of powerfulness.

Competition does not lead to growth into more highly developed spirituality.

Parenting at its best is not about competition, but about the higher central values humans have developed over our evolutionary history. We can easily see that at their best, all spiritual traditions have favored the cooperative parts of our heritage over the competitive parts. Spiritual or religious traditions support cooperation and caregiving, and they attempt to control individualistic striving for power. The teaching that we should do to others as we would have done to us is found in some form in all the major religious traditions as is the value on love and compassion rather than aggression toward others. In many religious traditions the higher spiritual life includes withdrawal from the competitive world. Though his followers have had difficulty duplicating it, Jesus rejected divine kingship in favor of a very high form of caregiving—suffering on behalf of others.

Apparently the evolution toward caregiving spirituality and away from spirituality based in domination has been a difficult task in our collective psyche. Parenting has not escaped the complex intermixture of the competitive instincts and the cooperative instincts. Both gods and goddesses have demanded that they alone may assume the role of all-powerful parents. They have demanded complete submission and child-like obedience from their subjects. Like dominant human beings, the gods were constantly on the alert for small signs of rebellion. They have called upon their worshipers to offer blood, body parts, and sacrificial death. At times the parental gods and goddesses have demanded that their subjects sacrifice their own children as propitiation for divine anger or as a guarantee of further divine protection. Even today, submission to divine will is one of the easy (but unhelpful) answers offered by uncomfortable friends to bereaved parents: "It is God's will, and you have to accept it;" or worse, "God loved your child so much that He took her back."

In parenting, the dynamics of individual competition and individual power are transformed in a way that is ascribed to God in many traditions. The caregiver is powerful, while the one who receives care is subordinate and less powerful. Indeed it feels, in the child's heteronomy, as if the parent is all-powerful. Parents often feel an enhanced self-esteem as they sense themselves reflected in their child's dependence. In the parent-child relationship, caregiving is altruism, acting for the good of the other, not for the good of the self. Parenting is the exact opposite of power seeking. While being a parent brings a high degree of self-satisfaction, at its best, parenting is the most enduring form of altruism and so connects us with the best in each of the religious or spiritual traditions. In the contemporary West, most parents try to emulate the love of God, not the wrath of God in their bond with their children.

For many people, the birth of their child is an occasion for self-reflection, for vowing to be a better person, for a transformation in the meaning of life from power and acquisition to caring and nurturing. After the death of their child, parents often are overwhelmed by depression, anger, resentment, shame, envy, humiliation and self-doubt, that is, in the feelings and thoughts found in losers of the competitive struggle (see Nietzsche, 1967, pp. 24–56). Sometimes parents regress to the elementary emotional life of the competitive instincts. One of the challenges faced by bereaved parents, then, is to regain a cooperative life, to find ways in which the caregiving they gave their child can be transformed into forms which maintain the parents in the higher parts of the genetic inheritance. We will see, especially in the chapter on community, the ways in which parents meet this challenge. If there is a central message in the Bereaved Parents self-help process it is that the best way to heal grief is to help others. In forming a self-help group, the parents in this book have opted to find the resolution of parental grief in the spiritual resources of the bond they had with their living child. In these words from the "Credo" of the Compassionate Friends self-help group, we can hear the sense of community with other bereaved parents within the bonds to their dead children:

> We reach out to each other with love, with understanding and with hope. Our children have died at all ages and from many different causes, but our love for our children unites us. . . . Whatever pain we bring to this gathering of The Compassionate Friends, it is pain we will share just as we share with each other our love for our children.

☐ Parents' Continuing Bond with Their Child

On Angels, Saints, and Bodhisattvas

While both Eastern and Western traditions build their philosophies and mystical traditions on the direct experience of transcendent reality, in both we find beings who bridge the gap between transcendent reality and everyday reality because they participate in both realms. The spirituality of lay people is often more concerned with these mediating beings than with the high gods or with less accessible spiritual entities. In the Western traditions angels and saints connect heaven and earth. In Buddhism the bodhisattvas move between levels of reality or between the worlds. The largest Mahayana Buddhist sects are

Pure Land, in which devotion to Amida is the central reality around which ritual is built. In Chinese religions, the Shen are beings who reside in heaven, but with whom humans can interact directly.

The spirits of the dead are among the mediating beings in both Eastern and Western spiritual traditions. Elaine Pagels, one of the leading contemporary scholars in religious studies, found that her bond with her dead husband allowed her to understand the relationship between humans and spiritual entities in the ancient world.

> In 1988, when my husband of twenty years died in a hiking accident, I became aware that, like many people who grieve, I was living in the presence of an invisible being—living, that is, with a vivid sense of someone who had died. . . . In the ancient Western world, of which I am a historian, many—perhaps most—people assumed that the universe was inhabited by invisible beings whose presence impinged upon the visible world and its human inhabitants (1995, p. xv).

In some cultures, only a few of the spirits of the dead are available for interaction. For example, in Islam, the tombs of Sufi saints are a focal point in local devotion. In Orthodox and Roman Catholic Christianity, it is easier to communicate through a saint who has a particular interest in the devotee's problem than to communicate directly with God. The Sufi and Christian saints once lived as humans, but they became so well developed spiritually that they became immortal. In some other cultures, virtually all the dead, not just the saints, are available to the living. In Japan, for example, dead ancestors are available to the living as aids in present difficulties and as mediators of the sacred. Ancestors are the spirits of those who are individually remembered by the living. After that, the dead become part of the generalized family dead (Smith, 1974; Plath, 1964; Gilday, 1993; Klass, 1996).

In the Western religious traditions, historical scholarship seems to show that the more authoritarianism is introduced into religion, the more interaction between the bereaved and the dead is likely to be restricted or tightly controlled. For example, in the middle ages, as Rome extended its control over the Church in central Europe, the cults of the saints became less local and became centered on saints important to Rome. The doctrine of purgatory was developed and resulted in contact between the living and the dead being mediated almost exclusively through Church sacraments (see Geary, 1994, pp. 89–92; Finucane, 1996, pp. 49–89). Contemporary scholarship seems to indicate that in ancient Israel before the Deutronomic reform (621 BCE) ritualized interaction with the family ancestors was common. But in the reform, all such veneration was to be given to God alone, and, thereafter, the dead "were doomed to a meaningless existence in the eternal darkness of Sheol" (McDannel and Lang, 1990, p. 11; also see Bloch-Smith, 1992).

After each era in which interaction with the dead is suppressed, contact with the dead returns in a form that either supports, or at least does not offend, the religious and political establishment. For example, interaction with the dead was ended in the Protestant reformation as purgatory was denied and the saints devalued. But a few centuries later, when Protestant Christianity was under siege by scientific rationalism, Protestants used Spiritualism, with its ethereal ghosts and messages from beyond the grave, to argue that, even if transcendent reality could not fit into the new scientific worldview, the presence of the dead proved that a truer transcendent reality could be known in intuition and feeling.

Spirituality and the Bond with the Deceased

Bereaved parents' spiritual experience of transcendent reality, establishing or maintaining a worldview, and affiliating with a healing community are all intimately intertwined with the parents' continuing bond with their dead child. Just as the parents' bond with the living child was part of their bond with the transcendent, and just as the bond with the child activates the most highly evolved human interactions, so too the spirituality in parental bereavement is intertwined with the parent's bond to the child. Like angels and bodhisattvas, the spirits of dead children bridge the gap between transcendent reality and everyday reality because they participate in both realms.

In their continuing bonds, parents no longer have an outer relationship with the children. Instead, they maintain the children as an inner representation that they can call on in difficult times, which comforts them in their sorrow and provides a means by which they can access their better self in their new and poorer world. We have inner representations of a living person that are constantly being reinforced or modified by our continued interaction with the person. When someone dies, we stop seeing and touching them with our bodies, and our conversations with the person no longer include her or his objective otherness. But the person is still a part of us, and our conversations with the person can continue.

Inner representations of deceased people, then, are complex and dynamic elements of our selves and of the world we have constructed. The representations are not simply pictures, ideas, or feelings. Inner representation is our full experience of who that person was to us when they lived, and who the person continues to be to us now. In her definition of children's representation of parents, Ana-Marie Rizzuto said:

> The term is meant to include the totality of experiential levels gathered in the course of growing up under a given name, whether it be father, mother, self, or God. Representation of people always include visceral, proprioceptive, sensorimotor, perceptual, eidetic, and conceptual components (1982, p. 359).

The contents of the inner representation are the characterizations or thematic memories we have of the person. But the representation also includes those parts of ourselves that are actualized in our interaction with that person. And the representation includes the emotional states connnected with our characterizations and memories, and connected to those parts of ourselves that we knew best in our relationship to that person. In their continuing bonds with their dead children, bereaved parents are again who they were with their children when the children were living; and, for the parents, the children are again who the living children were with the parents. As William James said:

> Such is the human ontological imagination, and such is the convincingness of what it brings to birth. Unpicturable beings are realized, and realized with an intensity almost like that of an hallucination. They determine our vital attitude as decisively as the vital attitude of lovers is determined by the habitual sense, by which each is haunted, of the other being in the world. A lover has notoriously this sense of the continuous being of his idol, even when his attention is addressed to other matters and he no longer represents her features. He cannot forget her; she uninterruptedly affects him through and through (1958, p. 71).

Phenomena which indicate interaction with the inner representation of a deceased person are: a sense of presence; seeing, hearing, smelling, touching, or talking to the deceased; belief in the person's continuing active influence on thoughts or events; or incorporation of the characteristics or virtues of the dead into the self. These phenomena, like other spiritual experiences, have about them a sense of the uncanny, a sense of mystery, wonder, and awe (see Dawson, 1989). It feels to the parent as if the child is still active in the parent's world. Although they fully know that the child is dead, parents also know that the child remains immortal.

These phenomena may be experienced in altered states of consciousness. Parents often use phrases like, "It was like a dream." Or they may be experienced in ordinary states of consciousness and accepted as part of the everyday world. Interaction may be consciously sought or it may seem to come unbidden. Interaction with the inner representation of the dead may be continuous with the self or the interaction may seem apart from the self-representation as the parent says that having such thoughts and feelings is "just not like me."

Interactions within the continuing bond with the dead child have the character of both outer and inner reality. It is not simply an objective presence, for the meaning of the experience is strongly personal. Neither can it be said to be simply subjective. Many parents in the study argue strongly against reducing the experience to a psychic reality, or as one person said, "Don't tell me that this is just in my head." Yet, at the same time, they are usually able to grant that the meaning of the child's presence is very personal and not necessarily applicable to other people's lives.

The message and meaning of the interaction with their dead children are self-evident to the bereaved parent. It does not matter to these parents whether, with the help of the spirits of the dead, parapsychologists can bend spoons. Their children appear, act, speak, and influence. The intense meanings they feel within the bond with their child are quite apart from rational proof or disproof.

Inner representations of the dead and continuing bonds are not simply individual matters. They are maintained and reinforced within families and other social systems. The dead child is often a part of the bond within the family and is an integral element of the bond between members of the Bereaved Parents. Parents consciously work to maintain the bond with the child in their own lives and in the communities that are important to them. Several families do this by including the picture of the dead child on family portraits made after the child's death. Others do it by consciously evoking the memory of the child on significant occasions. We can see the inner representation of the child stabilizing in the parent's life as it becomes stabilized in the family in a mother's report on herself written four years after her son's death:

> I am just now learning to include my son into my life in a way that comforts me. Emily goes with me to the cemetery, and we talk about life and death. At four, she is curious about her little brother. . . . I never expected sibling rivalry; and at other times she surprised me with her fiercely protective reactions. As she grows, Jason becomes more real to her; as he becomes more real to her, he become more precious and more real to us all.

A father who strongly participated in the pregnancy wrote about the continuity he feels between the bond he had with the child in "my" womb and the bond he now feels with the child who never lived. Though the child was stillborn, for the father the child is "born still."

> But you lived for me all the time in the dark chamber of my womb, and when I think of you now, perfect in your little death, I know that for me

you are born still; I shall carry you with me forever, my child, you were always mine, you are mine now.

In the resolution of their grief, parents maintain the bond with their dead child, albeit in new forms. Maintaining a bond in the resolution of grief, as opposed to doing grief work to break the bond with the deceased, will strike some readers as pathological because for most of the twentieth century the purpose of grief has been seen as withdrawing emotional energy from the deceased, thereby freeing the survivor to make new attachments in the present. It is clear, however, from historical research and from psychological research on the survivors of many kinds of death, that people do not do as the theory said they should, and that their continuing bonds with the dead are resources for creative, healthy living in the present (see Klass, Silverman, and Nickman, 1996).

☐ Conclusion

In our attempt to define "spiritual" we have ranged from the world's mystic traditions to evolutionary psychology. The range has been so wide because, except for those people at the concrete operations developmental level, there is no separate sphere that can be called spiritual as opposed to everyday reality. Like depth perception or color vision, the spiritual aspect of our own experience and the experience of others is an aspect of reality that we can choose to see or to ignore. Neither have we been able to separate *spiritual* from *religion*. The reality known in spiritual moments is perceived using symbols from religious traditions and maintained over time using symbols, rituals, and affiliations that have a religious character.

We found three characteristics that could be applied to all the world's religious traditions and be useful in understanding the lives of real people living real lives. The three characteristics are: (1) Encountering or mergering with transcendent reality; (2) Finding a worldview, that is, a higher intelligence, purpose, or order which gives meaning; and (3) Belonging to a community in which transcendent reality and worldview are validated. Those three characteristics will be the basis of the next three chapters.

Then we turned to look at the spiritual aspects of the parent-child bond. We noted that the parent-child relationship is the most common symbol for the relationship between humans and the divine. In their bond with their child, parents feel connected to transcendent reality and the defining values of the society. From an evolutionary point of view, parenting is an expression of instincts toward cooperation and caring that developed later than did our individualistic instincts toward competition and dominance. We noted that all the world's religious traditions, at their best, support cooperation and caring as opposed to competition and domination.

Finally we looked at a special form of spirituality that we will see as central in bereaved parents: the continuing bond parents maintain with their dead children. For many parents, their children function like angels, saints, and bodhisattvas in the world's religious traditions, bridging the gap between transcendent and everyday reality because they participate in both realms.

As we have attempted in this chapter to find a definition of spirituality adequate to the many religious traditions of humankind, adequate to the awful reality of a child's death, and adequate to describe the journey parents make toward resolution, we have found ourselves not in a separate realm. Rather we have found ourselves in the midst of a web of bonds and meanings. The spiritual lives of bereaved parents are played out within this web, within a series of mutually interdependent bonds and meanings that are in constant interplay.

> How the universe works
> Place and power of the self
> Bond with the child
> Bond with transcendent reality
> Meaning of parent's life
> Meaning of the child's death
> Community/family membership

We can diagram the web as follows.

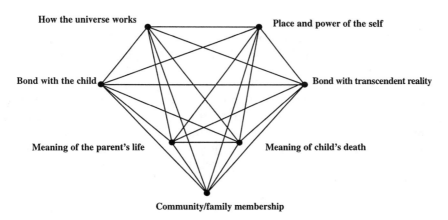

FIGURE 2.1. Spiritual lives are played out in a web of bonds and meanings. If any one of these bonds and meanings change, there is a corresponding change in each of the other bonds and meanings.

There is no spiritual realm that does not include the physical, the biological, the social, and cognitive realms. As our eyes have followed the finger pointing to the moon in this chapter, we have found ourselves pointing to the complex web of interconnecting processes. We will find the spiritual lives of bereaved parents within this web of bonds and meanings. If any one of these bonds and meanings change, there is a corresponding change in each of the other bonds and meanings. For example, the meaning of the child's death is found within the larger question of how the universe works. If the parent cannot make sense of the child's death, then the parent's understanding of how the universe works needs to be modified to accommodate the new reality. The place and power of the self in the universe and the meaning of the parent's life are often defined in terms of a long-standing sense of connectedness in the bond with the transcendent and in terms of community and family membership. The bond with the child is often felt as continuous with the parent's bond with the transcendent. If the parent feels cut off from God, the meaning of the parent's life, the quality of community bonds, the bond with the child, and the place and power of the self in the universe and in the community must be recast. When bereaved parents find a community in which their grief can be expressed and in which their bond with their dead child seems to be socially real, then the universe may seem to work in a new and better way and their bond with transcendent reality may seem more sure. As they learn to use the bond with their dead child to live more creatively in their world, they may develop a new and stronger sense of their place and power in the universe.

For the next three chapters we will look closely at the spiritual life of bereaved parents. We will look at community bonds first, because it is within community that the transformations of parental grief happen. Then, we will look at parents' experience of transcendent reality. We will find that transcendence is largely found in the continuing bond with the child and that the bond brings solace in a world made forever poorer by the death of the child. Finally, we will examine how parents maintain or rework their worldview in the face of the reality that their child has died. It would be nice if our tour through parental bereavement would lead us to a purer, more wonderful world where we could stand inspired. But like the parents' journey toward healing, our journey toward understanding will happen only when we open ourselves to their pain.

Community and the Transformation of the Parent-Child Bond

She died in late winter, a few months before her 17th birthday. Not knowing what else to do in the haze of their early grief, her mother and father did their usual spring work on the flower gardens around the house. The second spring, as they were buying bedding plants they saw a concrete angel. They looked at each other and with hardly a word exchanged, they knew they should buy it for the garden in the front yard. Somehow the angel reminded them of their dead daughter. Sometimes, as they passed the angel on the way into the house, it seemed to them that the angel was smiling, and at those moments they felt connected with their daughter. It was important, the mother said, that the angel was in the front flower garden, because she wanted their angel/child in plain view. They wanted others to remember the child, and they wanted others to know that their daughter was still a part of their individual lives and a part of their family. The neighbors were sympathetic, though, mostly, the concrete angel in front of the house marked the boundary between the world of bereaved parents and the *civilian* world. When most neighbors saw it they reminded themselves that such a tragedy couldn't happen to them, and sometimes they remembered how uncomfortable they felt as they groped for words when they met the parents at the mall. Some people were able to step across the boundary line and be part of the parents' world. High school friends developed the custom of waving goodbye to the angel when they left the house after they came to visit as they had before their friend died. The parents were thrilled when their daughter's best friend asked if she could include a rose from the angel garden in her wedding bouquet. A neighbor whose sister had died when she was young became a close friend in a way she had not been before. Other bereaved parents understood, and told about their own symbols of their dead children, and how they did not fit into the neighborhood in the old way either.

☐ Introduction: Death, Loss, and Continuing Bonds

The Anatomy of Pain

After a child dies, the parents are in incredible pain. The pain has two interconnected sources. First, the child is gone; a piece of themselves is missing; their every day interactions with the child will never happen again. Second, the parents know death in a way they have not known it before.

First, the child who was a center part of their lives is no longer there. They will never hug the child as they read bedtime stories. They will never banter about whose baseball team is better or whether the music is too loud. The reciprocal quality of the bond with the child has ceased. They speak, but the child does not answer. They listen, but hear only silence. Everything that they did with the child, they now do without the child. What they did because of the child, they no longer do. "She was always hanging around the kitchen when I cooked dinner, and she was just starting to be able to help," one mother said at a meeting. "The family really got tired of frozen dinners after a while, but that's all I could handle." Another said, "I used to take off work early for her soccer games. Now I work late and try not to think about it." Parents report that they are exhausted, but, when they lay down to sleep, their mind is flooded with images and feelings that keep them awake. "I can remember the feeling in the early morning," a mother said, "when I would awaken and think that everything was all right, and then the reality of the situation would hit me like a brick wall." She said she had four or five migraine headaches a week. Her physician prescribed antidepressants and antianxiety drugs, but with the drugs, "the veil over life became even heavier."

There is an empty place in their soul that will never be filled. At first, everything reminds them that the child is gone: room, clothes, television programs, vacation photographs, meal time, shortened shopping lists, and especially holidays. As grief matures, parents become habituated to the everyday reminders. It is not that it doesn't hurt, but pain is integrated into their daily routine in a way that it is hardly noticeable. But what one parent described as "potholes," things that sharply remind them of the child and of the reality that the child is dead, remain. The parents are just going about their business when out of the blue something "brings it all back" and it is as if the death were yesterday. "You just can't predict what it will be," one mother said. "It could be a song on the radio or just some kid wearing a sweater like hers, and pow, there you are knocked off your feet again, and just when you thought you were getting better." Sometimes the pain cycles with the calender. A father whose son was killed in a car accident Friday night, the 15th of the month, said that he became more emotionally volatile during the week as Friday approached, and increasingly volatile as the fifteenth of the month approached. "When the fifteenth fell on a Friday I was a basket case," he said.

Even years after the child's death, what would have been significant events in the child's life bring back the pain. Newsletters in the fall always have reflections on watching other children go for the first day of school. A father whose son had been dead for three years said he found himself looking intently at the faces of the graduates in the procession expecting that his son would be in the line. Birthdays and death anniversaries are important days, though often, as the years go by, parents find themselves marking the day alone.

The second source of pain is somewhat less distinct. Now they know death and knowing death puts them in a whole new relationship to life. Most people know about death, and have a fascination with it that keeps their fears at bay. Local television news is a daily dose of fatal accidents, the results of street violence, medical news on how to live longer, and reports from the eternal youth of sports. But when a child dies, the parent does not just know about death, the parent knows death. Children can die. It can happen to them. Now the news is no longer pictures, but people like themselves with cameras in their faces during their worst moments. Bereaved parents are no long protected by the illusion that death only happens to other people.

Suddenly, to others, the parents represent the reality that children do die. Bereaved parents live at odds with a world that denies death, that deems a corpse socially acceptable only after it has been cosmetically *restored*. Newly bereaved parents find themselves bombarded with messages that it is not as bad as others fear: "You are doing so well. I don't think I could handle that." As if the bereaved parent can, or has the choice. People feel crazy when the world does not appear to them as it does to the larger society. It takes some time before bereaved parents realize that what they know is true: that children die; and that people who think it can't happen to them are living a delusion. The question of who is crazy is a hard one for bereaved parents who live in a culture that reinforces the delusion so strongly.

Life After a Child's Death

After a child dies, the parents must learn how to be bereaved parents, that is, how to go on with the essential parts of life when they can no longer predict how they will respond in social situations, when they often feel alienated from those around them because their reality is so different and because their presence makes others uncomfortable. "You know why I come to these Bereaved Parent meetings?" a man asked me. "Because once in a while it is nice to feel like everybody else." Children's birthdays are still important, and as we will learn, parents learn to celebrate them differently.

Seemingly simple things, like what to say when a new acquaintance asks, "How many children do you have?" reach deeply into the pain. For the person asking, it is just everyday information. For the bereaved parent, however, it raises the profounder question, what does it mean to have a child? If they exclude the dead child from the answer, they have denied that the child remains real to them. If they include the child they face the possibility that the other person will retreat in the face of the parent's pain or that the death and grief will intrude into other matters between the parent and the new person. Bereaved parents need strategies to protect themselves from falling apart in those moments, so parents devise functional guidelines for themselves. One woman, for example, said that if the new person might be a continuing relationship, she says, "I *had* three." If the other person picks up on the past tense, it is up to the other person to ask what it means. Often that is enough, because other people back away from discomfort without being aware they are doing so. But if the other person asks about the children, she tells about the living ones first and then adds, "And my son was killed in a car accident five years ago." Then the other person can choose to acknowledge the death, can focus on the living children, or can withdraw from the conversation. If the new person does not acknowledge the death, the woman puts the person in her "we won't be close" category. If the other person acknowledges the death, then the relationship may turn to friendship, depending on the same factors as she used before her child died. If, however, the other person is not to be a continuing relationship, for example, that person is sitting next to her on an airplane, or if she needs to have a business relationship with the person and the other's discomfort would interfere with her career needs, then she says, "I have two," and gives a short summary of the current status of each of her living children. After bereaved parents have learned their new world the daily glitches become more manageable.

At a deeper level, losing the illusion that death only happens to other people means learning to live in the world less fearful of death, and learning how to integrate the transformed bond with the dead child into the parents' everyday lives. To live less fearfully of death is to live life more fully. When parents say they have grown in their grief, they mean that they have new priorities about what is important to them and what is not. They also mean that their own lives and deaths have meanings that they learned after their child died. One year, three long-time leaders of Bereaved Parents faced their own deaths. For each of them, their response to the prospect of dying was related to the death of their child. Dying was not what they wanted, but it was not the hardest thing they had done. They could come to terms with their own death because they had come to terms with the death of their child. A woman who had cancer said that she wanted to live, but that she had learned in Bereaved Parents that "you never know when death will come." She told me she had gone to a cancer support group, thinking the self-help would be good since she had found the self-help process so useful after her son died. She said that maybe the reality had not hit her yet, but she was "not in the place where the people there are." As people went around the circle, she said, they all said that this was the worst thing that had happened to them and they did not know how to cope with it. "Well, I didn't say it there, but I thought, no, this is not the worst thing that has ever happened to me. I survived that, and I have grown from that. My own death is not so bad. I mean I want to live. I really have a good life. But if this is what I am given, then that's OK." She thinks of herself as having faced the worst. Her child died and she is not overcome by the prospect of her own death.

A man who had led the group during one of its early transition periods was diagnosed with an aggressive cancer that did not respond to treatment. Over the years, he and I had met occasionally for lunch and talked over the meanings of life, especially after his divorce. I talked on the phone with him a week before he died. He wanted me to know that he had fought hard to live after his bypass surgery. But now, he was ready to die. He said, "I just want to go to sleep and not wake up." His thoughts of his own death were also about his dead daughter. He said, "I don't know if I will see Kate and be with her again, but I am not afraid to die now." He said he did not need to talk to me, but that he was concerned about his friend who cared for him in his last days.

At the funeral I talked to a longterm leader who had a brain tumor. He said that he was not afraid of what would happen, and that he was glad that he had the time to get his financial affairs in order for his wife. He said that considering all that the bereaved parents he had met in the group had been through, he did not find this too hard. He said,

> I don't know if you know about this, but I spent a long time after Lenny was murdered angry at God. I would curse Him, even out loud. But I am not doing that at this (the tumor). Maybe I resolved it or something with Lenny, so this is not a time to be angry at God. What comes is what comes. I just take things one day at a time. I know I have survived the worst, so I know I can do this. I have really been impressed at the great support I have gotten from the people in Bereaved Parents. I mean, I learned to express feelings, and they have been wonderful in their expressions of support. I mean, we have been through so much that it is like they understand.

Several months later I remembered my conversations with the Bereaved Parents leaders facing death when I was interviewing American Buddhists about their griefs. The Buddhists said that the truth they found in their grief is the same truth they worked so hard to find in their meditation—that everything is impermanent. As a young man, the Buddha had seen an old man, a sick man, and a dead man and he knew the first Noble Truth he would later teach, that all life is suffering. Within their grief, bereaved parents come to know that noble truth. We all live our lives in the face of death, although most of us live as if we do not know it. For bereaved parents, death has the face of their child, so they live their lives in the face of death differently than they did before.

Continuing Bonds

The couple who put the concrete angel in their front garden ritually symbolized their continuing bond with their dead child and provided a focus for a small community to maintain a bond with the child. These parents were demonstrating that, although bereaved parents know death in a new and profound way, they also know that even if death ends a life, it does not destroy a bond. Their child is dead. The pain will never go away, and, indeed, the pain of parting with their child reaches the bottom of parents' souls. Within their pain, however, the members of Bereaved Parents find that they are bonded with their child in a new way.

Grief has been defined for most of the twentieth century as breaking an attachment. The advice given to bereaved people was to mourn their loss, let go of the dead, and move on to form new attachments in the present. Clinicians assumed, with virtually no supporting data, that grief was pathological or chronic if the bereaved held on to the dead or maintained their bond. The model of successful grief was the young widow who freely expressed her emotions for a few months after she buried her husband, but who then learned to do the things he had done like balance the checkbook or fix broken faucets. After a few years she would be over her grief, as evidenced by a new romantic relationship, preferably with a man whose wife had died about the same time as the widow's husband. Grief after a death was often assumed to be similiar to the grief after a divorce. After all, both were the loss of a relationship. Bereaved parents were judged and treated within the grieve-and-move-on model.

But, the fact is, the members of Bereaved Parents do not detach from their child. They transform the bond in ways that enable them to keep the child as an important element in their lives. My experience with bereaved parents has convinced me that denial is not an element in their grief. They know the child is dead. But as their grief progresses, they find new ways in which the child continues to play an important role in their lives and in their family systems. In this chapter and in the following two chapters, we will be exploring how the parents transform the bond and what roles the bond plays in their life.

Tony Walter says that the purpose or goal of grief is "the construction of a durable biography," both of the dead person and the living person, "that enables the living to integrate the memory of the dead into their ongoing lives; the process by which this is achieved is principally conversations with others who knew the deceased" (1996, p. 7). In the Bereaved Parents, as we will note, the conversation need not be with people who knew the children when they were alive, because one of the core dynamics of the group is that the bond between members includes the bond each has with his or her dead child and grows to include bonds to each other's children. The process of rebuilding their lives after the death of a child is conversation in which the pain of the child's death and the bond with the child are both real. The continuing bond with the child provides solace, the basis for a durable worldview, and the bond within a healing community.

The transformation of the inner representation of the child is, I think, the key to understanding the spiritual lives of bereaved parents. For their parents, when the bond is transformed, children become like angels, saints, or bodhisattvas, that is, beings who mediate between the realm of the sacred and the realm of living humans. The transformation happens in community. We noted in Chapter One, the three characteristics of spirituality are membership in a community, a sense of transcendent reality, and a workable worldview. Because the bond with the child is transformed in community, and because the transformed bond with the child is a central component in solace and in maintaining a worldview, the first characteristic of spirituality we examine in detail is membership in community.

☐ The Transforming Community

This chapter is about community. We will trace the complex interchanges between the continuing bond with the dead child in the parent's psychic world and the continuing bond with the child in the parent's social world. Bereaved parents can feel pain alone, indeed, their pain alienates them from their usual support networks. Learning to live positively with their new knowledge of death, however, and especially transforming the inner representation of the child is a social function. Transformations of the bond with the dead child take place in a community, that is, in a self-help group, it happens in relationship with others. Healing is not an individual task. In the individualism of modernity, we tend to talk about grief as if it were an internal process. Contemporary clinical lore uses a plumbing model of grief: all we need to do is to unblock the natural flow of feelings, and grief will run through to the sewer where we don't have to think about it any more. Grieving is, however, not an individual internal process, it is interpersonal. It happens, as Walter says, in conversation. When the reality of the child's death as well as the reality of the parent's continuing bond with the child are made part of the socially shared reality, the inner representation of the child can be transformed in the parent's psychic life.

The social scientific literature focusing on individuals uses the term *social support*. Social support, however, is not an adequate concept because it implies that the parents are going through an internal process aided by the care and concern of others. Resolving grief takes place within reciprocal interactions between the bereaved parent and the communities of which they are a part. Social support does not convey the reciprocal quality of the interactions by which healing takes place. I think community is a better concept within which to work.

Grief and the resolution of grief, it seems, are an integral element of our social bonds. From an evolutionary point of view, grief is by nature social. Averill (1968) says grief is a biological reaction to ensure group cohesiveness in species where a social form of existence is necessary for survival. Cohesiveness is maintained by making separation from the group, or from specific members of the group, both psychologically and physiologically stressful. Averill argues that grief is a form of altruistic behavior; it is not for the good of the individual, but for the good of the group. He says that behaviors resembling human grief are more likely to be found in species in which groups are based on bonds between individuals (as opposed to aggregations of animals, e.g., birds all breeding on the same cliffs, or anonymous groups, e.g., schools of fish).

Only in the modern world have death and grief become private matters. The deaths of children seldom have public meaning, so parents are left on their own as they try to make sense of their child's death. In Bereaved Parents, members create the social bonds, missing in the modern world, within which they can transform the inner representation of their dead child.

> The search for meaning is, in part a personal project. . . . It is also a collective cultural project, shared by all bereaved parents who face the imbalance in world-view created by the child's death. This re-constructive project involves not only a reappraisal of the concept of mortality, but also asks other fundamental existential questions concerning the "fate" of the dead child, the point of a parenthood cut short and the purpose of life itself (Riches and Dawson, 1996, p. 144).

The fact that bereaved parents' bonds with their dead child are embedded within their bonds to a wider community is not as unique as it might seem. From the time a baby is conceived, the parent-child bond develops and is affirmed and supported within the parent's larger community. The quality and nonambivalance of the early parent-child bond depends a great deal upon the quality of the social support the new parent has. The interactions by which a baby is introduced into a community such as at the office or in a gathering of neighbors, is similar to sharing the bond with the child in Bereaved Parents. Each adult in turn holds the new baby and attempts to elicit an interaction with the baby, thus in a small way bonding to the child. Soon the baby tires from the effort to respond to so many faces and the child is passed back to the parent who is affirmed as the child's primary bond. Parents who do not have such a community are more likely to have trouble establishing a clear bond with the child (Anisfeld and Lipper, 1983). So too, bereaved parents have trouble establishing their continuing bond with their dead child if the bond is not a part of their social world.

In Chapter Two we cited Paul Gilbert's work (1992) on the evolution of human instinctual life. Gilbert says that the major challenge to human social life is managing the interplay between the early individualistic power-seeking instincts and the cooperative, caregiving instincts that evolved later. We noted that in their better moments spiritual traditions support love and compassion over competition and domination, though religions do not often live up to their ideals. Gilbert says that, in individuals and societies, competitive instincts can override cooperation and care-eliciting/caregiving especially when a person or social system is under stress. The death of a child is a stressor to both the individual and the social support network. Gilbert says that feelings of depression, anger, resentment, shame, envy, humiliation and self-doubt are responses to low rank in the individualist/power-seeking struggles. That is, these feelings are responses to loss in the power struggle. These are the very feelings that overwhelm parents as they begin to come to terms with the death of their child. We might understand the swirling emotions of anger, resentment, guilt, shame, and self-doubt in early grief as simply the phylogenetically programed responses to the loss of a sense of competence and power that is a part of parenting.

> The ability to nurture is evolution's most precious gift to humans. But like all gifts it is easily lost, atrophied or wasted. In all problems where there is a consistent failure to nurture, we find the inhibition of friendly love and compassion and the need to engage the world as if in a struggle. . . . The psychobiological changes help to lock attentive and coping styles into defensive strategies (Gilbert, 1992, pp. 195–196).

We know that, when a child does not receive adequate nurturance, it is difficult for the child to develop good cooperative and parenting skills. It appears that there is a reciprocal dynamic in parents. When deprived of the object of their nurturance, parents revert to the negative feelings of more primitive instincts. Such regression, it would seem, would be more pronounced in an individualistic culture, such as we have in the modern West, in which intimate bonds with the child are not shared within the larger social world, and where the death of a child is not easily integrated into the dominant cultural symbols.

If parenting is on the more highly evolved side of the struggle between competition and cooperation, and the death of a child throws parents back to the lower side, it would seem, then, that parents would resolve their grief best in a community where cooperation and caregiving/care-eliciting are well developed.

> To learn that one is an agent of value and has something to contribute which is valued by others can be enormously beneficial in overcoming deep senses of alienation, hatred and envy. It may be that our genes are selfish; . . . and it may also be that the wish to leave some contribution after our death, to leave the world a better place than we found it is a defense against death anxiety. . . . Be this as it may, the fact is that

humans are deeply committed to contribute to the welfare of others and to the development of human social culture. And it seems to me there is generally a great preference to do this co-operatively rather than individually (Gilbert, 1992, p. 208).

The interactions we see in Bereaved Parents are cooperative and nurturing. When the members consolidate their individual functioning at higher spiritual levels of cooperation and caregiving, they often associate the change with their bond to their dead child. A continuing theme in the group is that, "We are not a religious organization." The group is very firm in disavowing any shared religious beliefs. Religious doctrine is seen as a potential basis of controversy. In keeping with spirituality in a pluralistic culture, religious beliefs are defined in the group as personal matters. Yet, the members say that their bonds to their children and to each other are spiritual. We will see that participation in the group facilitates the transformation of the inner representation of the child and provides a community in which that transformation can be validated. Group membership nourishes the experience of solace, and provides a forum in which worldviews can be remolded or reaffirmed. As an organization, Bereaved Parents derives the energy upon which it runs from the shared inner representations of the dead children of the members. So the modern distinction between spiritual and religious is useful to the group. The group is not religious in the sense that it bridges rather than maintains theological boundaries, but still, the resolution of grief takes place in a community which feels to the members like a spiritual bond because it operates on a cooperative level, and because it grows to include their continuing bonds with their children, bonds that are for them a direct connection with transcendent reality.

☐ Newly Bereaved, Into Their Grief, Well Along in Their Grief, Resolved as Much as it Will Be

Though it is obvious that grief changes over time, it seems reasonably well accepted today that there are no easily defined stages in grief. Stage theorists claim that, just as there are stages of individual human development (Freud's oral, anal, genital or Piaget's cognitive stages for example), grief also must have stages. Scholars looking for stages posit that grief is an innate set of feelings and thoughts which are triggered by the environmental cue of the death of a significant other. This view of grief sees it moving toward resolution in a preprogramed sequence of feelings and thoughts (see Klass, 1987, 1988, pp. 193–214). Unfortunately for stage theorists, no one has been able to show that grieving people go through stages. That is, at this time there is no stage theory of grief that can be demonstrated as true using any scholarly tools available. It would seem then, that as we trace the resolution of parental grief, we have to accept a more messy world than if we had well-defined stages into which we could pour our data.

In the rest of this chapter, we will describe the ways the inner representation of the child is transformed in the inner life of the parent and in the social reality of the community. We need to find a way in which we can trace changes over time, but not get caught in misleading stage theory. The solution I propose is rather simple. We can use a working scheme the group members have developed themselves. Over the years, members have evolved some language by which they locate themselves and others in their journey. They define members of the group as "Newly Bereaved," "Into Their Grief," "Well Along in Their Grief," and "Resolved as Much as It Will Be." It is not a formal system; it is just a way to describe where members are now and where they see others in relationship to themselves. Other terms may be used, for example, "Into Their grief" can also be "That first year." And at the end they may be "Pretty much resolved." Because the system was developed by the parents themselves to explain their own experience, I have appropriated it as a way of organizing this chapter. But the terms may not describe griefs other than those within this one self-help group. In each of these phases we will discuss the representation of the child in the parent's inner world and in the communities of which the parent is a member.

Newly Bereaved: The Parent's Inner World

None of the parents in this book, even those whose children had been diagnosed with terminal illnesses for several years, was prepared for the death of the child. While there may be such a thing as anticipatory grief, for parents, their children's death is an awful truth that seems unreal.

Dissociation

Jeffery Kauffman (1994) pointed out that the initial response to traumatic death is not denial, but rather dissociation, and that the mourning process is best conceived as an interplay between integration and dissociation. Kauffman seems right. We will see in resolved grief a complex mixture of integrations. The newly bereaved experience a great many things, but the reality that their child is dead is undeniable. The initial response to death is shock in which the reality of the death is experienced over and over. From the first, they realize that their child is dead and that a part of the self has been cut off. One woman in the group wrote about the reality that would not go away. She said that every night she slept as long as she could, but in the morning the baby had still died. It went on, she said as days turned into weeks and weeks into months. And it kept on going.

> It wouldn't stop.
> It kept on having happened.
> No matter what I did, it refused to not have happened. . . .
> To this day it has happened.
> It will never tire of having happened.
> It was more than one day. It was more than one week.
> And it was more than months. It was more than years.
> And it knew it—All the time.

Out of Touch with the Child

Just as parents are dissociated from parts of themselves, they are out of touch with their children and they want to have the children back, to have the world back as it was before. Writing for the newsletter, a woman described how, as she woke up to a beautiful day with the sun shining into the bedroom windows, she seemed to resist awakening fully because it seemed that her child's death might just be a bad dream. So, she checked his room, and the empty room symbolized for her the empty place in her life to which she had awakened. "He wasn't there when we went to bed; he isn't in his bed this morning. It can't be. . . . Our hearts are left with an empty room that will never be filled again." The room, she said, is full of her dead son's presence, so the sense of presence only reminds the family that he is gone. The family does not know how to integrate the new meaning of the room and the new reality of the boy's death. She concludes,

> Today is a bad day. The door is closed. Someone is pretending it never happened. Will it be open again tomorrow? It's hard to say as we are just trying to make it through today. So we turn our heads when we go by. The urge to beat on the door and cry out, "Please come back," is almost too much to bear.

Anticipation of Continuing Bond

As the shock of the reality is hitting them, parents often anticipate the continuing bond they will have with the child. In a newsletter poem a mother describes a recurrent dream in which it seems "as though you were still there." But when she reaches out to touch, the child disappears. The mother's interpretation of the dream is that the child is sending a message that the child has not yet gone and is still with her. We can see that the child and the parent are not separated, for the poem shifts from the parent's dream to the child's dream, and she feels herself in the child's dream just as the child is in hers.

> For in your dreams each night,
> God lets my love shine through.
> God sends you all the pictures,
> for in your mind to view,
> of all the precious times we had,
> and all the love we knew.

In the poem, the mother knows that death is real and that she will not see her child again in her lifetime. Though at this time the parent does not experience the presence of the child, that presence is projected into the future. She looks forward to heaven when they will be reunited.

Linking Objects

During this early grief, parents often establish a connection with the dead child through a linking object (Volkan, 1981) that will transmute over time, but which will be long lasting. Three years after her 21-year-old daughter died, a mother reported that what had been the girl's room had recently been changed to a computer/word processor room. But on the top of a book shelf sat two nearly-worn-out Raggedy Ann and Andy dolls. She remembered that she had tried to throw the dolls away several years earlier, but,

> My then-teenaged daughter indignantly rescued them from the trash. "Not Ann and Andy!" she cried, settling them in her room. . . . E is gone now . . . her beautiful promising young life snuffed out by a drunk driver. . . . Our lives have been changed, and so has E's room . . . but many of the reminders are still there—including Raggedy Ann and Andy.

Newly Bereaved: The Parent's Social World

Isolation

The disequilibrium and dissociation that parents feel in their inner life is also their experience in their social world. Newly bereaved parents care whether other people share the loss. Parents report if people came to the funeral, if there was a memorial planned at the school, if they see other people deeply affected by their child's death. Unfortunately, for a significant number of parents, the pain they experience is not felt within their community in a way that allows the parent to know that the community is sharing their pain. It often seems to the parents that neither the child nor the child's death has social reality. They find people will not mention the child's name in their presence, that inquiries about how they are doing imply that it doesn't hurt as bad as it does, that the child can be replaced by a new baby, or that God loves the child in heaven better than the parent could have loved the child here. When a child dies, it seems to the parents that their lives have stopped while other people's lives go on.

A mother whose child was born with a defective heart and died a few weeks later wrote in a newsletter about how differently her community responded to the news of her pregnancy than to the news of her child's death. When she was expecting, everyone told her that this was the most blessed of life's events and that her baby was a new person, a unique individual, different from anyone else. She was told that this new person would change her life forever.

> And yet when this most blessed and unique person dies, everybody acts like it's nothing. "Oh well, better luck next time." "It's better he died before you got to know him." "You'll have more babies.". . . So parents who lose a baby will generally try to hide their feelings of grief from others for fear of ridicule, disapproval or stern lectures about how lucky they are—to have other children or the ability to have new (and obviously improved) babies.

Inadequate Support Systems

One of the reasons for the group's existence is that the symbols of the mainline culture and of the parents' community affiliations are not adequate help in making sense of their experience. Those symbols do not meld the reality that the child is dead with the reality that the parent is still bonded to the child. A continual theme in newsletter articles is an appeal to friends and family to understand and to accept the parents' feelings and behaviors. The appeals are often written in the first person plural, because one of the early discoveries is that other bereaved parents are treated in a similar way.

> Please don't tell us to turn off our memories, to snap out of it, that he/she is dead and life has to go on. But our love for them doesn't end with death. . . . Yes, we fully realize that he/she is dead, gone forever, and that's what hurts.

Please have patience with us. Try to understand why we are acting or feeling the way we are today. In a small word or gesture let us know it's all right with you for us to love, to cry, to remember. We aren't doing it to make you uncomfortable or to gain sympathy. We are just trying to cope.

For those who will affiliate with the group as the vehicle of their resolution, the group becomes a central community in their lives during this chaotic time. At an alumni gathering of parents who had been central members of the group but who no longer attend, people consistently referred to the group as their lifeline for several months. "It saved my life." "I just lived for those meetings for a long time." There have been up to five different monthly meeting groups within the chapter, and many people remembered attending more than one meeting a month. The importance of the group for them was not in the program, but rather in the connection to other people when they did not feel connected to others in their natural support system. Although it was a large gathering, the alumni arranged chairs in a circle to reenact the ritual that begins every meeting, going around the circle and giving their names, their children's names, and a little about themselves and their children. As they went around the circle, these veterans would name the people in the group who were important to them when they were active. Many reported that they have few memories of the first year after their child died, yet many of them could tell about their first meeting and the name of the first person in the group they met and connected with. Several looked across the circle to another person and noted the person was at the first meeting, or remembered something of the other person's grief that struck them as like their own.

Into Their Grief: The Parent's Inner World

Separating From the Living Child

As parents "move into their grief," the complexity of their bond with the child becomes expressed in the complexity of their grief. In parenting, the inner representation of a living child is an important part of the parent's self. This has survival value since the child's welfare depends on many years of parental altruistic activity. Many bereaved parents must spend time separating from inner representations of the living child, and some must spend time separating conflicting inner representations of the child from each other. Separation of the self from the inner representation of the child is difficult and in some cases, impossible.

> [If] one's image of self is contingent upon the availability of another
> . . . dependence demands continuing interchange as a requisite of main-
> taining an image of the self as whole and acceptable. The death of the
> dependent figure initiates a pathogenic shift in self-image from that of
> being strong, caring, and worthwhile to discrepant images of being weak,
> uncaring, and incompetent (Rynearson, 1987, p. 491; also see Horowitz,
> Wilner, Marmor, & Krupnick, 1980)

All parents in the group have parts of their self-definition and parts of
their self-functioning dependent on the child, so almost every bereaved
parent feels weak, uncaring, and especially incompetent after the child's
death. For a few parents, self-functioning had been highly dependent
on the availability of the child. In those cases, the inner representation
of the child was integrated directly early in the grief in a way that
maintained the child in the self system. The transformation of their
bond with the child, then, can also be a rather dramatic change in self-
functioning. For example, one recovering alcoholic whose 15-year-old
daughter, Mindy, was shot as a bystander in a holdup, was having
trouble maintaining sobriety in the painful months after her death.
From her childhood, Mindy had been the one in the family who "could
tell me off when I was being stupid. She would just say, `Dad, cut the
crap.' She loved me and didn't back off like the boys did. When she
told me to stop it, I did." He and his wife came for counseling within a
few weeks after the murder. As he talked through the history of his
bond with Mindy, it became clear to me that this child played the
same role in his life that his mother, on whom he was also highly
dependent, had played in his childhood.

About six months after the death, he was standing at the grave
when he heard a voice, "Dad, why are you acting this way? This is
what you were like when you were drinking." Within a week Mindy
was his constant inner companion helping him control his rage and
maintain his hard-won sobriety. In one counseling session I asked
him how it was going and he replied,

> Boy, she was really on my case today. I started to blow up at Sam
> because he left a mess when he cleaned up the kitchen. So, I just got out
> of there, and then some guy cut me off on the highway. I could just hear
> her there telling me to calm down because it wasn't worth it.

Over the next two years, a strong bond with other members of group
allowed him to separate himself from the direct dependence on Mindy.
He took on some projects for the group and was given a great deal of
positive feedback. He soon took it as his responsibility to make sure
that men who came to the group for the first time were not left alone
while their wives talked to other women. As he became active in the

group, Mindy became more than just the voice telling him to control himself. She became part of his good self which was expressing itself by helping other bereaved parents. As he learned how to be a bereaved parent, he learned new skills in inner dialogue and in sorting out what was important and what was not important so he could control his responses better. About two years after her death, we were having a cup of coffee after a meeting when he told me about his new boss who, in his opinion, had been very arbitrary in disciplining some of the workers. "Before I would have given him some shit," he said,

> but I just told myself that kids die, so don't sweat the small stuff. It wasn't directly affecting me. I know those guys. They were just testing him. So a couple weeks ago we were alone for a few minutes, and I asked him how he was feeling about the new job, and he said that being in charge of people was harder than he thought, but his boss was being real helpful. I think he will catch on. He is really a pretty good guy. People can change you know, even me.

We see differences in the way the child is integrated into various parts of the parent's self, and thus into the different social systems in which the parent participates. Those differences continue into the parent's grief. The more the activities of parents' daily psychic and social worlds are part of their interaction with the inner representation of the child, the more difficult it is for parents to separate out the inner representation of the child. A crucial issue is how the child's death affects the work life. In most families today, both father and mother are employed, so the workplace provides both the test of the bereaved parent's ability to focus on tasks and one of the important social networks to which they belong. For some parents, work is an island in a stormy sea; tasks and relationships on the job seem normal. Other parents find work difficult and their performance diminished. The difference seems to be the degree to which their selfhood at work involves the child. For parents who can focus at work, the transition from work to home is often marked by a surge of emotion. A midlevel executive said she functioned well at work, though she was occasionally teary. During the drive home, however, she became overwhelmed by the thought that her son was gone forever. She had the same surge of thoughts and feelings returning to her hotel room when she was out of town.

Some difficulties in marriages grow out of this dynamic. One salesman felt he had to control his grief severely because he was expected to be his old self with clients. He often entertained clients. It was difficult for him to be upbeat all the time as he had been. He was supposed to use his baseball and hockey tickets to take important clients to the games, but he found that he just wanted to give the tickets away because he could no longer care about the game. At first, he reported, everyone was very sympathetic. There were flowers from his customers at the funeral. But as time went on, people stopped knowing how to relate to him. He realized later that, in their discomfort, they backed off from him. He was fired from one job because his grief impaired his production, and he had a hard time finding another job. His wife kept her job, but was moved to a position where little was expected of her. On his new job, the husband was afraid of the financial consequences of grief. With his wife not producing at work, he was afraid that she would be let go, as he had been. So, he was very conscious that he not be as affected by the grief as he had been at first because he feared he would be only one of the couple employed. This brought prolonged conflict in the marriage. His wife could not understand how he could turn off feelings which were, for her, so uncontrollable. It seemed to her that he could not have loved the child as she did.

It is a difficult task, then, for the parent to transform the bond in a way that the child remains a continuing reality in their lives. The bond with the child is complexly intertwined with core dynamics in the parent's psychic structure, as in the case of the recovering alcoholic. The bond with the child is a part of many other bonds and activities in the parent's world as we have seen in looking at parent's work lives. The parent must learn how to live without the continuous presence of the living child. The alcoholic had to internalize his daughter's voice rather directly and later transform the bond with the child in an interior way, because his self-functioning was so dependent on the child. The salesman had to separate the self he was with his clients from the self that he had been with his child because otherwise, it seemed to him, he could not provide for his family. The salesman traded his close bond with the living child for his self-image of good provider. One of the consequences of that trade was increased tension between him and his wife. The child is dead, but life goes on. Parents learn to go on for themselves in their child's memory, because they have other children, because they don't know what else to do, or because they are afraid if they commit suicide they will be prevented from ever seeing their children again. For whatever reasons, they go on and learn to go on in a world that no longer includes their living child.

Connecting with the Child's Pain

As parents begin to separate from the inner representation of the living child many parents find that their first point of connection between them and their dead child is the pain of their grief and the pain the child knew. I interviewed a woman whose two-year-old daughter died after several months in the hospital. The child had blood drawn many times and feared the procedure because it always hurt her. A few months after the death, the mother went to the clinic to have blood drawn.

> As I went in, I found myself saying over and over, maybe even out loud, "Look at mommy, she can have them take blood, and she'll be a big girl so it won't hurt. See, Judy, mommy is going to be a big girl." When they stuck me it really hurt. I have given blood a lot, and it never hurt like that. I mean, it never hurt before, but this time it really did. When I told my mother about it she said, "This may seem strange, but I think that was Judy who was hurt." I think she is right. I cried all the way back to work, and I knew what she had suffered. The next time I had blood drawn it was like always, just a little prick.

One of the men in the group had taken up oil painting a few years before his son was killed in the car accident. He had done wild life paintings, a few landscapes, and occasionally a still life. He stopped painting when the son died, but about a year later he kept having dreams of the scene his son saw as the car came over the hill to meet the oncoming 18-wheeler. The dreams were very vivid, and the man felt compelled to paint the scene several times. The last painting was of the sky as he imagined his son seeing it when he lost consciousness. The paintings were, he told me, as close as he could come to knowing the pain of his son's dying. After that series, he said, he stopped painting. I do not know if he ever started painting again.

The child's pain can be in many forms. A young adult woman who had an incurable degenerative disease committed suicide when her mother and father were away for a long weekend. Her mother told me, "I never let myself experience her pain," because the medical staff had urged the mother to be the voice of hope and determination. When her daughter cried and wanted to give up, it was the mother who insisted she get up and try again. The mother so fully adopted the role assigned to her by the physicians that she started giving talks to community groups on maintaining positive attitude. "Well," the mother said in an interview, "I know the pain now." Several other parents whose children suicided used the phrase, "Suicide is a way to pass the pain."

Dealing with Ambivalence in the Parent-Child Bond

As parents come to terms with their inner representation of the living child, they often must come to terms with the ambivalences in the attachment between parent and child. Inner representations that are of the less-than-good self or which are extensions of attachments to negative figures in the parent's history produce more difficult griefs. Separating these inner representations of the child from each other can be simply a matter of purging stressful memories and holding the child in an idealized way. Most parents do this to some extent. We typically find them describing the dead child in glowing terms.

Ambivalence can also reach deep into the parent's psyche and the parent-child bond. Orbach demonstrated the complexity of parental grief nearly half a century ago in his article "The Multiple Meanings of the Loss of a Child" (1959). He gave one detailed case of a woman whose son by her second marriage died. The child's death was part of a string of deaths experienced as repetitions of a grandmother's death when the mother was young. It was also associated with the death of a close supportive brother who died during the pregnancy, a brother after whom the child was named and of whom she believed the child to be a "carbon copy." There was a strong intimacy between the mother and the child, and an estrangement between the mother and the father. The mother had hoped something bad might happen that would make the husband closer to her, so she prayed that her own child would become sick and thought her prayer caused the child's death.

It is not unusual for severe marital conflict to grow from ambivalence and guilt in negative inner representations of the child. For example, the son of a strict Pentecostal couple died of a drug overdose. His mother attributed his behavior to the father's strict discipline and distant emotional relationship to the boy. She blamed herself only for acquiescing in her husband's child-rearing ideas. She had been taught that wives should be obedient to their husbands, but she now thought she should have been assertive about the father's discipline. The fault was the husband's, not the son's. The difficulty was resolved only after the mother, in her anger at her husband, sexually acted out a part of her own *bad* self. In coming to terms with the resultant guilt, she was able to reconcile herself to her negative inner representation of her son. She quoted the scripture that "all have sinned and fallen short of the glory of God." God forgives sinners, she told me, and now she could both accept His forgiveness and forgive her son as she knew God did. With some difficulty she could forgive her husband too. She could not, however, return to her role as obedient wife, and the couple eventually separated and divorced as they could not rework their respective roles in the marriage.

Purging inner representations can also take the form of coming to terms with guilt stemming from what the parent now sees as less than adequate parenting or of anger at the child or the child's other parent for the child's behavior and attitude. Most parents talk directly to their child in their mind, but it seems to help parents who are full of anger and guilt to write their thoughts down as a way of working through those feelings. Near the end of several months of weekly counseling sessions, a mother, whose dead teenage son had sided with his abusive father rather than with her after their divorce, wrote a letter to her son telling him all the things that she never got to say to him when the son would not talk to her for months at a time.

> I told him of my anger over his death, my love for him, apologies for the ways I failed him if he felt that I did, and the guilt I had about his death. I told him that I had done the best that I could in raising him, and that I would always love him.

She kept the letter for a few weeks wondering what to do with it. We devised a ritual in which she would burn the letter at the grave. I offered to be there with her, as did her new husband, but she decided it was a matter between her and her son, and that she would do it by herself. "The tremendous guilt that I had been carrying around for six years was released as I burned the letter on his gravestone," she reported. "Part of my future has been taken away with R's death, but finally being able to communicate with R in this way, I made my peace with him." When I was the speaker on anger and guilt, at a meeting I seldom attend, a woman said that the minister to whom she went for counseling suggested that she write as a way of expressing her anger. She said she got a spiral notebook and that she would write to her son every day. She found that if she wrote in the evening, she slept better because the thoughts were on the paper, not just in her head. She strongly recommended the technique to others in the meeting. A few years later she approached me after I had again spoken at her meeting. She reminded me of our interchange, and I remembered her story of the notebook. She said that she had finally gotten over the anger, and that at the end she learned how to forgive her son. "I burned the notebook. Nobody else ever read it, not even him," she said, nudging her husband beside her. "Those thoughts were just for me and Kirby. I let go of the anger, and I didn't want to keep the book."

In the most difficult cases, the inner representation may be purged almost completely in a way that the parent hardly maintains a continuing bond with their child. A sociopathic young man, whose parents came for psychotherapy, died in a holdup attempt. His mother had supported him, but to do so, she repressed memories of his violent episodes toward her and toward his siblings. In the therapy those memories returned. In the third year after he died, she went through four months of seeing her son. Once, she was convinced that she had seen him in a truck in the parking lot under my office. She trembled as, at the end of the session, I walked her down the stairs and through the parking lot looking for the truck on the way to her car. She thought he was coming back to hurt her. She lived near a street used by emergency vehicles and was sure one night that the sirens were because he had caused an accident in which people were hurt. For two months, she was obsessed with the idea that the body in "that box in the ground" was not her son. She had not seen the body because it was badly disfigured and the father was so angry at the son that he said he wanted the casket closed with only a service at the grave. I called the police captain who had been on duty after the killing and asked how the body had been identified. He said that several of the officers knew the son very well from previous arrests and that they had a warrant for him because he had been identified in another holdup a few days earlier. There was no doubt in the captain's mind that the body in the casket was the woman's son. I reported my conversation with the captain to the mother in great detail. She missed a therapy session two weeks later. She told me the next week that she had left work to come to my office, but then she found herself an hour later lying on the grave at the cemetery. As she became aware of where she was, she stayed lying down for a long time. She sensed that the bad side of her son was in the box and safely in the ground. Gradually over the next few weeks, she found she no longer saw him lurking around, and she learned to feel safer. Her new feeling of safety took an interesting turn a few months later when she attended a company retreat lead by a psychologist who wanted the group to "get in touch with their feelings." In a small group she shared some memories of her own childhood that, she told me, she had never had the courage to share before. Only two other people at work, however, knew about her son. She told me that she had stopped telling about him a few years before he died. "People don't know what to do with it," she said. "I have to work with them everyday and get things done. You just can't have them looking at you that way. Tom (one of her oldest co-workers) knows about all of it and that's enough."

As parents settle their business with their living child, they come to terms with the ambivalence in their bond with the child. There are no perfect relationships, no perfect children, and no perfect parents. Every parent must come to terms with the guilt and anger they felt in their bond with the child. Some ambivalence is very deep seated and when it is, coming to terms with ambivalence can mean purging the inner representation rather throughly. Parents can repress, forgive themselves, or forgive the child. In the end they construct a durable biography of themselves and the living child that they can carry for the rest of their lives.

Into Their Grief: The Parent's Social World

Shared Bonds in the Self-Help Group

As parents separate out the living child from the self and come to terms with ambivalent bonds with the child, they are aided by integrating their bond with their dead child into their social world. Among the unique aspects of a self-help group of bereaved parents are expressions of the shared bond they have with each other's children. Thus membership in the community means membership as a bereaved parent, a person whose life is not as it was before, and a person who is to be related to differently than before. And membership in a community means that the dead child is also a member of the community, that the child is valued, remembered, celebrated, and loved.

Being There for Each Other

Sharing the bond with the child begins with sharing the pain that the death of the child has brought. "The mutual disclosure of pain and the sharing of their children's lives enables parents to discover a narrative through which to account to themselves for a seemingly senseless loss" (Riches and Dawson, 1996, p. 150). The sense of sharing pain is summed up by a phrase that continually reoccurs in members' accounts of what they need from people: "just being there." Being there means being with the parent in a way that the reality of the child's death and the reality of the pain are not the parent's alone. They say the only people who can really understand are other bereaved parents, for they have *been there.*

Being there for bereaved parents, metaphorically, and often literally, means being at the grave. Most cultures have periodic community rituals at the graves of their dead. As the twentieth century has progressed, however, there has been a marked decline in graveside gatherings. Modern cemeteries discourage decorating graves because it interferes with the power mowers used the cut the grass. Decoration Day and Memorial Day have lost much of their association with the dead. As grief has become more privatized, visits to the grave have become more and more individual and less communal. A notable exception is the Viet Nam memorial that provided healing and reconciliation in the nation at the same time the memorial provides a place that individual families bring presents to the dead soldiers.

Every parent of a dead child has experienced the incredible loneliness and devastation of the graveside. Yet, the grave is also where, for many parents, the child can be found. They go there to weep, to remember, to talk, and sometimes to listen. In Bereaved Parents, members need not be alone at the grave, and in a sense the children in the graves need not be alone either. One of the meetings in the chapter has a cemetery tour on a Saturday in the Fall. During that tour they visit the graves of each other's children. When the idea was introduced at the business meeting, there was widespread approval. One of the long-time members of the steering committee said that one day she was at the grave and saw a friend from many years earlier. They did not know that their children were buried near each other. Since that time, she always visits the other child's grave when she visits that of her own child. Several others at the business meeting said they, too, knew of other children buried in the same cemeteries as their children and that they visit the other graves.

The group gets a van for the cemetery tour, so they can all be together for the day. People sign up week earlier, so a route can be mapped out. At each grave, the parent of the child there gives a presentation to introduce the child. Favorite stories are told, and some parents bring pictures, tapes of songs, or artwork. After each presentation, the group spends some time at the grave before moving on to the next. In the middle of the day, they all stop for lunch. Then they go back to the tour until all the children have been visited. At the parking lot where the cars have been left, the day ends with many hugs and thanks for a wonderful day. At the business meeting when the activity was reported, there was long laughter at the description of the waitress's befuddled look when the group answered her innocent question about why they were having lunch together. The group laughed, because everyone there knew that being a bereaved parent puts them outside the normal world, and they have learned that they are all right within the group. If others cannot be there for them, they can be there for each other, and even be there with each other's children at their graves.

As a community in which pain is acceptable, many kinds of pain that can accompany grief at the death of a child are acceptable within Bereaved Parents. There do, however, seem to be some limits. The grief from socially unacceptable deaths, for example suicide or murder by a friend or lover is acceptable in the group. Murder by a stranger is regarded as similar to auto accidents, one of the hazards of modern living. It is common for parents whose children have suicided to wonder, sometimes aloud, whether they fit into the group, because their child chose to die. Often, but not always, these parents have been through some very difficult times with the child before the suicide. So the question of whether they will fit in with a group of other parents is not a new one for them. When suicide parents voice their questions, the answer is best given by a veteran parent whose child committed suicide but if one is not present, the answer is usually given by a member of long standing. Grief is grief; they say, and though there may be some issues in suicide that the group does not share, the children are still dead. They are welcome to share in the group. Many parents of suicides have stayed, and a few have taken leadership positions.

Some of the pain when children are murdered seems to fall outside what can be shared in Bereaved Parents. This pain is not from grief or trauma, but rather because the way contemporary culture construes crime and punishment brings so much extra pain to parents of murdered children. Those parents must contend with the criminal justice system in which they have no legal standing (see Klass, 1988, pp. 125–138). Until quite recently in human history, it was the family's obligation to exact retribution for the wrongful death of a family member. In many parts of the world, the family still carries that obligation. But in the modern West, the legal case is the State against the accused. The family has been reduced to sitting with the other spectators. If they might be called as witnesses, parents may not even be allowed to sit in the court room. If they are called as witnesses, they can be cross-examined by the defense in ways that might call their positive sense of their child into question. The Bereaved Parents have been very open to having parents of murdered children as members. When the Parents of Murdered Children was formed as a national organization, the local chapter grew out of our Bereaved Parents group. The main reason the new organization formed was to support each other in the criminal justice system. The two groups have maintained cooperative relationships over the years in activities that focus on grief. A representative of the Parents of Murdered Children sits in on the business meeting of Bereaved Parents, both groups are listed as sponsors of the Holiday Candlelight Memorial Service, and new leaders of the Parents of Murdered Children have attended the Chapter Effectiveness Workshops of Bereaved Parents where they learn skills at facilitating meetings. Many parents attend both Bereaved Parents and Parents of Murdered Children for the first year or two. These people say that they deal with their grief in one group, and the problems of the justice system in the other, but probably the division is not so clear-cut as they make it sound.

As parents share their pain in meetings, there is both a tendency not to compare pains and also a tendency to recognize that there are some differences and that some pains are more difficult. On the one hand, all the members share the pain that their children have died. When the group first formed, people wondered about whether it was harder or easier if a child died early or late, or if a child died suddenly or after a long preparation. As the questions were discussed, a consensus emerged that although there might be differences, there is no future in comparing pain. "If you hurt more than I do," said one person, "it does not make me hurt less. And both of our children are still dead. Dead is dead." At the same time, there is a recognition that there are differences in coming to terms with different kinds of death. Every year or so, the larger meetings break up into smaller groups based on the kind of death: accident, illness, suicide, etc. The basis of the divisions is to some extent planned ahead with small group leaders assigned in advance. But it is also a decision the group facilitator may make on the spot depending on who has come to the meeting or whether there are enough newly bereaved who need a group of their own for the night.

The death of a child can be compounded by other circumstances. Some members have had multiple children die, either in the same accident, from the same genetic disorder, or seemingly from random fate. With these people, the group members recognize their more difficult circumstances and offer what help they can. For example, a young woman, whose husband committed suicide six months after their child died of SIDS, sobbed all through a meeting. The woman next to her, a veteran in the group, spent most of the meeting gently stroking the woman's back. Almost as soon as the meeting closed, a couple whose adult daughter, a hospital social worker, had died only a few months earlier went to her. They made sure she had their phone number and made arrangements to meet the next week for an afternoon. Although the older couple often felt helpless themselves, they knew how to relate to the young adult. It did not appear to me that they needed to discuss for more than a moment that they would take on this project. They knew that her pain was different from theirs, but in identifying with the young woman's pain, they could also be in touch with their dead adult daughter who they knew would have taken this young mother into her heart. Several couples who have had multiple children die have become leaders in the group. "As long as God has been so good at making me a bereaved parent," a man said ironically to me, "I might as well be a good one." A man who was severely handicapped in the auto accident that killed his daughter took on the task of contacting all the social service agencies to make sure they knew about the group. It seems that, if people suffering these more complex circumstances can identify the pain of their child's death with the group, and if they can adopt the group's philosophy of seeking a positive resolution of their grief, then they become a part of the group.

Sharing Practical Solutions

Sharing the pain also means sharing ways to relieve some forms of the pain, especially in the parent's social world. Often, meeting time is devoted to practical issues. For example, how to include the child in the holidays. The November meeting topic is usually "Making it through the holidays." There are several ways these practical issues may be solved, but each answer is really a stance, that is, an attitude, a way of being-in-the-world. One mother whose child's name was not mentioned at family gatherings made a holiday wreath for the front door with many colored ribbons, including a black one. "It is there," she said. "If they want to see it and mention it, they can. It is not me that didn't bring it up." Because the same solutions work, members discover that they can use the solution someone else suggests, they realize that others have pain like them.

A major practical problem is how parents develop new stances within their family and community. It is common for parents to report that they are the ones who have to teach family and friends how to relate to them. Often what they teach is what they have learned from the group. A member wrote a note addressed to those who would help her:

> Please listen to me, just hear what I'm saying—not just the words that come from my mouth. Don't just listen with your ears. If you insist on giving me good advice and telling me not to worry, I'll think you don't understand. So please, accept my problem, be here with me, and cry with me. Then I'll know you've truly listened.

Part of learning to be a bereaved parent is learning how to integrate the grief into other social networks. A woman told about having to work on a Saturday. A man, with whom she did not usually interact, came by her cubicle where she had pictures of two grandchildren, her daughter, and her dead son on her desk. The man commented on the grandchildren and she responded with proud remarks. Then the man looked at Rich's picture that showed him by his Corvette and asked who was the young man with the sports car. She said that was her son and that he had died nine months ago. She started to cry. The man said he was sorry for bringing it up. She said, "No, I want people to know about him. It is okay if I cry because I miss him. But I still like it when people ask about him. My tears are part of what he means to me now." She reported at the meeting that after that day, whenever the man was in her area he would give her a smile. She said she still doesn't know much about him, but it feels good to her that he understands what she said to him and that he seems to care.

Practical problems, then, range from what to do with Christmas stockings, to how to introduce the child in new relationships, and to how to respond to family criticism of how the parents are grieving. Both God and the devil are in the details of life. Learning to live in the world without the living child, in a world that now includes death, and in a world that does not easily include the transformed bond they have with their dead children, involves many practical issues. As parents find solutions to those issues and share the solutions with other bereaved parents, they discover that they share the same pain because the same solutions work.

Validate Interaction with the Dead Child

As the dead child is integrated into the social network, the experiences by which parents maintain contact with their children can be socially validated. Seeing, hearing, and sensing the presence of dead children is not easily integrated into the social reality of modernity. Yet, for many bereaved parents, such experiences are a part of their daily routine. Most of the members have linking objects. To validate linking objects, members may tell each other about them. Parents often report holding an item of clothing and smelling the child's odor. It is common at meetings for parents to tell about the solace they feel from their linking object and to have that experience mirrored as they hear about other parents' linking objects.

Over the years there has been a development in the way experiences which fall outside socially-sanctioned reality are brought into the group. Early on, the group did not have a language to talk about these phenomena, and the attempts to share them were often very tentative. With time, the group integrated these nonordinary experiences into their shared beliefs. At the same time, a steady stream of discussion was taking place in the popular culture about near-death experiences (see Zaleski, 1987) and to a lesser extent, post-death contact. For the last several years, these experiences are routinely reported and integrated into the group's fund of knowledge about grief. The group maintains the principle of not holding to any doctrinal position, yet, at the same time, the group validates the experience by saying that the experiences are real although different for different people, and that what is learned in the experience is for the parent, not for everyone. Nearly every year, one meeting is devoted to these experiences, and several members have become well-read on the topic. At national and regional meetings, sessions on nonordinary experiences are well attended. As a conclusion to this chapter and as one way of summing up the complex dynamics we are tracing, I will give a rather full account of one meeting on unusual experiences and happenings.

Well Along in Their Grief:
The Parent's Inner World

Exchanging Pain for a Positive Bond with the Child

As members begin to find a new equilibrium in their lives, they find it in terms of the inner representation of their child. The movement is often cast in terms of letting go and holding on. The logo of Compassionate Friends, the self-help group in which our chapter grew, has a circle with a child figure distant from a pair of hands. One mother reported that her four-year-old asked why the child was so far from the hands. She replied that because the child has died and the hands are mommy's or daddy's reaching for the child. The four-year-old disagreed, "I think you're wrong, Mom. I think the hands are letting him go." For the mother, the child's interpretation was right.

> She made me see that I was still reaching. It has been two years since Michael was stillborn, but I continue to reach for something. Just what that something is, I don't know, but I'll know what it is when I find it. Perhaps then a part of me can let go.

The "something" she is reaching for is a positive bond with the child. The idea of letting go of the pain in exchange for a clearer, comforting inner representation of the child is one of the central insights in Bereaved Parents. Rather than identifying with the child's pain, the parent identifies with the energy and love which was in the living child. In a speech at a holiday candlelight service five years after her son's death, a mother reflected on her progress:

> I was afraid to let go. Afraid that I would forget the details of him, the peculiar color of his eyes, the shape of his nose, the sound of his voice. . . . In a strange way, my pain was comforting, a way of loving him, familiar. . . . Finally, I had to admit that his life meant more than pain, it also meant joy and happiness and fun—and living. The little voice in my heart was telling me that it was time for me to let go of him. . . . When we release pain, we make room for happiness in our lives. My memories of Colin became lighter and more spontaneous. Instead of hurtful, my memories brought comfort, even a chuckle. . . . I had sudden insights into what was happening to me, the pieces began to fit again, and I realized Colin was still teaching me things.

One of the cliches of bereavement work is that grief is the price we pay for love. A father worked through the balance, "If the price I pay for loving Deanna is the pain and sorrow I now have, I still think I got a bargain to have had her for thirteen years."

Connect the Bond with the Child
to the Parent's Own Healing

The developing bond with the dead child is often quite explicitly linked with the parent's thoughts about their own healing. A father reported that when he began running, his 17-year-old daughter encouraged him to keep it up by registering both of them to run a five-kilometer race. She was killed in an accident two weeks before the race. He thought about quitting running but did not because he thought she would have been disappointed to think she had caused him to abandon running in general and the race in particular. He ran wearing her number. After that, she became part of his running routine. As he settled into the pace "alone with no distractions but the pounding of my feet," he "could focus on her and my feelings." He would think about his daughter for a few minutes and then check on how he was dealing with her death. He would visualize the goal of his healing as a light toward which he was running. Then, he

> often moved on to report silently to her about what I'd been doing lately, about what I thought of the weather, how my conditioning was going, what her younger brothers were up to. Frequently, I sensed she was nearby, cruising at my elbow, listening.

Finding new equilibrium in life in terms of the transformed bond with the child is often complex, especially for those parents whose bond with the child has been ambivalent. Often, they must reconstruct the durable biography of themselves, of the child, and sometimes of the marriage. We can see some of the complexity in Barbara and Fred, a couple who came for counseling three years after her daughter, Abby, died at age 20, and three weeks after Barbara had attempted suicide. She said that the suicide was an attempt to stop the pain, not an attempt to rejoin Abby. Barbara had a long history of abuse and neglect. Her father was very physically abusive. Her mother very passive, probably depressed. Abby had been born with a congenital defect, and, though a series of operations offered a long shot at full functioning, she was not expected to live into adulthood. Beginning at age 13, Abby had rebelled against her terminal diagnosis in a series of sexual escapades, including activities in a local college fraternity house that were reported to the police. Barbara in one sense approved, because Abby was rebelling against convention in a way Barbara could not when she was a teenager. But school principals and juvenile authorities shamed her, and she could not admit that she admired her daughter's rebellion. Abby's behavior reminded Fred of the "trash" his father had so despised, so Barbara was often caught between Abby and Fred.

Early in our therapy, Abby became a part of Barbara's inner world as an ally in her healing. In our first session, Barbara said Abby was now a voice in her head telling her good things, though Barbara had difficulty saying what the good things were. Before the suicide attempt, Barbara had not felt in touch with Abby at all. In our second session she reported a dream of a phone call from Abby who said she was in the South of France and doing fine. But then the call was cut off. That same session she reported that she and Fred were going for a week's vacation in Florida.

Barbara and I had individual sessions for an intensive four months. She saw a television program with John Bradshaw and began reading a book on healing the inner child. She saw that there had been no play in her childhood and she began teaching herself to play. She especially enjoyed blowing bubbles on the deck. As she recalled her own early memories which were often very painful, she linked those memories with Abby's pain. She also recalled times when she was a competent parent, for example, a time when she had gone to the school and demanded better services for Abby.

As she talked about her anger at Fred's disciplining of Abby, she reframed it as Fred's way of showing that he loved his daughter. At that point, we invited Fred to join us, and we did weekly couple therapy for several months. As Fred talked about the meaning of his life, he described an angry, demanding father. Fred tried to be a good son. His father's message was to care about what neighbors would say. His father was often angry at Fred and his mother for small acts that his father thought were like those of "white trash." As Fred learned to describe his father using words, he could distance himself from having to live up to such a father's expectations. In couple work, Fred reframed his understanding of Abby's behavior into heroic rebelling against death and affirming life. Abby's rebellion, was not against him, but against death. He began to see her sexuality as her quest for what life she could have before she died, and her rebellion and manipulating men as her exercise of power in the face of her powerlessness at her certain death. He recalled when Abby was in the hospital at age 11 and seemed to have made a decision that living life would mean defying death. Fred was a passionate automobile racing fan. Abby's attitude toward death could be like the drivers he admired. He could identify with his daughter when he saw her in this *masculine* attitude toward death. He began to laugh at her antics, and to reflect on his own childhood, especially on his father's demands on him and his father's toleration of his brother's rebellious behavior. This positive representation of Abby could be shared between Barbara and Fred, later with Abby's siblings, and then with a new daughter-in-law. Barbara and Fred's growth continued as they constructed new durable biographies of both themselves and Abby, but we will pick up their story in the chapter on worldviews, because they have more to teach us there.

Well Along in Their Grief: The Parent's Social World

Stabilizing the Continuing Bond

The socially shared bond with the child stabilizes the parent's continuing inner bond with the child. One mother whose living children had moved away reflected on how she keeps the bond with all her absent children, including the one who is dead. She found she does it in similar ways, but that, while she can hold her living children on her own, she needs the group to hold the bond with the dead child. She said that in the group, mentioning the child's name does not cause an awkward gap as it does in other places where people do not know that the child is real to her, that the child is in her heart. Sometimes, she said, she wants to scream out loud that her child is real and that his name can be said in her presence. She told about stopping at a traffic light and seeing a boy in the next car put his hand on his chin in a gesture just like her living son makes. She made a joke as she talked about the question of how many children she has.

> My daughter is married and living in New York. And the boys? Well, one will always be four and a half. I heard him laughing the other day in the giggles of some preschoolers. And my oldest son? I told you . . . he made sergeant? And that I saw him in the gesture of a boy waiting at the traffic light?

Sharing the Continuing Bond in Rituals and Customs

As the bond with the child is made part of the parent's membership in Bereaved Parents, the inner representation can be more fluid and thus can be transformed within the parent's inner world. As the group has developed, members have devised rituals and customs by which the continuing bond is transformed and symbolized. We can see many of the dynamics of the self-help process in a newsletter article written by the coordinator of the annual picnic. She says there will be good food and games, but

> these are the sidekicks of our picnic. The center, the best, the reason we come back year after year is simply to be together. Whether meeting

new people, talking to old friends, playing, or just being there, it is the gathering that makes this event so special for so many of us.

If our gathering is the center, our children lost are the heart and soul of our picnic. It is for and because of them that we have come, and it is for them that we have our cherished balloon release, a time set aside in our day to remember and include our special children.

Helium filled balloons are passed out, along with markers, giving us all one more chance to tell our children the things we most long to say—mostly "I Love You." And then, oblivious to the world around us, we stand as one, but each involved in his own thoughts, prayer and emotions as we released hundreds of balloons to the sky and they disappear to a destiny we are certain they will reach.

The children are the heart and soul of the group, because it is the shared inner representations of the dead children which bond the members to each other. The children are in the midst of the group, not simply within each of the individual parents. Yet the children are also wherever balloon messages are carried. The ritual provides a means by which the parent can both reach out to the dead child and feel the presence of the child within. They "stand as one, but each involved in his own thoughts, prayer and emotion." Because the bond with the child is shared within the group, the parents can be in touch privately with the individual inner representation of their child. Because the group shares in the strong bond with the child, there is tremendous strength within the group. Because there is such strength within the group, the bond with the child feels surer. One balloon sent into the sky would seem a lonely and fragile message. Hundreds of balloons, each addressed to an individual child, are sure to get through.

In meetings the pain is shared and in that sharing, the bond with the child is shared. In the ritual with which each meeting begins, all around the circle introduce themselves, giving their names and then their children's names and something about their children's death. Often parents add a sentence or two about how good or bad a month it has been or tell if there is a significant date such as a birthday or death anniversary near. If both parents attend, usually one of them tells about the child while the other just says, "I'm Mary, Joan's mother." At the end of the introductions, the cumulative effect of all those names and all that pain is a deep quiet punctuated by the soft sobs of some newly bereaved.

The dead children are included in the community in many activities. As they connect with each other, parents include their bond with the child in the conversation just as parents of living children talk about their children when they meet new people. At a regional meeting, I overheard an extended conversation in which a man and a woman tried to figure out if their children could have known each other since they were at the same university for three years. What were their majors? Where did they live? What activities did they join? Both children were dead, so most of the data to answer the question was unavailable, but that did not seem the point of the conversation. It was very clear to me, as I eavesdropped, that the conversation was enjoyable in its own right. Nearly every year, for a meeting program, everyone brings and passes around pictures of their children and tells stories about the child. At national and regional meetings, there are long lines of picture boards. Parents from around the country often begin talking as they stand looking at the pictures of the children. Cards and phone calls come on the children's birthdays. One of the meetings had a program at Christmas at which people brought a present they would have bought for their child. The presents were then given to a children's home. People said it gave them an opportunity to buy a present for their child. One woman whose child has been dead for 10 years brought two big bags of presents. She said she had wanted to buy presents for him all these years and this was her chance. She was pleased that her 14-year-old son went shopping with her and, when they were at the cash register, asked her to wait while he went back and bought his own present for his brother. She felt good that her living son also shared the bond with her dead son.

Helping Others as an Expression of the Continuing Bond

For those who become core members and then move to leadership in the group, work in the group connects them with their child in a way that both the child's better self and the parent's better self are actualized. At a meeting effectiveness workshop that I help lead every few months for the facilitators and core members of the meeting from different parts of the city, we had many new facilitators who did not know each other. I suggested that we begin by having everyone introduce him- or herself to the others by telling how each still feels connected to his or her child. In doing so, all connected their leadership in the meetings with their relationship with their dead child. One woman said she feels her daughter is fully a part of her while she is doing Bereaved Parents work. She said that in Bereaved Parents she is "continuing who Beth was." She described Beth as a person who was always helping others. She has many memories of Beth being on the phone talking to friends who needed someone to listen. She remembered once waking up in the morning and finding Beth with the telephone cradled on her shoulder having fallen asleep listening to a friend.

So, now, while the mother is a helper in Bereaved Parents, and especially while she talks on the phone to the newly bereaved, she continues the kind of person that Beth was.

The facilitator of a newly formed meeting picked up that theme and
talked about her son as helper. He had been in a peer counseling
group and had spoken at places on behalf of DARE, a drug prevention program. So helping others was part of who her child was, and
therefore, her helping others makes the child real in her life. She said
she sometimes feels her son looking over her shoulder saying, "Come
on mom, you can do it." She felt challenged getting the new meeting
going. At that time, there were few attending her meeting. She had a
daunting task ahead of doing the organizational work, the publicity,
and still running the meeting. But her son is behind her, saying, "Go
for it, mom. You can do it." Her son is a kind of cheerleader in her
life.

A third meeting facilitator talked about her son as the one who
brought the vitality into the family. It was the anniversary of the
child's death, so she was in pretty bad shape during the early part of
the workshop. She said she really missed the vitality. He was the one
who organized things. If he said, "Let's go skiing," they went skiing.
She said, now when she gets blue she thinks of him as the one saying,
"Come on, let's get going." She said,

> You know, sometimes I just sit downstairs at the computer. I call it my
> nothing time because I just play the same game over and over. I hear
> him, almost pulling at my chair, saying, "Come on mom, get your ass
> up; get going mom: get your ass out of here; get doing something." So
> I want to just sit still and do nothing, but I feel like he is the one pushing
> me to get involved in this group, to do something, to get out of my
> lethargy.

The facilitator for the infant-toddler group had two stillborn children, so her children could not have been models for her helping now.
But she identified with the other leaders' children. She said,

> I don't have the kind of memories of the children pushing me like that,
> but I have always been the kind of person like your daughter and like
> your son. I have always been the kind of person who reached out and
> wanted to help, and so I am doing that now.

As a way of closing the introductions, I later asked the question
"How do you feel about each other now that you have shared your
children in this way?" The answer was, as one person put it, "I feel
close to you. Now that I know your children, I know you."

Including the Continuing Bond in Other Communities

As they learn to share the child within the group, members find ways to include the child in their other communities. One woman reported that, six years after her daughter's death, she decided she wanted the child included in the family Christmas gift exchange.

> Last year, 1991, I shocked my sister, who usually organizes the name exchange. I called her ahead of that day and said, "I want Phillip's name in the exchange too." Well, there was silence on the phone. So I began to explain—whoever gets Phillip's name can make a donation to a charity in his name. Yes, his name was included, and for the first time since 1985, I felt he was part of things.

In a few cases, the parents must do a little fictional work in creating the biography of their child and themselves. Until recently in this society, a miscarried child had not been regarded as real, so the miscarriage was not treated as a real bereavement. Very early in the life of the group, there was ambivalence about miscarriages, but within a few years after the formation of the infant/toddler group, neonatal losses were treated like the deaths of full-term babies. An interesting development has occurred, as parents who miscarried before the chapter was formed have come to meetings. These people reframed their situation using the group's definition, rather than the definition the wider society had given. They report they have been able to express and work through feelings for which they had hitherto found no outlet. One such mother, for example, wrote in a newsletter about telling her teenage son for the first time about a miscarriage when he was small. She had been sent home from the hospital not even knowing the sex of the dead child. Her son suggested they name the baby Cory, a name which could be either a boy or a girl. She wrote that even though she does not have a gender when she weeps, she does have a name, and she sees a face. The inner representation is thus established as a personal reality and within the family's social reality. The grief can then be focused. Though the mother has never seen her child's face, she can supply the face and know the child, even as she feels the hole in her life and family that the death of the child created.

In the beginning parents did not know how to include the dead child in their own lives, although they had a deep sense that they would. Often their communities did not know how to include the dead child because modern families and neighborhoods no longer have ways of doing that. They learned in Bereaved Parents that the child could be part of their social world, and as parents are well along in their grief, they find ways to integrate their bond with their children into the bonds they have with their neighbors, families, and coworkers.

Resolved As Much As It Will Be: The Parent's Inner World

Living with Sadness

Members are adamant in their conclusion that "you don't get over your grief." They often add, "but it doesn't stay the same." The message to newly bereaved parents at their first meeting is unequivocal, "It will always hurt, but it will not hurt the way it does now." What, then, can resolution mean?

At an alumni gathering the group went around the room doing the ritual of introduction. There was a lot of humor. The fourth person, who had been a group facilitator a few years earlier, paused for a moment after she introduced her child and said, "Gosh, it feels so good to say that and not cry. Look, we are doing this and we are sitting around laughing. Isn't that really nice to do?" There was a lot of agreement. Several said they were moving on with their lives, noting with a laugh, "We are not even on the mailing list any more." A man said, "The first time I went to candlelight, I didn't think I could stand to be there. I went because I needed to. After five years, I was one of the people who read the names. And do you know what? This year it skipped my mind. We forgot about it. I guess that shows how far we've come." Several said they remember their child regularly, and that it is a good feeling. Occasionally, they still cry, but that's OK too. Their sadness is part of them, and they can recognize it and not be afraid of it.

In a newsletter, a mother wrote about "older grief."

> Older grief is gentler
> It's about sudden tears swept in by a strand of music. . . .
> Older grief is about aching in gentler ways, rarer longing, less engulfing fire.
> Older grief is about searing pain wrought into tenderness.

Fully Established Continuing Bond

The bonds we have with our children are complex, so transforming that the bond can be a long and exhausting task. But eventually, the parents in the group are able to reestablish the inner representation of their dead child as part of their ongoing life. One of the paradoxical feelings often mentioned in meetings is that finally completing grief is itself a kind of loss. Moving on with life has its own ambivalence for bereaved parents, but the ambivalence is somewhat mollified by the reestablished inner representation of the child. As she talked to her child in a poem, one mother reflected on how hard it was for her to take advantage of some new opportunities that were opening to her. She had wanted just to be a mom, but that was no longer an option. She closed the poem with a request:

> If you can't make this earthly journey through time with me,
> Will you then come along in my heart and wish me well?

The parents often tie the resolution of their grief to their bond with their child. The parent's newfound interest in life is often described in terms of the child as an active part of their inner life. As the child comes along in their heart to wish them well, many report that the peace they have found in their resolution is what their child wishes or would have wished for them.

> It was an unmistakable thrill
> That moment I first noticed
> I think more about his life now
> Than about his death!
> It's just what he would have wanted!

Continuing Bond Guiding the Better Self

Dead children are often melded into the parent's better self in a way that makes the children seem like teachers of life's important lessons. We might say that the dead child is part of the parent's realization of the spiritual truths of cooperation and caregiving. The father of a child born with multiple congenital heart defects, but who lived "2,681 days," ties his present activity in Bereaved Parents to those lessons.

> He not only taught me the importance of what really matters in life, but through his death, also how we can make even more use of his life.
>
> Because of Timothy we make ourselves available to other bereaved parents who are at some point on death's desolation road. . . . So, whenever people ask if I'm done grieving for my precious son, I answer with much conviction, "Most assuredly so. But I will never be done showing my appreciation for having been blessed with such a gift."

Resolved As Much As It Will Be: The Parent's Social World

Making the Child's Life Count

Part of the resolution of grief is making the pain count for something, or, put another way, of making the parent's life, especially the experience of the child's death, count for something. In making their own life meaningful, the parents' inner representation of the child is made real. One of the ways parents' lives can count, and the children be real, is to help others, that is, to return to the cooperative and caregiving interactions which characterizes parenting. The organizational life of Bereaved Parents depends on some people staying and leading the group as a way of expressing the change in their lives that their child and their grief made. A man who led the committee planning the candlelight ceremony wrote, "I wanted most to do it for Carla. All that I do now I do to honor her memory and her life." He continued,

> We do need to find a positive outlet for all the anger and pain. Find a charity, or a cause that has personal meaning; get involved with Bereaved Parents; plant a garden; get into shape; do something that illustrates the positive effect that your child had on you—even if you are the only one to see it.

The dynamic creates some moments of irony, as happened when one person was honored for extraordinary service to the national organization. After he got a long standing ovation at the convention, he said, "I just had a funny thought. I thought, if Dirk were here, wouldn't he be proud. But if he were here, this wouldn't be happening." But the irony is not expressed too often, because the interactions in the life of the group have an authentic feel. The tasks are important and difficult. Members take long calls from the newly bereaved, spend two days a month with a small group folding and labeling newsletters for mailing, or make calls all over the city to have donations for the picnic which will include the balloon release. Meeting facilitators prepare for several days and then spend hours debriefing each other as they try to keep abreast of members' progress and the complex interactions in the meetings. The organization has proved itself to these parents. Affiliation with other bereaved parents gave them a path toward the resolution of their grief. In giving back to others, their experience is part of their better selves and an expression of their bond with their dead child.

Reintegration into Wider Communities

Early in their membership, parents found they could be bonded with their children in their affiliation with the group. Over time that bond changes. As the bond with the child becomes more secure in their life, the bond with the group becomes less focused. In a meeting of a committee rethinking the organizational structure, a discussion centered on the idea that the group works best when there is a steady turnover of meeting facilitators. Two former facilitators said that they just knew when the time in their grief had come for them to move on from that job. A woman whose daughter had been dead two and a half years and who had recently taken on the task of facilitating a meeting said, "I don't understand. The time I give to Bereaved Parents is my Anna time." She thought of the energy and care she gives the group as care and energy she would be giving to the child. She worried, "So, what does it mean to move on? Do I lose my child? Does that mean I won't have that any more?" A veteran who no longer attends meetings, replied,

> No, you don't lose that. It has been thirteen years for me. I was like you when I was facilitating the meeting. That was my connection with Paul. It was real direct; when I was doing Bereaved Parents work, that was for Paul. I can't say exactly when it changed or how, but now he is there all the time. He is just there; he is part of me. It isn't my connection with BP that connects him to me. But Bereaved Parents gave me something important when I needed it, and I want to give something back. Sometimes it is good for me to be very involved, and other times it seems like I should pull back more. Right now I feel like getting more involved again. But that is because it feels right to be part of something good. Paul is part of that, but Paul is part of many things in my life.

Early in their grief, parents searched for community in which they could keep their bond with their children. They were angry when their children were not included in their interactions with the family. An important element in transforming the bond was sharing the bond with the child with others. For those who stay with the group as leaders, the bond with the child remains part of their work in the group. As their grief resolves, parents find that the bond with the child is a natural part of many of their social affiliations. At a meeting a father, whose son had been dead over 10 years, reported that early in his grief people seemed afraid to talk to him about his son. But as he is more resolved, the boy becomes part of many spontaneous conversations. At work he keeps a piece of metal from his son's welding class on his desk as a paperweight. He reported that even people who could not have known what the object was used to avoid asking about it.

> For a couple years there, you could just see them trying not to look at it, let alone mention it. Now someone will see it and ask, and when I tell them what it is and why I keep it there and what it means to me, they just accept it and seem comfortable with how I feel about my son.

And then the conversation moves on to business. Thus, the inner representation of the child is integrated into the parent's social world in similar ways the inner representation of a living child would be.

Nonordinary Phenomena in the Everyday World

The phenomena which indicate parents' active interaction with their dead children, a sense of presence, hallucinations (parents might argue that "hallucination" is an inappropriate word here), belief in a child's continuing active influence on thoughts or events, or a conscious incorporation of the characteristics or virtues of the child into the self, are no longer occasions for the parents' concern about their own sanity. The phenomena are accepted as positive part of everyday living. On the twentieth anniversary of her son's death, Margaret Gerner, the founder of the St. Louis chapter, reflected in the newsletter on his place in her life and sent him a message of love and care.

> Arthur is still a big part of my life even today. As a family . . . we don't hesitate to mention him, even to strangers, if he fits into the conversation. . . . We tease about him. Pictures get crooked on the wall and we say "Arthur's been at it again. . . . We ask his help. Something big is in the wind for one of us and we tell Arthur "get working on it. . . ."
>
> Arthur's death has had a tremendous impact on my life. His death has been an impetus for positive change and growth for me. . . . I had Arthur for only a few short years, but he has given a special love to my life. He can't receive my love, but, none the less, I can send it to him by giving it to others.
>
> Arthur, years ago, in my heart, I let you go—to run and play in Heaven and not to have to worry about how I'm doing.
>
> Now, on the twentieth anniversary of your death, again my heart is stopping by Heaven's playground to just say Hi! and to tell you how much I love and miss you.

☐ Conclusions

In this chapter we have traced the complex interactions between the inner worlds and social worlds of bereaved parents as they transform the inner representation of their dead child. We have been talking about a complex task and trying to understand. We have been trying to get inside the lives of the parents as they reconstruct the durable biographies of themselves and their dead children. We have been trying to follow the progression of the relationship between the parents' inner world and their social worlds. I realize that I have asked readers to open themselves to the lives of bereaved parents, and that when people do that they often find themselves with strong feelings and thoughts. The feelings and thoughts both help us to understand and hinder our clear, orderly thinking. I will close this chapter by offering two conclusions. The first is a schematic summary of what we have seen in the inner and social worlds of bereaved parents as they move through the self-help process in Bereaved Parents. The second is a slightly-edited version of my notes from one meeting on the nonordinary phenomena in which parents still feel bonded to their dead children. I have decided on these two ways of ending the chapter because neither seems complete without the other. If we end with a nicely arranged outline, we understand what is happening, but we miss the wonderful complexity of how it happens. If we end with field notes in all their complexity, we can get a sense of how the process is happening, but we have little grounding in what is happening. As an information medium, one of the advantages a book shares with the Internet, as opposed for example to film, is that the user controls which items are used, how much time to spend on items, and the order in which the items are accessed. I think I have made heavy demands on readers in this chapter, so I trust that readers who have made it this far will use the conclusion(s) they need to get ready for the discussion of solace in the connection with transcendent reality, the discussion of the making sense of the the child's death and the parent's life by maintaining or remolding a worldview, and the discussion of how professionals can help parents along their way.

Conclusion One

Bereaved parents' pain is like an amputation. A part of them has been cut off. They have lost active interaction with their living child, and now they know death as they have never known it before. The interactions within Bereaved Parents are commensurate with the cooperative and nurturing, rather than with the competitive, interactions that characterize parenting. The dynamics by which grief is resolved by parents in Bereaved Parents are transformations of the inner representation of the dead child in the parent's inner world and in the parent's social world. As the reality of the child's death, as well as the reality of the parent's continuing bond with the child, are made part of the socially shared reality, the inner representation of the child can be transformed in the parent's psychic life. The end of grief is not severing the bond with the dead child, but integrating the child into the parent's life in a different way than when the child was alive. Phenomena which indicate interactions with the dead child change from being mysterious to being an everyday part of life. The group seems a temporary affiliation in members' lives in that the group is the social bond in which the pain can be shared and the bond with the child acknowledged and honored. When parents stop active participation in the group, however, it is not because they have moved away from their dead child. At the end of their time in the Bereaved Parents, the child is part of their ongoing inner life and part of the social bonds in which they feel at home. There are no stages by which grief moves toward resolution, but members of the Bereaved Parents have developed an informal schema by which they locate themselves and others: newly bereaved, into their grief, well along in their grief, and resolved as much as it will be. We can summarize what is happening in the parents' inner world and in the parents' social world in the Table 1.

TABLE 1. BOND WITH THE DECEASED CHILD IN THE INNER AND SOCIAL WORLDS OF BEREAVED PARENTS AS THEY MOVE TOWARD RESOLUTION

	Inner World	Social World
Newly Bereaved	• Dissociation • Out of touch with the child • Anticipation of continuing bond with the child • Linking objects that evoke the presence of the child	• Isolation from usual social networks • Inadequate symbol systems by which to interpret the new reality
Into Their Grief	• Separate from the living child • Connect with child's pain • Deal with ambivalence in parent-child bond	• Share bond with the child in self-help group • "Being there" for each other • Share practical solutions • Validate interactions with dead child
Well Along in Their Grief	• Exchange pain for positive bond with the child • Connect bond with the child to parent's own healing.	• Stabilize continuing bond • Share continuing bond in ritual and customs • Helping other bereaved parents as expression of the continuing bond • Include continuing bond in other communities
Resolved as Much as it Will Be	• Learn to live with sadness • Continuing bond guides the parent's better self	• Make child's life count • Reintegrate into wider communities. • Accept non-ordinary phenomena as part of the everyday world

Conclusion Two

As a way of trying to give the flavor of the interactions in the group, the following pages are notes I made after one of the "unusual experience meetings." As I have done with other extended accounts, I have taken out the names and have changed some details to disguise individual parent's identities. It was a large meeting, with over 40 people attending. As usual, the conversations did not follow any straight lines, and reports of experience were fully intermixed with interpretations of what the experiences mean to the individual, and interpretations about the *scientific* validity of the experiences. In keeping with the group's style, there was no attempt to reach consensus, so contradictory interpretations could exist side by side with no need for reconciliation.

The meeting began with short reports prepared by two families who had met with a person claiming to be a medium. There had been some features in the press about the medium, so the group was interested in the reports of someone they knew who had been to see him. The first report was from a leader of the group who met with the medium along with her ex-husband (her dead son's father), her mother, and her surviving son. The medium had named her son, her deceased father, and then a roommate of her son at college who later died. The mother reported that family members differed in their response to the visit, but that all felt it to be a positive experience, that is it felt good to hear about her son and to talk together as a family about him. But the family members retained various degrees of skepticism about whether they were actually in touch with him. The mother believed she had been in contact with her son, but her mother and son were noncommittal when she pressed them.

An older couple reported that they had visited the medium together. The husband was very skeptical. He thought the medium's answers were those which could be given by any intelligent person. He talked of "how much we want to be in contact with the children, so we will take any evidence we can get." His wife, who is a believer, said several times that he should listen again to the tape they had made. He said he had. It was obvious that we were hearing an interchange they had been over several times before, and that the couple was comfortable with differences of opinion, so the meeting started with an openness to both experiences and to differing interpretations. There were no further reports of anyone visiting a medium.

The meeting went to parents sharing more spontaneous experiences. A woman who attends, though her husband does not, said her husband is a "doubter," so he waited three days to ask if she had slapped him on his hip in the night. She said no, so both now think it was their dead daughter. One man told about sitting at the bedside while his dying son had had a long near-death experience. The son seemed to be having an interview. The parents only heard the answers, not the questions. The son said "Yes. No, I didn't do that. Yes, I did that." Then the child said he was having a hard time getting in because, "It is too narrow, it is too high." The father did not know what the experience meant to him now, except it seemed proof that there is "something more."

The conversation in the meeting then turned to coincidental events. One person talked about going through the house screaming after coming home from a trip a few weeks after the son died. She was just overwhelmed by the reality that he wasn't there. Then she got a call from the boy's father to whom she was no longer married. She said that was just the person she needed to talk to. She is convinced that it could not have been that the boy's father knew how she was feeling, because when they were married he did not read her feelings well. It must have been something else that made him call just when she needed him. It must have been the son, she thought, who made the father call right at that moment. Another mother talked about coming home from the funeral and smelling her daughter's perfume. She smelled all her bottles and then went to the daughter's room, checked all the bottles there, and found that none had been opened. So she was convinced that the daughter was there with them.

One couple told about a dog that seemed to have been a gift from their son. This couple has always had full-size schnauzers. Just before the son died, they had to euthanize one of them. One day a little girl came up to them when they were in the yard and asked if they knew the dog she was carrying. It was a miniature schnauzer. The mother found it significant that the dog's ears were floppy, not clipped upright, just like the dog that had died. A check of the neighborhood, found no one missing the dog. When the dog had barely been in house, after they decided to keep it, the father had to run an errand, and the dog darted through the kitchen into a breakfast room to look out the window at the father walking out. It was as if the dog knew the house. Both the parents felt quite uncanny at that happening, and so are convinced that the dog is a gift of the dead son.

One person reported a preschool child throwing things out of his room, saying he didn't want any of the things the dead older brother had given him. Right then, an ornament on the Christmas tree started working again. It was a little person who sawed a log as the ornament turned. The mother reported that the arm had been broken and the ornament had not been working for some time. The arm was fixed and the ornament was working and still works. They reported the meaning they gave to their living child: "See, Jackie doesn't want you to be mad at him. He really wants to be friends with you." The same person reported that the same child looked out the window and saw the dead child helping an older surviving child mow the grandmother's lawn. Lawn mowing had been the dead child's job, and now the child was helping the sibling who had inherited the job.

A person who had been in the group for some time asked another to share a story that had the same sense of the uncanny. At that request, a woman told how her family has cardinals as linking objects, that is, they sense the presence of the child when they see cardinals. When the child was alive they watched cardinals outside their windows. One time cardinals built a nest right outside the window and the child watched them raise their young. Now, many times cardinals have appeared when the parents need them. One time, as the mother was really down, she saw a cardinal looking in the front door glass. Her husband reported a few minutes later that there was a cardinal on a bush looking in the basement window. Another time, when she was frightened during the pregnancy of a subsequent child, she looked out and saw 15 mixed male and female cardinals on the front lawn. Another person in the group noted that cardinals don't flock together, and it would be extremely unusual to see that many at one time. The mother responded that, at that time, they did not have a feeder. Now, they have a sunflower feeder, and she has never seen more than four or five cardinals, even with the feeder. So, the unusual natural event is for the parents a proof of the dead child's presence.

After reports of a few more very dramatic experiences, several people reported that they used to wish for the dramatic experience, and that, right after their child died, they wanted a visitation or a vision, but none ever came. "But, you know," said one person, "when I stopped looking for the dramatic experiences, that's when I really got him. Little things would happen." She talked about a sense of presence at times when she was down and when good things would happen in her relationships with others. Those times were, for her, when she felt the bond with her dead child most intensely.

A woman who was taking yoga lessons lost her four-year-old daughter. The little girl's love was gymnastics. As the mother does yoga, she has a sense of the child's presence. "That's because I'm in touch with my body just like she was in touch with her body." She reported three different vivid experiences during yoga. The first time was an especially strong sense of presence. The second time, she was learning a difficult position and the child said, "Here, mommy, like this," and the child showed her how to do the position. The last time, she was bent over forward and the child kept tapping her on the back, and she said to the child, "Now you go away now, this is mommy's time." With a laugh she said it was just like when the child was alive; sometimes she just needed the child to stop pestering her so she could have her own space. At that, the woman who had told the story of the miniature schnauzer said that it is true that children retain their individual characteristics after they die. Once she really felt the son's presence as she sat in the upper story of her house. As the experience ended, she heard the toilet flush downstairs, apparently before he left. "Well that would be like him. He certainly spent enough time in the library," she said.

The husband of the woman taking yoga lessons reported that he had visualized his daughter at a group meeting a few months earlier as the members did some relaxation techniques together. He said, "She is with me all the time, and I think about her a lot. But she was right there (holding his hand in front of his face). I don't do that kind of stuff. I don't believe in that. But all I know is that she was right there."

Then there was a lot of sharing of what little children had said. There was a consensus that children are not contaminated by adult notions, so they really do understand what is going on. For example, a grandmother reported that her grandchild said to her mother (the dead son's sister), when driving home, that she wanted to drive fast to get home because Jim promised he would come back tonight. At that, the mother pulled off the road and asked what the child meant. The child reported that Jim had come last week, and that he had said he would return tonight. Interestingly, Jim's mother did not then have a report of any visits that night. It hadn't occurred to her to follow up on that until she reported it at the meeting. The woman next to me said that the previous week her six-year-old grandson said he had a conversation with her dead son, the child's uncle. The woman said that her grandchild came to her saying, "Grandma, it is really important that you know that Will is with Jesus." She didn't know what to respond, so she gave a mild reassurance. So the grandchild persisted, "No, it is really important for you to know that Will is with Jesus." The woman now feels the reason the child was so persistent is that she had some sort of message.

As the meeting drew to a close, people offered a few possible interpretations of the experiences that had been shared. A woman who had said nothing so far said, "You know we always think that heaven is up there—far away. Maybe we are wrong about that. Maybe heaven is right here where we are. It is just another dimension." A man said, "We can't see radio waves; they go right through us. So the idea of the child being here doesn't have to be crazy."

One of the core members of the group said she never had direct experience of her son, but it made sense to her because he was an independent person who was very much on his own at college where he died. But, she said, when she was at the Botanical Garden, she had felt compelled to go to a spot where, she later learned, there is a tree planted in honor of the child of another person in the group. The connection with each other's children was the opportunity for the group facilitator to introduce a closing thought that the dead children of the group are together, and that the bond with the children is part of the bond with the group. An older woman who had not spoken before then said, "Well, for you who have younger children. My son was always complaining that these little kids were hanging all over him. Some children would call him daddy, some would call him grandpa." So she wanted the others to know, "If any of you are worried how your young children are, don't worry. My son is up there and he takes care of kids just fine. So they will be just fine."

Then the meeting ended as usual with many people staying for about an hour talking over coffee and cookies.

CHAPTER

Solace: Comfort within Devastation

☐ The Parents' Pain

"I walk around all day feeling like somebody just kicked me in the stomach," a bereaved mother said in a meeting. "I just hurt all over, all the time," said another. The reality that their child died is inescapable. In the first year, a few moments of relaxation, or a day of relative calm is an achievement. For the first few months, many parents report, they feel numb. The pain is there, but they are protected by the early sense of shock. Then the numbness wears off. "I have cried every day," a mother said in a counseling session three and a half months after her daughter died. "But today it came all the way from the bottom. I pulled the car into the McDonald's lot and cried in a way I have never cried in my life." A piece of them has been amputated and every inner and interpersonal nerve ending fires in protest. Months into their grief, parents report that the pain surges up again as if it were new. Potential triggers for the renewed pain are all around: an advertisement for a store in which a teenager bought a favorite sweater, a line of preschoolers moving down the sidewalk. "You think you are okay, and life is starting to move along, and then, 'Bang,' one of these things just hits you out of the blue, and it is like you are right back at the beginning."

Even after two decades of being with bereaved parents, I do not think I can comprehend, much less describe, the pain of early grief. I hear the words, and I have heard them enough to respond in helpful ways, but as a nonbereaved parent I find nothing in my experience that seems faintly similar. The members of the group insist that only others whose children have died can understand. It seems to me that their claim should be taken at face value. The baseline of the spiritual lives of bereaved parents is their pain.

The first lesson bereaved parents share with each other is that "you never get over it." The pain changes, but it never goes away, they say, because "you never stop loving your child." Bereaved parents do find resolution to their grief in the sense that they learn to live in their new world. They *re-solve* the matters of how to be themselves in a family and community in a way that makes life meaningful. They learn to grow in those parts of themselves that did not die with the child. One mother wrote, "Being a bereaved parent will always be a part of our lives—it just won't be the most important or only part." They learn to invest other parts of themselves in other tasks and other relationships. But somewhere inside themselves, they report, there is a sense of loss that remains. A bereaved father wrote in a newsletter:

> If grief is resolved, why do we still feel a sense of loss on anniversaries and holidays and even when we least expect it? Why do we feel a lump in the throat even six years after the loss? It is because healing does not mean forgetting and because moving on with life does not mean that we don't take a part of our lost love with us.

☐ Definition of Solace

The defining characteristic of solace is the sense of soothing. Solace means pleasure, enjoyment, or delight in the face of hopelessness, despair, and sorrow. For bereaved parents, solace comes in the sense of transcendent reality experienced in the midst of devastation. Solace comes into the heart of the pain. Solace is found within the sense of being connected to a reality that transcends the self. Among bereaved parents, their interaction with their dead children is merged into their other experience of transcendent reality. Like the saints and angels in the Western traditions and the gods, buddhas, and bodhisattvas in the Eastern traditions, the spirits of their children bridge the gap between the worlds of the living and the dead, between the realms of heaven and earth.

To console means to alleviate, but not to remove, sorrow or distress. "The angel of consolation follows the angel of tears," say the Sufis. Samuel Johnson said,

> Consolation, or comfort, signifies some alleviation to that pain to which it is not in our power to afford the proper and adequate remedy; they imply rather an augmentation of the power of bearing, than a diminution of the burden (Webster's New International Dictionary of the English Language, 1913).

The modern world is built on denying pain, or at least on making all pain curable. So old phrases like "gladden the heart," come to mind as we try to define solace.

Parents do not get over their grief. In the face of irreparable loss, bereaved parents find solace by getting in touch with transcendent reality within a world that has, for them, fallen apart. To find solace is to find comfort, to find relief, hope, or strength amidst affliction or sorrow. Bereaved parents are often angry when well-meaning friends say things that try to take away the pain in a way that diminishes the meaning of their bond with their child. For example, they may say, "Be thankful that you still have other children." They are angry because, although they do not want to be in such pain, their pain is a link to their child; it is the present form of their love. The solace bereaved parents find does not take the pain away.

Paul Horton (1981) finds that the majority of people have a history of solace that they nurture. Most adults can easily identify a solace-filled object to which they repair when they need soothing, a memory of a special place or person who is no longer physically present, a piece of music or art, an imagined more perfect world, a sense of divine presence. Horton says solace seems necessary to participate meaningfully in a community. In his clinical practice he found that psychopathic criminals had no sense of solace in their lives.

D. W. Winnicott (1953, 1971, pp. 1–25) finds that the earliest form of solace is a child's transitional object such as a security blanket. The toddler is learning to live as an independent person in a frightening world after the secure sense of the mother's protection is gone. The transitional object provides security that helps children explore new situations and adjust to unfamiliar environments (Passman, 1976; Passman & Weisberg, 1975). Winnicott connects spirituality in its many forms to this early solace. He finds that our ability to participate in cultural, artistic, and religious symbols and myths is an extension of our early transitional objects:

> The task of reality-acceptance is never completed; . . . no human being is free from the strain of relating inner and outer reality, and . . . relief from this strain is provided by an intermediate area of experience which is not challenged (arts, religion, etc.) This intermediate area is in direct continuity with the play area of the small child who is "lost" in play (1971, p. 13).

The language of one mother writing in the newsletter shows that she already knew the part of herself where she now feels connected to her child.

> I cannot open my eyes to see his smile. I close my eyes and listen to my heart, for it is there that he lives. I must dig deeper inside myself to a place that I ever knew existed to feel the joy this child brought.

Just as little children feel comfort with their security blankets in strange or threatening environments, so in the terrifying aloneness of parental bereavement, solace comes within a bond that transcends present space and time. The child's sense of the mother's presence is, of course, in the concrete form of the blanket. We will see that many bereaved parents also have objects that call forth the presence of their transcendent reality; but we also will see that most adults have developed bonds with transcendent reality at higher cognitive levels and more highly-evolved emotional levels. The sense of transcendent reality, then, is multifaceted. That is, it is experienced in many ways and on different developmental levels at the same time. While Buddhist practioners work to realize nondual reality, they sit in front of a statue of a bodhisattva that provides a physical symbol of movements between the levels of suffering. The Christian mystic who knows that the reality of God can only be defined as a being greater than can be conceived, may also offer daily prayers to a patron saint who intercedes with a God that feels like a judgmental father.

Transcendent Reality in Religious Traditions

Solace is grounded in the experience that is at the core of spiritual life: the encounter or merger with transcendental reality, that is, in those moments when there is an opening between the realm of the sacred and the realm of the profane. In a trance, the shaman communicates with the spirits in order to heal problems in this world. Mohammed goes to the cave where he is given divine words to recite to humanity. The yogi transforms physical energy into spiritual energy. Perhaps such high experiences are rare. Still, most people have, at points in their lives, felt touched by something beyond themselves, by, as Kant said, the starry sky above or the moral law within. Like Luke Skywalker in the film *Star Wars*, many people feel the Force is with them. When in *West Side Story*, Tony's love for Maria transcends the boundaries of peer group and ethnic divisions, he can sing that the sound of her name is "like music playing" or "almost like praying." Psychologically, in these moments our usual ego boundaries become more permeable; we no longer feel alone; and we feel joined to those we love, to our people, to nature, or to God (see Smart, 1994, pp. 58–73). In these moments, as Martin Buber said, we leave the I-it and move into the I-thou.

In Western spiritual traditions the experience of transcendent reality is most often conceived as an encounter with the *Wholly Other*. Scholars of comparative religion have found useful Rudolf Otto's distillation of Western religious experience (1923, pp. 1–40). Otto wrote that what makes an experience religious is the "peculiar difference of *quality* in the mental attitude and emotional content of the religious life itself" (p.3). Otto names that quality the "holy" or the "sacred." We know the holy, he says, in a mental state

> which is perfectly *sui generis* and irreducible to any other; and therefore, like every absolutely primary and elementary datum, while it admits being discussed, it cannot be strictly defined (p.7).

At the core of the holy is the *mysterium tremendum et facinans*, a mystery which is overpowering and fascinating. Before the mystery, he says, we feel awe—which for Otto means speechlessness. The mystery, he says, overpowers us so we behold the majesty of the divine who is "Wholly Other." Yet, he says, even as we are overpowered, we know we are creatures in the presence of our creator.

> I am God and not man,
> the Holy One in your midst,
> and I will not come to destroy (Hosea 11:9).

Not everyone has such dramatic encounters, but many people have moments that seem to softly echo Otto's *mysterium tremendum et facinans*. "Indeed much of religious ritual is designed to express and to stimulate such feelings" (Smart, 1996, p. 59). The pilgrim at Mecca calls, "I am here, Oh God. What is your command?" The sinner at the close of a revival meeting sings, "Just as I am without one plea." The audience stands while the words, "And He shall reign for ever and ever" pour over them. A few moments after the delivery, a father and mother giggle as they examine their newborn's hand.

In the Eastern traditions this experience is most often conceived as "nondual." The distinction between self and other drops away. In the nondual there is no other. Indeed, at the highest levels of awareness in Hinduism, the true self (Atman) is understood to be a part of the universal spirit (Brahman), and in Buddhism, the real self (Atman) is understood to be an illusion (Anatman). True perception, Nāgārjuna says, does not discriminate between thisness and thatness. He says,

> The dualism of "to be" and "not to be,"
> The dualism of pure and not-pure:

Such dualism having abandoned,
The wise stand not even in the middle (in Suzuki, 1963, pp. 100–101).

Everything, including me, is one. In meditation or yoga practice, the distinction between inner and outer is overcome. In Zen, I learn that my hearing and the bell are not distinct from each other, but rather that reality is the hearing experience, that it is an interaction between me and the bell. In the same way the goal in meditation (if it can be said to have a goal) is to know that my conception of my self is an illusion, that I make a false distinction between a "me" inside the skin bag and a "not me" outside the skin bag. The goal is to know that I am an interaction of many interactions which are happening in the now. So, at the end of the spiritual disciplines is a new, nondual, way of being-in-the-world.

Such flashes of enlightenment may be out of the reach of those of us who are still attached to this world, but many people experience moments when the distinction between inner and outer, between then and now, or between me and you are blurred, if not erased. From the top, a hiker surveys the mountain world where once the ancients thought the gods lived, quietly watches a hummingbird attracted to a red backpack, and then a golden eagle soaring on a thermal from the valley below until, as a speck in the sky, it disappears. He knows at that moment that he is a part of the earth in this place, and then he remembers that the words, "Now he is part of the earth" were said the year before when his friend's casket was lowered into the grave.

The transcendent reality, either the holy other of the Western traditions or the nondual of the Eastern traditions, is hard to express in words. In North American and European cultures, we tend to talk more about belief than about experience or practice when we discuss spirituality. So we have limited language for describing these transcendent moments. It is difficult, then, for bereaved parents to share the meaning of their spiritual lives with each other. It is especially hard in a pluralistic society, where many worldviews are represented. But when bereaved parents talk about their faith, they are often talking about their connection with transcendent reality. "I know that not everyone can say this," said a woman in the group, " but I am so thankful that I never lost my faith." By "faith" she does not mean theology or belief. She means the feeling she has when she prays that God is close and protective. It is, she said, an inner sense she can remember having as a child when she went to church with her grandmother. At a meeting, a parent said, "After Melody died, I lost my faith. I never got it back, but I got a new one." The new faith is not simply a different set of beliefs, it is a new connection with transcendent reality.

☐ Solace within the Continuing Bond

Among bereaved parents their interactions with their dead children are an important part of their other experience of transcendent reality. Their children are like saints and angels in the Western traditions and the gods, buddhas, and bodhisattvas in the Eastern traditions. Their children bridge the gap between the worlds of the living and the dead, between the realms of heaven and earth because they are citizens of both worlds. Parents find solace within their continuing bond with their dead child. We will look at four common ways Bereaved Parents interact with their dead children that bring solace: (1) linking objects, (2) religious ideas and devotion, (3) memory, and (4) identification. The ways are not exclusive, because the experience of transcendent reality is multidimensional. Bereaved parents can retain the linking objects from early in their grief while at the same time finding the presence of the child within religious practices. They can memorialize the child at the same time they incorporate the child into their identity, their own sense of selfhood.

Linking Objects

Linking objects are objects connected with the child's life that link the bereaved to the dead; in so doing, they evoke the presence of the dead (Volkan, 1981). Linking objects function like relics of the saints in which "any personal possession or part of a person's body . . . can carry the power or saintliness of the person with whom they were once associated and make him or her `present' once again" (Sullivan, 1987, p. 51).

Parents often find their linking objects very early in their grief. In the early months after a child has died, many things provide both a sense of the child's presence and an acute awareness of the child's absence. When an adult daughter was killed in a car accident, her mother adopted one of the daughter's dogs. The mother reported that the dog, like the mother, often moped about and seemed to be awaiting the dead child's return. The mother found a home for the daughter's other dog, explaining that the dog she kept had a special meaning to the daughter, and besides, the other dog was too large and needed more room to run outside than she could provide. This same mother was very aware of her need for other linking objects. She and her daughter often shopped for clothes together and gave collectibles to each other as gifts. The mother was troubled that she was having problems getting her daughter's husband to let her take some items, especially stuffed animals that she could cuddle. The husband understood his mother-in-law's request, but still it was hard for him to take anything of his wife's out of the house. He was not ready to decide what he wanted to keep and what he wanted to let go.

Over the course of a few years, it is common for parents to rely less and less on the exterior presence of the linking object because they develop a more interior sense of their child's presence. For the months after her child died, one mother reported, a stuffed animal "was like a crutch for me. I felt that as long as it was near me as I went to sleep each night, so I could reach out and touch it or smell it, that Barry's death was not so final." One day as she cleaned, she put the stuffed animal in another room and found she didn't miss it. "By then the memories of Barry were ingrained into my mind so well I didn't need to look at a symbol of his life to remember him by." Six years after his child's death, a father wrote a birthday letter to him about a few linking objects that decorate the study.

> I haven't been able to part with the bicycle cart that I bought for you and your sister a few weeks before you died. It's never used anymore, but I keep it in my study at home. . . . I still see your smile as you sat there holding our puppy. . . . Your little windup toy, the one of Donald Duck sitting in a shoe, sits on top of the file cabinet in my study. I feel close to you when I'm close to your favorite things.

The sense of smell is particularly intimate. Parents often report that they hold their children's clothes which still have the scent of the child. One mother who miscarried wrote that it is not the usual newborn scent that links her to her child.

> So the flowers I place upon his grave
> Are the only scent I know.
> So when I smell a flower
> My son always comes to mind

The linking object need not be small toys or fast fading flowers. A father whose daughter had died five years earlier said,

> It's that old pickup truck. She used to ride around in it with me. She would lean against me on the seat. It has almost 200,000 miles on it, but I am not going to sell it. By now, I probably couldn't get anything for it anyway. I told the boys they could work on it and use it if they got it going. But I'll never sell the truck because I can sit in there and feel my daughter. It's great.

The linking object is a self-validating truth to the parent that, though the child is dead, yet, in a sense, the child lives. One parent had many memories of being at the beach with her child. They would look for sand dollars which the boy saved. Her memory of those times also include natural mystical experiences (Hood, 1977) in which her bond with nature and with the child are intertwined. In a newsletter article she wrote that the child "was especially awed by the setting sun and as we walked the beaches, always he would stop and watch the sun go down—I did too! I was so happy with him." In late winter she went to Padre Island and, acutely feeling her son's absence, walked the beach alone. "Just the sand, the sea, a beautiful setting sun, the screeching gulls, God and me." She talked to God and begged Him for a sign that her son still lived, even though she knew he was dead. She asked God, "Please send me a sand dollar." She knew it was the wrong season for sand dollars. She said the local people had told her that they had seen no sand dollars since the summer.

> But I only wanted just one sand dollar—just one! Watching the fading sunset and listening to the roar of the waves, darkness began to fall, so I turned to go back when there by my feet, the waves pushed up one lone sand dollar—a small but perfect sand dollar!
>
> That is exactly the way it happened and I cannot begin to tell you the feelings I had. My prayer had been answered.

The answer to her prayer for a sign that the child still lives is the linking object of the sand dollar. It links her to her child, to God, to the past she shared with the child, and renews her link to a place that has always seemed eternal to her. Sand dollars were out of season, yet one washed up at her feet. The sand dollar, coming out of the sea and onto the land beneath her feet, crossed the boundary between the living and the dead, between timelessness and change. She had, at that moment, a sense of the uncanny, a feeling often associated with religious belief and practice. No natural laws were violated, although a rare statistical probability happened. But it was a miracle for her, no matter what her scientific mind might have known. Now that she has had the intense experience of finding the sand dollar, the memory of this experience can be evoked, and the memory itself can serve as a linking object.

People in the child's world serve as linking objects. One mother wrote about the relationship she now feels with the members of her daughter's kindergarten class. "Each of them somehow is now a piece of Martha. Now these children seem to be part of mine somehow, for they hold in their presence a part of my precious Martha." A divorced father whose 25-year-old son drowned reported that some of his son's former girl friends came to his house after the funeral. They continue to invite him for a restaurant dinner, and to send cards on holidays and on his son's birthday and death anniversary. He probably reminds the young women of their dead friend. In a conversation after a meeting, the father said that, in the intimacy he feels toward the young women, he feels close to his son, and with pride he added,

> You just know what a special kid he was because these girls are very special people. You know, he told me that after he broke up with a woman, they stayed friends. Now they give that friendship to me. One of them even brought her new boyfriend over last month to meet me and have me show him Jay's swimming trophies, and have me tell him about Jay. He seems to be a nice fellow. I thought he would be jealous of Jay; but she says if he wants to go with her, he needs to know about someone special in her life. Jay was a neat guy. Now I even think about playing with this girl's children when she has them.

Linking objects can serve as an enduring communally-shared symbol. One family in the group found the child's presence at a place in a national park which the child had spontaneously called "just like heaven." The park is several states distant, but the mother's sister lives a hundred miles from the park, so part of their yearly vacation now includes a visit to the sister and her family and a day trip to that place. I had been there, so it was easy for the couple to tell me about it. A few years after they told me the story, I was cross-country skiing in the park and came to the spot they had described. For a moment, I knew that the child was right, it is a heavenly place. My experience was richer because the child did seem there for me, and I felt close to the parents as I leaned on my poles for a moment and let the beauty wash over me.

If passersby are given a reminder, even strangers can stand in the presence of dead children. Just off a back country mountain trail where it overlooks a magnificent valley and the peaks and glaciers surrounding it, I found a rock cairn with a plaque in memory of a young person who died in an accident several years earlier a little distance from there. The view communicates the youth's love of wilderness and links his experience to the experience of the backpackers who come across the monument. Like the young people whose names are on war memorials around the world, this young man need not be known personally to feel his presence. We can stand in awe and sadness at the reality of his death, connect our sense of awe with the overwhelming grandeur of the place, and know that his spirit and his memory are still in these mountains, just as these mountains and our experience here has become a part of our soul.

One couple shared a linking object that has an often unrecognized cultural symbolism. When I asked, "Do you ever sense that Rachael is still around?" a mother answered,

Every time I see a mourning dove. Mourning doves are magnificent. The day after Rachael died, Cliff and I were sitting in the den looking out the window and there was a mourning dove on the porch. I didn't know what it was at the time, so I got out my bird book and looked it up. It is m-o-u-r-n-i-n-g dove, not m-o-r-n-i-n-g. It was so ironic because here I'd just lost a daughter, and I'm getting out my bird book to look for mourning doves. It was phenomenal that we would see a mourning dove when we were mourning. It's got to mean something, right? So the two of us took this as, "This is Rachael. Rachael is with the dove." Then, a few days later, there were two doves there. Cliff decided that it was Rachael telling him that she had a friend with her. It's really fascinating because I'll find myself thinking about her, and I'll look around and see the mourning dove. That has become a symbol of Rachael. It was on the year anniversary when we were going to the cemetery and Cliff said, "I wish I could see a mourning dove." So I said, "Come over here, there is usually a mourning dove over here." And I'll be damned if there wasn't a mourning dove on the wire. He said, "That's a sign. Now I can go to the cemetery."

As their grief matures, parents feel less of a need to be in daily contact with the linking objects, but the linking objects remain just outside their conscious field of awareness. Almost all bereaved parents have a box somewhere in the house that holds the child's possessions that they have chosen to keep. They may not open the box often, but they know it is there, and that knowledge is itself a link to the child. The linking object is joined with a larger sense of the continuing bond with the child. The sense of the child's presence moved from the external reality of the linking object to a more internal sense of the child's presence. One mother wrote:

Our children will always be with us in spirit and in love, and we often feel a need to hold onto tangible items, such as toys or clothes, to maintain that feeling of closeness. But, intense grief work allows us to let go of the relationship we had in order to create a new relationship with our child. Our remembrances, love and feelings of oneness with our child can never be destroyed. I cannot see or touch my Allen, but I vividly remember him. I have completed earthly mothering, but I still have an intense mother-child relationship with my son.

As Volkan (1981) uses the term, a linking object remains a transitional object in grief. That is, the object provides a temporary sense of attachment while the process of mourning is adjusting the mind to the fact that the attachment is over, that the person is dead and gone. Thus, Volkan uses the concept of linking object to reinforce the model of grief that says the purpose of grief is to leave the deceased behind, thereby freeing the survivor to form new attachments. Bereaved parents, as we have noted, do not sever their bonds with their dead children, but rather they remold the bonds in a way that will remain with them for the rest of their lives. If linking objects are transitional for bereaved parents, they are part of a transition to a different kind of bond. A mother writing for the newsletter shows the linking object as the midpoint of the transformation of the inner representation of the child. "Yesterday, I held you in my arms. Today, I held your picture in my arms, for I needed to be with you. Tomorrow I'll keep you in my dreams, for I will always love you." If the linking object is transitional, the transition is from being bonded with the living child to having a secure inner bond with the dead child.

Prayer, Ritual, and Religious Ideation

Linking objects focus the presence of the child in a concrete and direct way. For many people, the sense of transcendent reality is found less concretely and less directly in prayer, ritual, and religious ideation. The inner representation of the child is merged with something bigger, but something of which the parent feels a part. In most cultures in human history, the memory or presence of the dead is a central element in religious devotion. In Tibetan Buddhist meditation, after the practioner's root teacher dies, each meditation session opens with the evocation of the teacher's presence. In Japanese Buddhism, rituals for people who have died within the last 33 or 50 years comprise the primary religious activity for everyone except those few individuals who have chosen to follow the austerities of the adepts. The major summer festival is *O bon*, when the dead come back to visit the living for three days. A Muslim student in my class said that his father had gone on pilgrimage "for my grandmother who had died. He loved his mother very much." In Judaism, the Kaddish, the prayer for the dead, is an important part of the high holidays. Although Protestant Christianity banished the saints, the flowers in the front of the sanctuary each Sunday are often in memory of a deceased person, and stained glass windows are often memorials. The great dead are buried beneath the floors of English and European churches and cathedrals, while in the villages, worshipers often walk through the graveyard on their way to services.

For some parents in the contemporary world, religious ideas and devotion can be provided within an institutionalized framework, usually in the tradition in which they were raised. The comfort and presence they felt as children can now be the vehicle by which they find solace and the presence of their children. One mother wrote a letter to her dead daughters describing the sense of presence at Catholic Mass.

> Every time I attend the sacrifice of the Mass, at the part where our Blessed Lord comes into our hearts, I feel so close to your angelic presence. What a divine experience! The only problem is that it doesn't last long enough. If only the others could share these feelings.

With the rise of the more individualized spirituality of modernity, many parents have developed religious ideas and a sense of transcendent presence in devotion that is outside the orthodoxy of churches or theological doctrine. Before her child's death, one mother had already developed a pantheistic spirituality in which God seemed to her to be everywhere she chose to see God. Her dead daughter could now have the same omnipresence. On the girl's birthday her mother wrote a letter as if from the child.

> I would have been twenty today, bound by earthly constraints. Do not cry, Mom. I am forever, I am eternal, I am ageless. I am in the blowing wind, the first blades of grass in the spring, the haunting cry of the owl, the shriek of the hawk, the silent soaring of the turkey vulture. I am in the tears of those in mourning, the laughter of little children, the pain of the dying, the hopelessness of the homeless. I am the weightless, floating feeling when you close your eyes at night; I am the heaviness of a broken heart. . . . Like an invisible cocoon I surround you. I am in the moonlight, the sunbeams, the dew at dawn. . . . Do not cry. Remember me with love and laughter and, yes, with pain. For I was, I am, and I will always be. Once Amy, now nameless and free.

The sense of the uncanny can also be an ongoing experience at those times when the parent feels the presence of the child. An article in the newsletter reported on experiences which seem to be unexplained to the bereaved mother writing. One morning, after a night when she had dreamed of a crying infant, she awoke to rainbow colors on the ceiling and then discovered it was sunlight coming though a crack in the curtains and refracting off the framed photograph of her child that she had just put on the dresser. She said she felt blessed all day. Another time, after a party for her sister's children, she found a butterfly inside the window and she was convinced it was her child attending the party. Yet, another time, she broke an egg and discovered two yolks and felt her daughter close by. "I could almost hear her giggle and say, 'See Mom? I'm still right here with you.'" Although others might interpret these events more scientifically, for this parent, these are not signs she has made up, but events that seem beyond simple chance. "Do you think it's all a coincidence?" she wrote. "I think not. I firmly believe there is life after life, that the spirit lives on in ways we could never comprehend." She concluded,

> For as long as I live, there are going to be times when I need a little extra reassurance. . . . And just when I need it most, my little girl reaches through that misty barrier of space and time, gently tugs on my heart, and whispers, "It's O.K., Mom. I'm here."

Almost all the parents in the study feel that the child is in heaven. Heaven is not a religious myth or an idea that symbolizes giving up the attachment to the deceased. Heaven seems to be a reality in the heart as much as it is a place in the sky. Some people in heaven are not lost to us; they are safely with us. The inner representation of the child as in heaven is held tightly by some parents in the initial shock and disbelief of grief, even before they can develop a sense that they have an active interaction with the child. The separation from the child seems too much to bear for many parents. So, even as they feel that their child is nowhere to be found in this world, they retain hope that they will join their child after death. Early in her grief, before she had put together an integrated inner representation of the child a mother wrote in her diary,

> There's a hole in me. You see, as part of me is missing. I keep looking for my son, and all I find are bits and pieces of him—something he wrote, a picture he took, a book he read, a tape he made, something he drew—but there is an emptiness in me that these bits and pieces cannot fill, that nothing will ever fill. . . . My son is gone and he is not coming back. I will have to go to him and someday I will.

Such a feeling early in the grief often gives way to a more immediate interaction with the child in a way that, while the hope of reunion after the parent's death is retained, the bond with the child in heaven is more consoling. The dead child is merged with other significant attachments and to other death-transcending connections the parent feels in the world. The child in heaven remains the child in the heart. Heaven is *out there* and for bereaved parents it is also *in here*. In more proper theological language, it is both transcendent and immanent. Several people in the group felt the child to be with another significant person who had died. One woman whose father had died four years before her child reported:

> It was hard after my father died, because I always had this sense that I didn't know where he was. But I was busy with Lois because she was so sick all the time. After Lois died, I was really bothered that I didn't know where she was and that somehow that meant that I didn't know she was safe. That lasted two years. One day I started crying, and I realized I

wasn't just crying for Lois. I was missing my father. And suddenly I just thought, "Daddy is taking care of Lois. She is OK because she is with him and that's where he is. It is like they are together." That sounds so simpleminded. I don't believe in heaven or afterlife. I think we just live on in memory. But it just feels like I don't have that worry about either of them any more. I know they are together.

She does not believe in heaven, but she knows her daughter and father are together there.

The relationship to a child in heaven can be a complex one. The parent can both be happy that the child is in heaven and even that the child is performing useful functions in heaven, and still miss the physical interactions with the child. A week before Christmas, Wayne's mother told me that she had attended the funeral of one of her son's friends. The newly bereaved mother sought her out after the funeral because she wanted to tell her about a vision the friend's mother had the previous day in which Wayne was in heaven welcoming her son. Wayne's mother believed the woman's vision, and it provided solace, but it did not take away the pain. She said, "Now I am even more sure that he is in heaven, but I still miss him. I just want to hold him." She is still bonded to the child who was living and still feels the amputation. Her bond with the immortal child feels secure as it is reinforced in her social relationships. It is comforting, but it does not take away the pain that sits like a stone at the bottom of her soul.

Some holidays, for example Memorial Day in the United States, *O bon* in Japan, or Day of the Dead in Mexico, have a specific focus on recalling the dead. Any gathering of the family to celebrate any holiday, however, often includes poignant reminders of the absence of the dead and evocations of their presence. One mother recalled that a few months before she was murdered, her daughter told her of a dream in which the daughter was looking in the window at the family gathered for Christmas. On Christmas morning, while they were opening the gifts that the dead girl had made and hidden away for them a few weeks before she died, her husband told her to look out the window. There were two rocking chairs on the porch and one was rocking back and forth.

> My husband reached over and held my hand, and it was at that moment I remembered what Alexandria had told us about her dream, and I realized then that her dream had become a reality. Alexandria was still with all of us and was indeed content at watching the family she loved so much sharing the joy of Christmas together.

The feeling of the uncanny seems to be akin to the feelings of awe, wonder, and mystery often associated with worship and revelatory moments. Parents often interpret the feeling as an indication that the child is communicating and supporting healing actions in their lives. The feeling of the uncanny indicates that events are not just a coincidence, but somehow were meant to be and are connected to each other by meaning beyond human comprehension. One mother reported that, when she and her husband were trying to decide whether to have a subsequent child, a relative suggested they go on a religious retreat. The retreat house was on a street that had the same name as their child. The next night the new child was conceived. "Chuck and I truly believe that Carolyn gave us this sign." She refers to the new child as the "miracle" baby.

Memories

While religious studies scholars Jacob Neusner, Ernest Frerichs, and Paul Flesher were editing the book *Religion, Science, and Magic* (1989) Frerichs' son died. They dedicated the book to him

> Whose sudden death, just after our conference,
> saddened our days
> and left us with the sharp pain
> of the knowledge of good and evil:
> How brief, how uncertain, things are
> but whose memory endures for us
> as a reminder of how much
> of us endures in love and hope and faith (p. v).

Bereaved parents can find solace in memory. Unconflicted and peaceful memory is often at the end of a difficult process of separating self-representation from the inner representation of the child. Memories are at first very painful, because they are reminders of the loss. One mother reflected on the discovery that letting go of the pain did not also mean letting go of the child.

> You know, I remember being afraid that someday I would wake up and my feeling of being bonded to Kelly wouldn't be there. I thought that when the pain left, she would be gone too. But now I find that I hope the memories will come. The times in the hospital are not what I remember. I remember the good times, when she was well. Sometimes I just look at her pictures and remember when we took them. I never know when I will look at the pictures, but I feel better afterwards.

This use of memory as solace seems similar to what Tahka (1984) calls "remembrance formations." He says, once the remembrance formation has been established, its later calling back to mind, reminiscing about it and dismissing it again from the mind, are invariably experienced as activities of the self taking place exclusively on the subject's own conditions. Although it is experienced as a fully differentiated object representation, no illusions of its separate and autonomous existence are involved. In contrast to fantasy objects possessing various wish-fulfilling functions, it includes the awareness that nothing more can be expected from it and therefore, in its fully established forms it has chances for becoming the most realistic of all existing object representations (p. 18).

One mother made the point more gracefully. Memories, she said, are like the perennials that bloom again after the winter of grief gives way to hope. Five years after her daughter died, a mother said:

I still feel the warmth of love when I think of Allison. I still laugh when I think of some of the witty and wacky things she said or did. I still cry when the loneliness of her absence pierces my heart, and I miss her as much as I did at the beginning of this journey. I have a new relationship with Allison. It is internal, redefined, relevant, valued. Our relationship and memory are captured within me always to draw upon.

Memory can be a part of everyday life. The quiet times remembering the dead child have about them a somewhat forbidden quality, but the memory time becomes a personal ritual around which to build a day.

Sometimes I pretend, when no one's around,
that you are still home,
creating your own special sound—
the car, the stereo, singing in the shower.

Many years after his daughter's death, a father reported about his own holiday, "Ellen's Day." He said that George Washington, Christopher Columbus, Abraham Lincoln and Martin Luther King were all very special people, and that, as a way of recognizing them, people set aside days and name them after them to honor their lives and their memories. So, a few years after his daughter's death, he decided to that he would set aside a day each year to honor Ellen's life and memory. As the years went by, a tradition built up. If it were a work day, he took the day off. In the morning, he would visit her grave to talk to her. He tell her what he had been doing with his life, what was happening in the lives of other people who were important to her, how the world was changing since she died, and what things endured. After the time at the grave, he does something special for the day. Each year he thinks about what the activity should be, because it should be something that Ellen would have liked, something that they might have done together, or something that brings out the part of the father that feels connected to Ellen. He was divorced when Ellen died, so it was a holiday for one. When he remarried, his new wife joined in the holiday rituals, even though she never knew Ellen. Ellen is a part of her new family, so she is a full participant in the rituals. The father said, "I don't expect the world to join in this celebration, but neither will I let the year be complete without this special day being included in the calendar of hearts."

Thematic memories, that is memories that catch the essence of the individual child, can take the parent out of the present and to a time when the world was better.

> I can still envision the surprised, happy look on his face that Christmas when he opened a gift and found a silver vest and pants to wear when he played his bass guitar with his beloved band. . . . I remember when he took me out to eat one Mother's Day, just he and I. . . . how handsome he was in his tux and top hat and how he introduced his date for the prom . . . how proud we all were at his graduation when he gave the welcome address. . . . Wonderful memories are something that no one can take away. Some memories just won't die.

Often the emotional states attached to the thematic memories carry the quality of solace. Writing nearly 20 years after the death of her daughter, a mother reflected on her memory of a beginners' ballet recital.

> I can't remember the details of that afternoon. . . . But I remember the feeling, somewhere between laughter and tears. I remember loving that small, beautiful person, my child. I remember my sense of admiration for her, and a fittingly stifled flood of pride. . . . I have forgotten so many things, but I remember the feeling. Always the feeling.

Memories are often social, that is, memories are held by families and communities. Too often, however, bereaved parents are left with memories that are not easily shared in the larger culture. Sharing memories of their children comes easily in gatherings of Bereaved Parents. At a business meeting, a mother shared a scrapbook she had made and talked about how different it is remembering her child in Bereaved Parents than in other settings. There is a company that sells supplies for scrapbooks (nonacid paper, high quality plastic clips, etc.) for people to hold their memories. Large groups get together for series of evenings spaced every two weeks to do scrapbooks. Most do it for living children. This parent did hers on her eight-month-old son who had died seven years earlier. The book had pictures and thoughtful comments written in calligraphy. The book went from birth, through hospitalizations and operations with some written memories of when the physicians removed tubes and other procedures. It included pictures of an air ambulance that took the child for specialized treatment. There were pictures of her and her husband in the funeral home standing at the open casket and pictures of the grave with the decorations they put on at his birthday and at Christmas. There were pictures of the Bereaved Parents picnic and balloon release, and recent pictures of the grave with balloons on his birthday. As she showed the book at the meeting, she said that making it was a healing process and that she liked the fact the book would now last long enough to pass down to children and grandchildren, because now her son would always be remembered.

As the book was passed around, she laughed and told about asking aloud how to spell Resurrection and Cemetery. When someone at another table asked why she wanted those words, she said that is where her child is buried. The other mothers making scrapbooks didn't know what to say. She reported that her whole table laughed because they were in on the joke, so she felt supported and accepted. At the meeting, she got more social support as the others shared how they preserve memories and laughed with her at the people who did not know how to respond to parents wanting to preserve the memories of their dead children.

Memory binds family and communities together. In Bereaved Parents, the members do not remember each other's children as living. It was the death of the children that brought members to the group. But the solace of memory is important in the group's bond. The group has developed rituals which express the bond with the child as part of the bonds within the community. Such rituals give permission to each parent to hold the inner representation without conflict. A significant portion of national and regional meetings are devoted to ritual activity, such as boards with pictures of the dead children. Bulletin boards line both sides of a long hallway or fill one large room in the hotel. Some parents just pin their child's picture on the board, but many prepare quite elaborate displays or collages that communicate their children's personalities or characters. The picture boards are popular gathering places during the meetings. As I walk down the line of boards, I often find myself filled with an intense sadness as, one after the other, I see this child, then this child, and this child. As I have reflected, it seems to me that I often protect myself from the parent's sadness, but what I feel in front of the pictures may be a small imitation of what the parents feel most of the time. The gathering of the bereaved parents is in the presence of this gathering of their children, and so it is a gathering of deep pain. Yet, as I stand back and observe parents moving along the bulletin boards, it is not sadness that is the predominant feeling. People look at each other's children, and then go back to their own child. Conversations often begin between strangers. "This is your child? My son had a car he loved too. He was killed in that car, so I feel pretty ambivalent about all the pictures he took of it. But he did love it, and he was never so happy as when he was working on it. How did your son die?" They bond with each other as they share memories, they feel comfort as they relive the times the photographs represent, and they feel comfort in sharing their child with others.

The continuing bonds of memory are most clearly expressed in the holiday candlelight memorial service, the largest gathering of the local chapter. Many of the members, including alumnae who no longer attend meetings, bring their children's siblings, grandparents, uncles, aunts, or family friends. The memory of the child is thus included in the holiday and in the family circle. Parents sign in and make sure their child's name is on the list to be read, they put their child's name on a colored ribbon. The ribbons are taken to the front of the sanctuary where they are attached to a lattice. As the sanctuary fills with people, the lattice fills with ribbons of many colors. At the end of the service, as the children's names are read, the parents and those who have come with them rise and light a candle. For a few years, while the parents stood holding their candles, a children's choir sang "Rainbow Connection." The parents hold their separate candles, but together they light a darkened room. The rainbow of the song is also the rainbow of colored ribbons on the platform. One of the meetings in the chapter is in an old river town. Their memorial service is of candles and roses. The candles are lit in a building by the river and at the end of the service, everyone goes to the river where a rose for each child is put into the current.

The ritualized memory in Bereaved Parents is similar to the rituals that many other cultures have for being with their dead. The difference is that in the modern West, bereaved parents must invent the rituals and, by and large, perform the rituals as individuals, while in other societies the interactions of the living and the dead are communal affairs that draw the whole extended family together. We can see the similarity if we look for a moment at ancestor rituals in Japan (see Klass, 1996; Klass and Heath, 1996–1997). *O bon* is the major summer holiday in Japan. Robert J. Smith (1974) describes the meaning of the traditional *O bon* festival as:

> The periodic merging of the two worlds (living and dead) strengthens the sense of continuity of the house and reassures the dead of the living's continuing concern for their well being. Neither death nor time can weaken or destroy the unity of the members of the house (p. 104).

The unfortunate choice of the English word "ancestor" to translate the Japanese *sosen* gives much too impersonal a sense of the relationship between the living and the dead in the Japanese rituals. The children of American parents retain their individual personalities as do Japanese ancestors. Smith tells of a nearly-deaf old man with whom Smith often passed time when he was doing his fieldwork in Japan. Smith was away when the old man died, and, when he returned, he went to the house and asked if he could burn incense at the family altar, a ritual appropriate for an acquaintance. The wife of house put one of the cakes he had brought on a dish and took it to the *butsudan*, the Buddha altar that is in every traditional home where the dead may be contacted. She knelt and said in a loud voice, "Grandfather, Mr. Smith is here" (p. 143).

In a survey of what Japanese people think is important in doing the rituals for the dead, comforting and cheering was listed as the most important (81%), and expressing gratitude (65%) was second (Offner, 1979). Comfort and cheering seem to be solace, but in the Japanese culture, so is expressing gratitude. Gratitude is the feeling inside the dependent relationships that characterize Japanese culture (see Doi, 1973).

The lanterns are lit at the beginning of *O bon* to guide the spirits of the dead back from the other side to their homes. As the spirits arrive, family members bow and say that they are pleased they have come. The end of *O bon* in many Japanese towns even looks like the Bereaved Parents memorial service. Candles are placed on small wooden rafts and lit as the rafts are put into the river. The community gathers on the bank, waves and shouts, "Bye. Come back next year." As each candle goes out, it is said that the spirit returns to the other world. "I live in their presence" a Japanese man reported, "and make a welcoming fire early and a sending-off fire late at *O bon*, so that the ancestors will stay longer" (Smith, 1974, p.150). When the new wife joined in the celebration of "Ellen's Day," she was joining in the relationship to the recently dead, just as a woman marrying into a Japanese family would do.

After the closing song at the end of the Bereaved Parents candlelight service, many parents seem reluctant to extinguish the candle. There is no rush to the exit, as many sit quietly, some alone, but many sit close to other family members. It is not a time the researcher should ask how they are feeling, but they seem to be cherishing the moment. Then people go to a large hall where there are tables full of homemade cookies and cakes, and other tables on which parents have placed pictures of their children.

Over the years, as members of the group have developed confidence in themselves and in the group process, they have become rather adept at creating rituals. At a January business meeting during the evaluation of the candlelight service, it was reported that the lattice on which the colored ribbons were hung had fallen off the truck and broken when it was being taken home after the service. So, with the loss of the ritual implement, the group needed to decide whether to build a new one, or do something else. Apparently some people had not really felt the ribbons helped them get in touch with their child, but, of course, had never said anything. So when the lattice broke, the group had an opportunity to do something else.

Someone suggested that notes be written to the children and put in a container up in the front. That got put into the context of an earlier discussion of long lines at the sign-in where people register their presence to make sure their child's name will be read, pick up candles, and take care of a few other details. So, in a very rapid interchange, it was suggested that the note cards could be handed out, and people could compose messages to their children while they waited for the service to start. At a point in the service, the messages would be collected and taken to the front. The question then came up regarding what to do with the messages after the service. They couldn't just throw them out. Almost immediately, the suggestion was made that, because our chapter does not do regular tree plantings to remember the children, we should start a spring tradition of planting a tree, and that the messages could be put into the hole when the tree was planted. The idea quickly developed to include a suggestion that the note paper would have to be easily biodegradable. Within a few moments, the proposed note cards had become cheap paper in the shape of butterflies, an important symbol in the group.

The concept of ritual comes easily to the leaders of the group, and, as the rituals have developed in the group, the group has developed a sense of how rituals should go and, so, invents them rather easily. The core members of the group have individually learned how the continuing bonds with their dead children fits into their ongoing lives, so they understand how the interactions can be acted out in ritual. Although the wider culture has few remaining rituals by which the living interact with the dead, a community of people finding solace in their memories develops rituals to fill the void.

Enriched Identification

In identification, the inner representation of the child is integrated into the self-representation in such a way that it is difficult to distinguish the two. Because the inner representation of the child is maintained less as a separate entity, solace has a somewhat different character. It is found in a sense of reinvigorated life, in renewed feelings of competence.

Often identification is found in a decision to live fully in spite of the death. One parent wrote, "I came to the decision that I was to try to use my gift of life to the utmost as my son had used his." Children often represent the parent's best self and seldom consciously represent darker parts of the parent's self. The inner representation of dead children often reverts to an ideal, just as saints, angels, and bodhisattvas personify values. The children can be models by which the parents and the community can live more authentic lives. The idealization of the child provides another element in the child's serving as a connection between heaven and earth, between perfection and reality.

To be sure, severe dysfunction can result if an idealized child is forced into a family system in a way that living children are judged against the perfect standard the dead child represents. It is very hard for living children to compete with a saint. But when parents, as they often do, use the hopes and ideas that were once projected onto the child as values around which to center their own lives, the parents' lives are richer and better, so they are better parents to their surviving children.

> There are persons whom we cannot think of except as being alive. They seem to resist destructions, even when dead. . . . Around them, even remembering them, whether away for a while or permanently, we feel the whole world a more vibrant as well as more interesting place (Harper, 1991, p. 89).

In a poem, a mother reflects on the long life her child might have lived. She decides that the child only lived the prologue of a story, and it would be her task to live out the meaning that the child's life began. Her child's message and meaning are love, devotion, joy, and knowledge. If she can live so those values are real in her life, then her dead child's life story will have been completed. She ends the poem: "These truths will speak / through my pages, / Making your prologue— / forever mine." Eight years after her child died, a mother reflected on her success at being a better person "for him" and how the better parts of herself are the ones that are like him.

> Sure, I miss my son and always will, but I can try to be a better person for him. He loved the birds, and so do I. He liked funny stories, and so do I. He loved people, and so do I. Life will go on for me, and I can be happy. I never thought it would, but it does!

After the deaths of their children the parents' lives go on; but life does not always go well. The continuing bond with the child can provide a new source of solace and meaning, and it can play other roles as well. A counseling case can illustrate the complex way the bond with the dead child functions in the parent's psyche. Several years after we had concluded long-term counseling following the death of her 10-year-old daughter, Meg, Rita called for an appointment. Her clinical diagnosis was depression that varied from mild to severe. It was a feeling Rita had carried most of her life, especially during her college years. In our sessions after her daughter's death, her physician had wanted to put her on antidepressants. I remembered her saying then, "Don't talk to me about depression. I know depression. I am a connoisseur of depression. But this grief thing is something completely different."

As Rita came back for counseling, she was again depressed. Our talk turned to what role her daughter played in her inner life now. Her continuing bond with her child plays a role in her depression, just as the child plays a role in her life when she is not depressed. When she is depressed, Rita identifies with those times she experienced her daughter as vulnerable, so the memories are of the painful times when she could not protect her daughter from pain. When she is not depressed, her memory of her child provides solace. Meg had always represented Rita's best self. When Meg was born, Rita knew that Meg would grow up to be the kind of person Rita wished she herself could be. In her depression, Rita was feeling very distant from her best self and from Meg. In our next several sessions, we found the way out of the depression through the bond with Meg. As she talked about her depression, Rita remembered a few times when Meg felt as Rita now felt, vulnerable and easily hurt by people who seemed to be rejecting her. She wished now that she could protect herself from being hurt, just as she wished she could have protected her child from being hurt. In her depression, Rita found solace in the fact that once there was a person who, as she wrote in her journal, was herself "redone . . . unfettered by hatred and evil."

> Oh, how I miss my Meg . . . I want to smell her hair and hold her and feel the essence of her in my nostrils and in my head and in my soul. She is (but not close enough to me) such a strong life for me. She was truly a butterfly, a free spirit who spread her love everywhere she went. She was so enthusiastic, so in love with life, she was an example for all the jaded, angry people in this world. That quality also gave her a vulnerability. I wanted, and still want when I see a child who reminds me of her, to shield her from hurt, from the hatred of those who are not lucky enough to have had what she had, who were not loved and cherished the way that she was. I could have killed anyone who laughed at her, who rejected her openness and who made her have that puzzled look which said, "Mamma, I don't understand their hatred. What do I

do now, Mamma? Why do they treat me cruelly?" I only saw that in her a few times, and it killed me that she should have to feel that. And I wanted to hold her and say, "Meg , it is not you, my darling, it is them. Don't take their hatred inside yourself or let it touch you. Let yourself remain free and open to the universe. I love you, my golden girl. For you are a precious gift to me. You are me redone. You are me unfettered by hatred and evil. Soar, my beautiful butterfly, as I could not."

After a few months of counseling Rita felt more competent. She identified less with the hurt part of her daughter, and she remembered the family fun they used to have. It helped when her teenage son came for two of our counseling sessions, shared his very positive memories of his sister, and spoke maturely to his mother about how he knew he could never be like a daughter would have been. He said that, when he compared her to his friends' mothers, "I have it pretty good." As Rita's depression passed, the solace in her bond with Meg changed. When she is not depressed, she does not need solace from a hateful world, only from a world that is poorer because her child is not here to enjoy it. Rita is close to her dead child both in her depression and out of it, but the closeness is more comfortable, like life in general, when she is not depressed.

The energy on which the self-help group runs is the energy parents identify as their children's and the energy that flows between them and their children. A very musical bereaved couple wrote a song about bereaved parents with the refrain, "Our children live on in the love that we share." One parent described the self-help process in the meeting as a circle of weavers in which the bonds that were with the child now become interwoven with the bonds between other bereaved parents in the group. As we noted in the chapter on community, the meetings begin by going around the circle with each person giving their name and their child's name and something about their child's death. The ritual evokes the presence of the dead children and the pain their deaths have brought. As the pain is shared, the parents' bonds with their children can be real in the group. We have seen that many of the members who go on to become leaders in the group feel that in turning their pain into helping other bereaved parents, they are living out the values their children embodied, they are being the kind of person their children were.

☐ Negative Solace: Revenge and Retribution

In the majority of the chapter we have looked at solace as a positive sense of the presence of transcendent reality. But there is a negative kind of solace: fantasies of revenge or retribution. We need to spend a few moments thinking about negative solace as a spiritual issue. In cases of wrongful deaths, especially murders, some parents take comfort in thoughts of the perpetrator suffering. A woman, for example, whose son had been murdered by his girl friend and her new lover, found that she could banish the visions of her son's battered body enough to go to sleep when she imagined in great detail the two murderers being subjected to medieval-like torture. Everyone has such thoughts when they are in pain that they think has been caused by another. All of us can identify with the hope that the one who hurt us will suffer for it, even if we cannot inflict the suffering ourselves. The fantasies give comfort. We have been hurt, and we think we would feel better if the one that caused our suffering would feel what we feel.

Such fantasies are based in our most primitive emotional inheritance and so have very limited possibilities for developing into healing. Like other solace, imagined or hoped-for retribution is based on a sense of being in touch with transcendent reality, albeit, at a very low developmental level. That is, the hope for retribution depends on the idea of some final justice, whether it be in this life or the next, whether it be by the criminal justice system or by divine intervention. In those moments, we feel isolated and we hope there is a power greater than ours—God, the state, or a super hero like in the movies—that can put the world right. That is, the fantasies put us in touch with at least the hope of transcendent reality, the hope that there is a being with greater power than we have to bring justice in a world gone wrong.

When Hamlet meets his father's ghost on the battlement, it is not to receive comfort in his grief. Rather, Hamlet is commissioned to bring justice for his father's death, and the plot of the revenge tragedy is set (see Jacoby, 1983). From ancient times until quite recently, ghosts were reported to come back to request or demand justice for their wrongful deaths (Finucane, 1996, pp. 22–26). I do not know why, but I have never heard from a bereaved parent that their dead child is supporting them in their revenge fantasies. The absence of the dead demanding revenge seems to be a new phenomena in modernity. It may be that as the duty to bring justice in wrongful deaths has passed from the family to the state, and because the family no longer has the power to extract revenge, the spirits of the dead don't ask. It may also be that such thoughts occur to people, but there is so little social support in the culture for such thoughts that they do not speak them aloud, even in the supportive environment of a self-help meeting. It may be that deaths like murder are such an assault on parents' sense of power and competence that the fantasies of doing harm to the killers function to restore the parents' sense of power, while not connecting very deeply with the bond to the child. For whatever reasons, in an age when the parent-child bond has become primarily emotional rather than economic and genealogical, the feelings of revenge seem no longer to be supported by the dead child.

The consolation of revenge or retribution fantasies, like actions of revenge or retribution, seldom grows into positive resolution because, as many spiritual traditions teach, hate harms the hater more than the one hated. It eats you up. After several parents who had just begun attending the Parents of Murdered Children meeting vented the rage they felt toward their child's killer and voiced their need to have the killer suffer as badly as their child had suffered, a woman whose son had been murdered 10 years earlier and the killers never found said, "After a while, I just had to give that up. One day, I just said to myself that they had taken enough from me and they were not going to take any more." Probably because the self-help group's purpose is finding a positive resolution of the grief, as time passes, virtually all the parents in the group find that hopes of revenge are a dead end, and they let them go. Some parents, however, do not leave their revenge fantasies completely behind. In telling me about how he decided that the hate was "killing me while it wasn't doing a damn thing to them," a father whose daughter was gang-raped and then murdered ended the conversation by saying, "Still, if I ever found myself where I could do it, I know I would kill those sons of bitches and never give it a thought."

Revenge for children's deaths can, in some times and places, take on political significance. The perpetrators of genocidal movements and protracted ethnic conflict in this century have justified their actions to themselves as the restoration of sacred honor of their dead that had been taken from them in defeat generations or even centuries ago. Ethnic, racial, or political membership is often infused with spiritual feelings. Indeed, for many people, God and country feel as one. Socially sharing a religious sense in the bond with the dead child can get merged with the sense of transcendent reality we feel in our ethnic, racial, or national membership. Ken Wilber (1981, pp. 87–109; 1995, pp. 171–173) calls such spirituality mythic/membership. He says it indicates a low level of spiritual development in which the individual has not differentiated the self from the social environment. But it is a kind of spirituality to which individuals and cultures regress when they are under stress. All peoples encourage a strong bond with the dead hero or martyr. Among the symbols which bind a nation together are the internalized representations of its young who so died that the nation could have its land, freedom, king, religion, form of government, or economic power.

Fantasies of revenge that come by identifying the dead with the nation or tribe become very destructive when the fantasies are acted out politically. In some pathological cultural systems which operate at the mythic/membership levels, or in historical situations in which there has been a regression to mythic membership, blood must be answered by blood. In those times, the fantasies of revenge and retribution that most people feel in their grief at what seems a wrongful death can be acted out in reality. In the name of those fallen for the cause, other people's children may be killed with impunity. It is difficult to stop a cycle of violence when each side merges the solace of the inner representations of the dead children with a spiritual feeling of peoplehood and with a drive for revenge which feels as if it has divine sanction.

☐ Solace and Immortality

In their parents' solace-giving experiences, the children become immortal, in the sense that the inner representation of the child remains a real, living presence in the parent's inner and social worlds. A poem in a newsletter makes the point that even as the ache to hold her child remains in her memory, for the mother the child is a living, comforting presence.

> You may say he is dead.
> I know he is very much alive. . . .
> What I have is memory,
> the mind's blurring pictures. . . .
> And now he is part of my heart,
> Resting softly on my mind.

Most modern psychosocial thinking about immortality concerns itself with the immortality of the autonomous individuality that forms the core of modernity. Because the worldview of modernity holds that the highest developmental stage possible is the separate individual who lives by the reality principle of rational thought, not the pleasure principle of fantasy and imagination, spirituality can only be understood as regressive (see Wilber, 1995, pp. 205–208). The questions for contemporary people seem to be, "Do I live on?" and "Does the reality that I feel my individual self to be last beyond death?" The modern quest for individual immortality takes us back to childish ways of being and back to a less differentiated sense of selfhood. Contemporary psychology and philosophy treat the sense of transcendent reality as a necessary illusion, a compensation people invent because they cannot face the pain of recognizing that this life is all there is. Individuals fear annihilation of the self and compensate, as one psychoanalytic scholar finds, by "regression to the union of the archaic idealized omnipotent figure in the death-transformation passage to the 'new existence' . . . based on symbiosis with the undifferentiated god" (Pollock, 1975, p. 341). That is, the transcendent reality we find in the face of death is a fantasy based in the undifferentiated sense of oneness we had as infants with our mothers.

We do not need to think, however, that immortality is so regressive. Robert Lifton (1974) thinks the sense of immortality is beyond our sense of autonomous individuality and is embedded in the many connections we have to our world. Immortality, he says, is "man's symbolization of his ties with both his biological fellows and his history, past and future" (p.685). To parents, their children already symbolize the parents' ties to their biological, personal, and cultural history. Bereaved parents often remind each other, "When your parent dies, you lose your past. When your child dies, you lose your future." Solace is for living in that poorer world. The immortal inner representation of the child maintains the bonds to history and future, to biology and culture. The continuing bond with the child is bound up, as Lifton says, with other bonds that transcend individual isolation.

The idea of spirituality being a regression to a preverbal sense of undifferentiated union simply does not fit my experience with Bereaved Parents. As soon as the group was founded, a newsletter was established so members could share what they had written about their grief and about their children. The meetings in the group are characterized by talking. It seems wrong to conclude that, in such a wordy process, the parents' continuing bonds with their immortal children are a regression to some kind of preverbal infantile narcissism. The parents in the group are constructing durable biographies of their children and of themselves after the deaths of their children. They are constructing those biographies, as Tony Walter (1996, pp. 12–19) says, through conversation. That is, they are using words. They are not regressing to a preverbal state. They are stabilizing themselves, and their children's places in their lives, in a very verbal inner world and a very verbal social network.

In many of his sonnets, Shakespeare asks how a dead friend or lover can live on. He seems finally to settle upon the immortality of his own words. If he can join the reality of the deceased to the "eternal lines" of the poem, then the dead person is made immortal. Thus Shakespeare locates the immortality of the dead in the words of his art, much the way bereaved parents locate their dead children in their experience of solace.

And every fair from fair sometime declines,
By chance or nature's changing course untrimm'd;
But thy eternal summer shall not fade
Nor lose possession of that fair thou owest;
Nor shall Death brag thou wander'st in his shade,
When in eternal lines to time thou growest:
So long as men can breath or eyes can see,
So long lives this and this gives life to thee. (Sonnet 18)

For their parents, dead children do not lose possession of that fairness they embodied, nor do they wander only in Death's shade. They have lived just the summer, but their summer does not fade. It remains eternal in a part of the parent's psyche and in the social system where the parent feels most at home. The parents find solace in linking objects which evoke the presence of the dead, in religious ideas and devotion which merge the child with other death-transcending connections of the parents' lives, in memories by which time can drop away and the parents can return to the world when it was a better place, and in identification by which the children become the best part of who the parents understand themselves to be. So long as this lives in the inner and social world of bereaved parents, it gives life to their children who have died.

Immortality in the continuing bond with the dead child is not the only immortality available. In the ancestor rituals of most cultures, the continuity of the generations is the most easily recognized element for outsiders to see. If the dead children have borne children of their own, like other grandparents, bereaved parents find a sense of their children's immortality and their own in the continuation of the generations. Shakespeare recognizes,

But were some child of yours alive at time,
You should live twice; in it and in my rhyme. (Sonnet 17)

Although parents plant trees in their children's memories, give donations to institutions so the children's names remains on scholarships, brass plaques, or even buildings, these external symbols of immortality feel less sure, and in the end, less meaningful, than the immortality bereaved parents find in the solace-filled bond with their children. Shakespeare again reminds us how this works.

Not marble, nor the gilded monuments
Of princes, shall outlive this powerful rhyme;
But you shall shine more bright in these contents
Than unswept stone, besmeared with sluttish time. . . .

So, til the judgement that yourself arise,
You live in this, and dwell in lover's eyes. (Sonnet 60)

At its core, immortality is a social reality, not an ontological reality. It is actualized in the continuing bond between parent and child, in the love that does not die. The reality of immortal children is not in an imagined better world outside this one. "Love and loss are constant riding companions in the rough and tumble of life's unpredictable splendor," says Allen Kellehear (1996). If life be merely a material reality, as it is in the concrete operations of lower cognitive and ego development, then death is final, and immortality is only a necessary fantasy in a cruel, hopeless, and ultimately meaningless world. The body is all there is. "The more sophisticated message" Kellehear says, "is that love is something that can emerge from, and triumph over, the complex and unpredictable nature of life's changing fortunes" (pp. 147–148). In the continuing bond with the parent's dead child, the child remains immortal in the parent's memories, and the parent makes the child real in the life the parent now lives dedicated to the child's memory. So long as this lives, the child lives in the Eternal Now.

Immortal children are present in the same world in which their parents live, not in another world. The solace children bring does not take away their parents' pain, but comes amidst their parents' pain. The world of suffering, *samsara*, and the world of liberation, *nirvana*, are the same. In another sense, their children are not of this world. If there be a heaven, the children are there, and the parents expect that when they die they will be reunited with their dead children the way it was before. In bereaved parents' spiritual experience, however, heaven and earth are connected. The children are both in heaven and in their parents' hearts. The children—like angels, saints, and bodhisattvas— are citizens of both worlds. When the children seem real to the parents, when it seems that they sense their children's presence, when they act on the values that were incarnate in their children, when events happen that seem to be the children still influencing their world, then the children are real in this world, and the Lord's Prayer comes true. For a moment, it is "on earth as it is in heaven." One woman summed it up in the final stanza of a poem:

Although my family's circle of life has been
    broken by death, it will be mended by love.
I will always love and miss Robert, but I know that
    he is waiting for me, somewhere very near.
All that we were to each other,
    that we are still.

☐ Conclusion

The immortal children are merged with other transcendental realities in their parents' world. In linking objects, in religious ideas and devotion, in memory, and in enriched identification, the parents remold their bond with their children into one that will continue through their lives. Parents make new attachments, but their children remain part of their lives. In their interaction with their dead children, bereaved parents move back to the time when life was better. They bridge the gulf of time between now and when the children were living. Bereaved parents know that their children cannot make the rest of their earthly journey with them, but they invite them to come along in their hearts and wish them well. In a new life that sometimes feels neither sure nor safe, the immortal children and the transcendent reality of which they are a part provide a solace-filled reality which feels both inside and outside the self, a reality that does not change, and the truth of which cannot be challenged.

5

CHAPTER

Worldviews: Finding Order in the Universe

The deaths of their children force parents to reexamine their worldview, to either reaffirm or modify their basic understanding about themselves and about the justness and orderliness of their world. The solace parents experience in the bond with their immortal child is intertwined with their discovery of an underlying order, purpose, or intelligence to which they align their lives. Sitting in meetings or in my counseling office, I sometimes feel like I am listening to the Old Testament story of Job. How, I often wonder, will they make sense of their lives after the nonsensical death of their child? Then the question broadens in my mind: What sense would any of us make of our world if we were in their place?

☐ Worldviews at the Grass Roots

Worldviews are the beliefs, myths, rituals, and symbols by which individuals and communities answer two questions: The first question is, How does the universe function? Does the power in transcendent reality impact on the everyday world of living people? Is transcendent reality friendly, hostile, or indifferent? Is it consistent or capricious? The second question is, What place do humans occupy within the universe? Do humans have any power to affect their destiny, and if so, how much and what kind of power do they have? If humans have power to affect their world, what are the means by which the power is accessed?

Most people's worldviews are not systematic, nor have their worldviews been subjected to rigorous critical analysis. Worldviews are experiential in the sense that individuals and communities use them to orient themselves. Worldviews are the maps of both visible and invisible reality on which individuals and communities locate external and internal events, from which they discover or choose religious, political, or ideological affiliations, and upon which they base moral judgments and actions. Worldviews allow individuals to "respond to what they see as true, as good, and as sacred in the realities they experience in this ever-changing, puzzling world" (Morgan, 1990, p. 1). Worldviews are the template by which individuals and communities find meaning in the events of their lives.

> What does it imply that something has meaning? Primarily it can imply that whatever I am searching for a meaning in, is possible to interpret and is understandable. Nonsense means non-meaning (Kallenberg, 1995, p. 55)

So existentially important is the worldview to the individual that Tillich (1951, pp. 155–159) calls it the "ground of being." Erikson (1963, pp. 247–251) says that for individuals, worldviews rest within the most elementary feelings and earliest human experience, the basic trust developed in the preverbal interactions between mother and child.

Worldviews can be maintained at any developmental level, and an individual's movement into a higher developmental level entails a change in the structure of the worldview (Fowler, 1981; Wilber, 1980, 1981). Within the same religious tradition, the worldviews of individuals and communities can be quite different if, for example, the myths and symbols of the tradition are interpreted at the literal concrete operations level or interpreted less literally at the formal operations level. Still, the task at every developmental level remains the same: to make the world make sense. In Bereaved Parents, we see people whose worldviews operate in childlike simplicity, and we see people whose worldviews are very sophisticated. Whether they are sophisticated or simple, however, all are trying to make sense of a world that has fallen apart after the deaths of their children, a world in which trust is very difficult, in which the foundations of their of being have been shaken.

Recently many scholars (Neimeyer, 1998; Neimeyer and Stewart, 1996; Walter, 1996) have adopted the idea of narrative as a way to think about worldviews of grieving people. Each person has a life story, a narrative of their experience as an individual over time. The assumptions we make about life set the general framework of our life story. If

I think of myself as lucky and living in a random world, then I can be free to take risks because things usually turn out well for me in the end. I would live a quite different story, on the other hand, if I think that the world is rigged against me, that I usually cannot control my destiny, and that the only satisfactions available to me are the short term pleasures.

Individual narratives are embedded in cultural narratives. In some cultures, the story an individual is to play out in life is tightly prescribed. When I talked to a young woman in India about coming to the United States for graduate school, she said that she would like to do that, but it really depended on whom her family arranged for her to marry. Although she knew that American women had "love marriages," her life story would not include the concept of free choice in selecting a mate. When she did marry, her role in the relationship would not be subject to negotiation. Her culture's narrative is restrictive. The single most distinguishing feature of the modern developed world is that individuals are more free to choose how they live their lives than at almost any other time in human history. A young American woman expects that only she and her prospective husband have a right to decide whether they will marry, and that after the marriage, it is up to the couple to decide what roles and responsibilities each will take. The woman in India knows what is to be a wife. Her task is to conform to the role assigned to her by the culture. In America, *wife* has very few absolute meanings now, so it becomes each woman's task to define the role for herself. In traditional societies, individuals act out the roles given to them. In the modern world, we are more like actors in improvisational theater. There may be parameters and limits given to us, but within those, we have a wide range of freedom in how to play out our lives. Each person, then, becomes responsible for constructing her or his own life story, and at the same time each individual becomes responsible for whether the story works out, especially in hard times. When a child dies in the modern developed world, few compelling cultural narratives that make sense of the child's death are available. Parents are left on their own to work out the meaning for themselves as individuals or as families.

The death of a child is a radical disruption of parents' individual narratives in the modern world. In other historical times, part of the expectation in having children was that some of them would very likely die at an early age. But at the beginning of the twenty-first century, very few people expect to be bereaved parents. The world changes when a child dies. The task confronting the parent is to make sense of the new world, especially to make sense of the new self that includes the experience of the child's death, and includes the deceased child in whatever roles the child continues to play in the parent's life.

In other times and places, the meaning of death and the actions that individuals and communities should take when death happened were given as clearly as the meanings and actions that were given within the role of wife or husband. The life narrative we construct is deeply rooted in our personal history, which is nested in the history of our families, which, in turn, is nested in the history of the communities to which we belong. So we make sense of the world using the templates provided by the symbols, myths, beliefs, rituals, and practices in which our lives are lived.

> Meaning construction involves the perpetual encounter of a meaning-seeking subject and a historically and culturally orchestrated world of artifacts . . . . Specifically, meaning construction is a Piagetian "assimilation" process whereby people employ old cognitive models as resources for making sense out of novel experience (Shore, 1996, p. 319).

The modern world provides very few templates by which to make sense of the world after a child dies. We have very few symbols, myths, beliefs, rituals, or practices that newly bereaved parents can simply live out. The consensus that seems to be emerging among scholars and clinicians is that the purpose or goal of grief is to construct a narrative story, a durable biography, that organizes and makes meaning of the survivor's life after the death, as well as the life of the person who died. The task bereaved parents face is finding the meaning of their lives and the meaning of the lives of their dead children. "What does life mean now?" is another way of saying, "On what assumptions can I now base my life?" "How do I understand the story of my life and the story of my child's life?" "How do I understand how my child has gone from my life, and how do I understand how my child is still in my life?"

In this chapter, we look at worldviews at a grass roots level. Our sources are not theologians, ritual experts, or masters of meditation practice who supply the information used by most scholars of religion. Our sources are common people whose lives have touched mine because their children have died. Some of them have had rather full instruction in religious grammar schools and high schools. Some have been active in their churches or synagogues. A few are even clergy. A few have explored religious and spiritual possibilities for several years. For the majority, however, religious questions have been less interesting than how to make a living or how well the ball team is doing. Only rarely had their worldviews been a pressing problem before their children died. Like most people, the questions of spirituality had not been foremost in their mind during their parenting years. The adolescent and college time of questions and answers is past. Their own death or their child's death seemed a remote possibility. The parenting years are a time of earning money to support the family and trying to fit many activities into a full schedule. At the grass roots level, one's worldview need not be an issue in constant focus. People live their lives following social expectations and rely on the assumptions implicit in the culture in which they live. Then their child dies. The questions of how the world functions and what place or power the parent has in the world are raised in a way that demands answers. They find, however, that contemporary American culture has very few answers at hand.

In the modern developed world, most people know that children die, but they assume that it will not happen to them. Their assumption has some rational/scientific basis. Children die less frequently now than in previous times. Their assumption also has less rational elements, and those are deeply seated in their minds. God has given them this child and will care for the child. Or, they are usually lucky, and life so far has been without hardship. Or, if they think bad thoughts, it might happen, so it is better not even to think of the possibility. People usually do not think about their assumptions, they act on them. They do not get up every morning worrying that today is the day it will happen. They allow their children to take reasonable risks. When the children are adolescents, parents may be anxious while the children take unreasonable risks, but they retain the underlying belief that death only happens to other people's children. When children die, assumptions about how the world works and about what power parents have in their world are tested. The questions are not intellectual, but personal ("Why was I not competent enough to prevent this death?"), or moral ("Why me?"), or social ("How can they let people like that out on the streets?"). The personal, moral, and social questions all lead back to the big questions: Does the world make sense? How do I go on now? How do I make sense of my child's death? How do I now make sense of my life?

People go about their daily lives based on the assumptions in their worldview. They find a mate, plan a career, choose a neighborhood, and anticipate their children based on their assumptions about how the universe works and what kinds of power they have in it. When a child dies, the whole world constructed on the basis of those assumptions is shaken. An example is one couple who came for counseling, both of whom came from troubled childhoods. Both thought their baby would cement their union and provide each of them a chance to live a life better than the one that had been given to them. The baby died at three months of an infection of unknown origin. The mother became anxious and dependent after the baby died. The father had resolved the poor mothering he had as a child by allowing his wife to mother him, but he did not do well when she needed him to nurture her in her grief. They got pregnant the next year. The father never really bonded with the child, and the mother did so only late in the pregnancy. Both said they needed to know the baby would live before they could pin the same level of hopes on the new baby as had been dashed when their first baby died. By the time the second baby was born, the father had found another woman who could care for him as his wife no longer could, and his wife had reverted to the extreme self-reliance of her high school years. Obviously the marriage did not survive the death of their child. The worldviews on which they had built the marriage had been tested and failed. An older worldview carried the mother through, while the father tried to replay the same script with a new partner.

A person holds a worldview not because it is true, but because it is useful. James Leuba said,

> God is not known, he is not understood; he is used—sometimes as meat-purveyor, sometimes as moral support, sometimes as friend, sometimes as an object of love. If he proves himself useful, the religious conscious-ness asks for no more than that (quoted in James, 1958, p. 382).

When children die, parents learn whether or not their worldviews help them make sense in their changed world, that is, whether their God is useful. Some parents find that their worldview proves adequate to the test, and others find that their worldview does not. As they move into their grief, parents begin to sort out their worldview, espe-cially as they give voice to their grief and see how other parents are handling their grief. As they are well along in their grief, or have resolved it as much as it will be, they solidify their worldviews, some more rigidly than others. They keep the worldviews that are useful, jettison those that are not, and modify or marginalize those that were partly useful or irrelevant.

The death of a child dumps the parent out in a world that is new. Parents may not know where they have been dumped until they have explored the place for some time. Parents sort through what they have been given in their own history and within their social networks that can withstand their grief. From the available fragments, they construct a worldview that shapes the durable biography they are constructing of themselves and of their child. Probably because worldviews are so complex and the changes happen over a long time, I have found myself relying heavily in this chapter on cases from my counseling practice.

Clergy Religion/Lay Religion

We will spend the next few pages looking at the relationship between bereaved parents and the traditions from which they come. To do that, we also need to look at the difference between scholarship on religious traditions and the task of this book: understanding spirituality in the lives of real people. A trip to any art or cultural history museum proves that worldviews through the history of humankind show amazing diversity. As we stare into the glass cases at the artifacts of peoples who lived long ago or far away, it is hard to understand how those people could have used those items or ideas to make sense of the world when their children died, yet we know that they did.

To understand bereaved parents in our day, however, we do not need to know the worldview expressed in the museum artifacts. Only a few worldviews are available to any person, even in the amazing diversity of the modern world. Worldviews are always rooted in a time and place. One of the possible roots of the word religion is the Latin *religio*, to bind. Worldviews feel as if they are objective. That is, our assumptions feel like they are a truth outside ourselves. They feel that way because they are given with our cultural inheritance and claim an authority beyond any individual's questioning. Worldviews are a central part of individuals' social affiliation (Bellah, Madsen, Sullivan, & Tipton, 1985, pp. 27–51). Religion provides the worldview that binds a society together.

> We belong to a group not because we are born into it, not merely because we profess to belong to it, nor finally because we give it our loyalty and allegiance, but primarily because we see the world and certain things in the world the way it does (Mannheim, 1936, pp. 21–22).

Scholars in comparative religion tend to think of worldviews as well-developed systems of belief, myth, and symbol. For these scholars, a worldview is usually held by a particular, easily distinguished, religious or cultural group. There are Christians and there are Buddhists. Among Christians there are Protestants and Catholics; and Protestants are divided into Methodists, Baptists, Episcopalians, and Pentecostals, and so on. Buddhists are divided into Theravada and Mahayana, and each of those, especially Mahayana, is split into many schools and sects. Scholars find it important that each religious subdivision has a cultural or sociological basis. For example, the Protestant break from Rome is rooted in emerging North European nationalism and the new merchant class of early capitalism (see Weber, 1958). Which god a person worships in Hinduism may as well be more an expression of caste, ethnicity, or regional tradition than personal piety.

Scholars also note that worldviews can be held within social groups with varying degrees of rigidity. Differences that seem insignificant, and often unintelligible, to outsiders are important enough to insiders to maintain the boundary between two or more groups. For example, among the theological disagreements in the split between eastern and western Christianity a thousand years ago were whether the Son was of the same substance as the Father or was of similar substance, and whether the Spirit proceeded from the Father and the Son or from the Father alone. Most Americans know members of Protestant denominations who can explain the differences between their beliefs and the beliefs of other Protestants in more detail than they can explain the difference between Christianity and Buddhism.

In some groups where religion is used to maintain strong boundaries, the demands on members to conform to a particular interpretation of a myth or to a particular interpretation of life's events can be very intense. Other groups are less rigid, and may even have abandoned the beliefs around which they first formed. It is difficult, for example, to find among John Calvin's Presbyterian descendants in American suburbs, people who believe Calvin's doctrine that God predestines who will be saved and who won't. Where beliefs are not so strongly in the service of maintaining boundaries, members may have more latitude in how they interpret the group's myths and symbols, and and how they interpret the meaning of what has happened, although they may also have fewer authoritative guidelines to use as they try to come to terms with hard times.

Scholars of comparative religion tend to focus on religious leaders or on authoritative written texts and tend to overlook the individual lives of those within the group. That is, scholars are interested in the content of the worldview, rather than in the actual experience of a person holding the worldview. David Chidester (1990), for example, has examined a great many religious systems, East and West, Primal and Modern, to find the ways of transcending death that religions provide. He finds four characteristic ways of symbolizing transcendence of death: Ancestral, Experiential, Cultural, and Mythic (pp. 13–27). In each religious system that he examines, he finds that all these ways of symbolizing transcendence are melded in different proportions into a unified whole. This also seems to be the case for bereaved parents. We can find all four ways, Ancestral, Experiential, Cultural, and Mythic, among bereaved parents. But, interestingly, none of the data in Chidester's study comes from actual bereaved people trying to come to terms with the death of someone close. Rather his data are the official beliefs, symbols, rituals, or customs of the groups he studies.

Scholars try to find the common ground among worldviews which developed in different parts of the planet. The scholarship seems to indicate that how rigidly or freely groups maintain their worldview is more determined by sociological and political forces than by the believers' spiritual needs. How well the worldview functions in individual lives does not seem to affect the immediate historical change in the worldview. For example, a recent sweeping study of twentieth century fundamentalist movements in several of the world's religions found common sociohistorical characteristics, even though the content of the beliefs and symbols were very different from each other (Marty and Appleby, 1991–1993). There are bereaved parents in all the fundamentalist groups in the study, but how the worldviews function in their lives does not seem to change the larger movements. The result is that despite the sociohistorical movements affecting the worldview of the culture to which they belong, individual bereaved parents must use whatever is available in their culture's worldview when the child dies. A rigid cultural worldview provides parents with firmer guidelines, but less latitude in how to interpret what has happened to them. A less rigid worldview offers parents fewer guidelines, but greater freedom in how to make sense of their changed world. A worldview, then, has two functions: it is used to maintain social boundaries, and it is used to help parents make sense of the the world, including the deaths of children. A worldview that serves well in either one of those tasks may or may not serve so well in the other.

It is difficult to know how worldviews at the grassroots level interact with worldviews of the more developed and abstract kind studied by scholars of comparative religion. We find both connections and disconnections between the religion of the theologians and the religion of the laity. In their personal lives, both theologians and lay people find that the test of their worldview is not logical coherence, but its usefulness in life's hard times. I saw an example of discontinuity between a theology and an operating worldview when the wife of a prominent Christian biblical scholar came to me for counseling shortly after her husband learned he only had a few months to live. When I talked to him, instead of Christian theology, I heard a strong stoicism by which he held his emotions in check so he could keep his intellectual strength in order to finish the book he had in progress. When I read that book later, I found little in it that reflected the stoic worldview with which he had faced his death. Apparently his theology and his living had little to do with each other. As he faced death, the God, whom he had made it his life's work to study, did not prove useful; but stoic philosophy, that he never seriously examined as a scholar, did. His wife, by the way, found her meaning in the Christian theology that her husband had not used to find his. Clergy's sermons and teachings, as well as the rituals they perform at significant occasions in individual and communal life, provide myths and symbols that the laity may appropriate with varying degrees of coherence. At the same time, symbols that have a deep meaning to clerical religion can translate to different meanings in lay people's religion. For example, a famous Zen image shows Bodhidharma meditating so deeply that his arms and legs have withered away. His body is shown as a circle. In a popular Japanese lay interpretation, the figure is seen as a "bop bag," one of those inflated toys weighted at the bottom so that, when it is punched, it pops back up. The esoteric symbol of focused discipline turns, in lay imagery, into an optimistic ability to bounce back after one of life's blows. In all traditions, great religious art is recast as kitsch.

Loss of Public Meanings of Death

The majority of people find their way in the world by adopting the map of invisible reality given to them within religious institutions and cultural affiliations. But in modernity, the death of the child often takes parents into what seems to be uncharted religious territory. The maps they find in their resolution are often beyond the scope of the conventional religion, beyond the scope of, as Goodenough (1986, p. 160) calls it, the "blueprint" provided by the institutional and theological cultural symbols which individuals bring to the death of their child. When we enter the lives of bereaved parents, we often find ourselves at the level of analysis that Luckmann (1967) calls the invisible religion. As Chidester says, "there is a sense in which the shared symbolization of death within a community reveals an essentially religious response to human limits that may not register explicitly in the organized institutions of religion" (1990, p. 14).

Historically, for most peoples and times, the spiritual or sacred were thoroughly interwoven with their sense of land and culture. When people were confronted with death, the myths, symbols, and beliefs expressed in the rituals of the culture functioned in three ways. First, they provided a framework in which the events in an individual's life could be interpreted and so made understandable. Second, they provided a way for the dead to remain integrated into the world of the living and at the same time to assume their social status as the dead. Third, because the myths, symbols, and beliefs were shared by everyone in the culture, survivors could be given the social status of mourners, and later, given the new social status brought by the death—widow, orphan, new matriarch or patriarch in the family.

The most obvious difference between this age and most others is the decline of overarching cultural worldviews that give meaning to individual lives. At the end of the twentieth century, the deaths of children have, for the most part, little public meaning. In the modern West, we live amidst competing worldviews, so there is no taken-for-granted framework in which to interpret life's events. The dead have been banished and the culture provides virtually no rituals by which the dead can remain integrated in the world of the living. The social roles brought on by death—mourner, widow, orphan, matriarch, or patriarch—have very little significance in a present-oriented consumer culture. Parents, families, and communities are now forced to make sense of the death on their own.

Perhaps the most notable exception to the decline of public meaning of children's deaths are the war dead. We can see how traditional spirituality gives meaning if we look for a moment at the public meaning of death in battle still found among all peoples. The death of young people, especially boys, as warriors is viewed as a glorious death (Warren, 1995). Death in combat confers instant immortality. The parents and family have a socially validated explanation of the death and share their continuing bond with the dead child within the wider community. If the war is popular, or if the results of the war facilitate a stronger sense of ethnic or national identity, the spirits of those who die are merged into the soul of the people and into the defining myths of the nation. At the dedication of the cemetery for the Union soldiers who died in the battle at Gettysburg, President Lincoln began his speech by putting the civil war into the wider historical meaning of a nation "conceived in liberty and dedicated to the proposition that all men are created equal." He said that the war was a test of whether a nation founded on those ideals could endure. He said that the young men in the graves around him had died for those ideals, but that their deaths could have meaning only if people still living dedicated themselves anew to the ideals and to the Union for which the soldiers had died. Although the individual mothers and fathers of the dead soldiers at Gettysburg carried their private sorrow, the deaths of their children had a public meaning; each child's name was on the monument in the town square, and every Memorial Day a parade and speeches reinvoked the memory in the service of national identity. As their deaths merge into tribal or national identity, the deaths of young people in war cease to be individual deaths, because it does not matter if they were draftees or volunteers, if they joined the army to avoid prison, to carry on a family tradition, or to see far away places with strange sounding names. Their deaths in battle take away their individuality and put them among the glorious dead. A World War II veteran, who had seen some of his comrades die, sat in my office as he tried to make sense of his grandson's death. It was difficult for him to bridge the gap between the deaths of soldiers in his youth and his grandson's death in an age when children's deaths have no public meaning. He said,

> It just doesn't add up. I remember when I came home and there were all those gold stars on the houses. It meant that the mother's boy had died. There was a reason. We were sad, but somehow that was not a bad thing. Richie just felt sick and went to the hospital and two days later he was dead. It just doesn't make any sense.

In cultures with well-established and all-encompassing worldviews, all deaths, not just the glorious war dead, made public sense. That is, all deaths could be interpreted within a sacred narrative to which everyone subscribed. All the dead, not just the war dead, were incorporated into the life of the community. In medieval Europe, communal life was carried on in the presence of the dead. Social life included continuing interactions with the dead.

> Death marked a transition, a change of status, but not an end. The living continued to owe them certain obligations, the most important that of *memoria*, remembrance. This means not only liturgical remembrance in the prayers and masses offered for the dead for weeks, months, and years but also preservation of the name, the family, and the deeds of the departed. . . . All the dead interacted with the living, continuing to aid them, to warn or admonish them, even to chastise them, if the obligations of *memoria* were not fulfilled (Geary, 1994, p.2)

Meaning of Death in the Modern World

The spiritual challenge faced by modern bereaved parents is somewhat different from that faced by parents for most of human history. In the modern world, in most cases, the task of interpreting the child's death, of making sense from potential nonsense, is no longer a cultural and communal task. It has become an individual task. Some vestiges of communal meaning remain. When the Viet Nam memorial was dedicated, those deaths could be integrated into the cultural myths and symbols, and individual families could find some resolution that had previously eluded them.

As a substitute for communal meaning, the mass media offers stereotyped scripts in which the deaths of some children become emblematic of larger social concerns. To some extent, the media do create a new kind of public meaning, but the media-created meaning seldom helps parents as they try to come to terms with the death of their child. By publicly showing the grief of some bereaved parents after bombings or violence, the media is creating a story line for the audience about the events in the news. For most bereaved parents, however, the meaning they make of the death is different from the simplistic and sensationalized media presentation. The lights of television cameras pointed toward the front door can become an invasion of privacy that adds insult to their grief. Despite the public outpouring of sympathy, the parents' grief remains intensely private. When the child's death becomes a media symbol, some bereaved parents may become media personalities, working out their pain on a public stage. After their life as media personalities, however, these parents seem still left with their grief. Over the years, a few of these parents have found their way to Bereaved Parents after their public life was over. It seemed to me that what they now shared in private was more complex than media story lines could allow, and that, when the cameras stopped, they were left to make sense of their children's death with the help of the other parents in the group.

The vast majority of children's deaths today have meaning only to the parents and family. Hence in the modern world:

> The most important task of a view of life seems to be to give the individual a framework for interpretation within which the reversals of life can reconcile and the individual ego be given a meaningful place with open-mindedness toward the future (Kallenberg, 1995 p. 57).

At the same time, the continuing bond which bereaved parents maintain with their dead children has lost its public meaning. In the modern world "the dead are banished from our society" (Geary, 1994, p. 2). Indeed with the rise of modern individualism in late industrial capitalism, a new way of thinking about grief developed. The purpose of grief work was to withdraw attachment from the deceased and to invest in new attachments which serve the present reality. In the modern world, the dead are gone and can be of no use to an individual making sense in the competitive world of industrial and consumer capitalism (see Stroebe, Gergen, Gergen, & Stroebe, 1992). In modern capitalism, parents' bonds with their children have largely ceased to have economic significance. Children are no longer assets to parents who need labor on the farm or in the shop. Children instead have become economic liabilities that may relegate executive women to the "mommy track." The DINKs (double income, no kids) can lead the lifestyles of the rich and famous portrayed in the commercials. Child rearing has become more and more an altruistic activity that has only personal meaning. At the same time, in a mass society, the parents' bonds with their children have become among the most important meaning-giving bonds in their lives. As meaning is increasingly found less in the public sphere and more in the private, having children becomes more and more significant to the personal meaning parents make of their world. When children die, then, their deaths have no public significance, but the deaths have intense personal significance to the parents. The parents' bond with the child had little public significance when the child was living, and, when the child is dead, the continuing bond with the child has almost no public significance.

Bereaved parents are faced with a private death that rips through the fabric of the world they have constructed. Individual survivors must make meaning within the family and community in which the death occurs. In their more fragmented modern world, bereaved parents can choose from among a large fund of religious and cultural myths, symbols, and ideologies as they come to terms with their children's deaths. Yet at the same time, the myths and symbols do not carry the indisputable conviction that they did in other times. Modern bereaved parents have many more myths and symbols than people had before, because, in a pluralistic world, virtually all religions of humankind are available to them. Still, within this wealth of potentially meaning-giving symbols, the search for meaning remains private and individual; only the individual can choose among the multitude of myths and symbols available.

Interactions with the Dead Child and Worldviews

In bereaved parents we see a great variety of worldviews and many ways by which parents interact with their dead child. But within all the diversity, we consistently find a strong connection between the solace-filled bond with the dead child and the parent's task of maintaining or remolding a meaningful worldview. As a way of focusing on the connection between solace in the bond to the now-immortal child and a parent's worldview, we can listen to a clergyman's report about how the key to his finding a renewed faith was a dream of his dead son.

> There he was! Walking toward me as if coming out of a mist. There he was—that lanky 17-year-old whose life I loved better than my own. He looked deeply into my eyes and with a grin on his face, the way he used to do when he was "buttering me up." Not a word was spoken, but everything was said that needed to be said for my turning point to come. It was time to resume life. I would not be bitter, but in loving memory, I would be better. I would live again because I knew that my boy lived again. My own Christian faith was to be retro-fitted. It offered meaning and purpose within the shadow of my loss. It asserted that, though God does not intend my sufferings, He involves himself in them.

> My pain and loss were not to be the end of life. Rather, it was to be a beginning—a beginning to a more compassionate life of quality and caring.

We notice that the boy is alive in this account; not just in heaven, but in the father's dream. The grin on the boy's face renews the bond between father and son, and at the same time, it seems, the grin allows the father to renew his own bond with the Heavenly Father who is involved in the father's pain. The clergyman father's renewed bond to transcendent reality and his deepened understanding of how his pain fits into God's care of the world help him to maintain his role in the community as the authoritative interpreter of life's meaning. The clergyman finds the turning point of his spiritual journey in his dream of the boy's presence, not in the sacred texts. Indeed, it seems, from his account, that his son's wordless presence marks the occasion for the sacred texts to speak to the father with a message that had not been so clear before.

Now, to be sure, this is a clergyman who has given his life to the myths, symbols, and rituals, of a well-developed worldview in an established religious tradition. So perhaps, the connection between faith and interaction with the dead child is clearer in this example. Still, as we explore the ways bereaved parents make sense of their children's deaths, we will find a consistent connection between the parents' bonds with their dead children and their finding or reworking worldviews that are useful them.

☐ Maintaining or Remolding Worldviews

Traumatic events challenge worldviews. Scholars studying the effects of traumatic experiences such as rape, physical assault, or bereavement on individuals have described the search for meaning in which victims often engage. Ronnie Janoff-Bulman (1989,1985) says,

> The coping task facing victims is largely a difficult cognitive dilemma. They must integrate the data of their dramatic negative experience and their prior assumptions, which cannot readily assimilate the new information. Victims must rework the new data so as to make it fit and thereby maintain their old assumptions, or they must revise their old assumptions in a way that precludes the breakdown of the entire system and allows them to perceive the world as not wholly threatening (1989, p. 121).

After a traumatic event, the worldview is like a Piagetian schema in the face of new information. The schema must assimilate the new experience. If, however, the new information can no longer be fitted into the structure of the mental schema, the schema must accommodate. That is, the schema must change in a way that allows the information to be part of a larger framework. Some worldviews prove adequate to assimilate the traumatic experience of a child's death. Some worldviews do not, so these worldviews must accommodate. That is, these worldviews change in ways that allow the reality of the trauma to make sense.

Early in their grief, it is not unusual for parents to make what Elisabeth Kübler-Ross (1969, pp. 82–84) called bargains. Often these take the form of an early readjustment of their faith in exchange for the return of the child. They want their life to be like Job's who, after he had passed the test of faithfulness, had his former life restored to him. Because the bargains are so stark and so simple, bereaved parents often confuse these bargains early in the grief with the long term changes that come with the resolution of grief. A month after her child died, a mother wrote in her diary:

> Today was so hard, it's been a month now. I think a part of me believed you'd be back by now. I kept saying to myself, "I can take this for one month, and then I want him back." The month is gone and you are not back. I want to scream, "The test is over. I pass, you jerk. Give him back, damn you, give him back."

The changes in worldview that we see in bereaved parents are longer coming and more thorough-going than a simple one-time test of faith.

Worldviews are very complex. Each person's worldview is deeply embedded in cultural history and in individual history. As we try to understand parents' worldviews, they do not reduce to simple yes or no questions such as, "Do parents believe in God more or less?" or, "Do they find the world less just?" Worldviews are made of symbols woven deeply into the parent's whole self and world. As I have listened to bereaved parents feeling their way along and to the accounts of their journeys after they had come safely through, it seems to me that there are some patterns. But the patterns are not in the content of the worldview. That is, what people believe does not seem the critical factor. There seem to be endless variations of belief, symbol, ritual, and action among bereaved parents. Every worldview, no matter what its content, is tested, and none is guaranteed to pass. In Chapter Two, as we tried to define worldview, we noted that Erwin Ramsdell Goodenough said that archetypical themes do not form the common element within the diversity of worldviews. Rather, he said, the common element is "the insecurity and universal anxiety which various peoples and individuals all experience, along with the equally universal craving for explanation and control" (1986, p. 18). It seems to me that, if there is a pattern in worldviews in the resolution of parental grief, the pattern is found in how parents' prior worldviews meet the challenge of the insecurity and universal anxiety as well as the need for explanation and control brought on by the death of their children. The question is whether and how the assumptions which the parent held before the child died hold up to the test, whether or not the God that the parent used before the child died proves useful now. The question is whether the parents can assimilate the experience of their children's deaths into their prior assumptions, or whether they must strike out on their own to construct new meanings for their life as well as for the lives and deaths of their children. The pattern we find is in how much the parents' prior worldviews pass the test and how much the parents' worldviews must be changed in the light of their new experience.

1. Some parents are able to retain the worldviews they held before their children died. The content of their worldviews does not seem a factor. We see both very liberal and very conservative viewpoints that work for parents. For some people, retaining their prior world-views depends on their being able to reinterpret the death of the child in a way that is consistent with these worldviews.
2. Some parents find new and compelling worldviews during their children's terminal illness, and all their experience after their children die fits into those worldviews. The crisis of caring for a dying child provides some parents with the experience of authentic communities on which they can base new worldviews adequate to their grief. The new communities include their children. The inner presence of the child as well as the memories of the living child can provide the parent with a model for a better way to live.
3. Some parents interpret symbols and myths within their worldview in new and profounder ways. The symbols and myths of religious traditions have deeper meanings than most people use. As people can discover meanings that they did not understand before in symbols and myths, their worldviews accommodate in a way that can include the experience of their children's deaths.
4. When the symbols or affiliation of the parents' worldview are not useful, some live in a divided world. They maintain a bond with the transcendent that is linked to their children. In other parts of their lives, however, they feel cut off from the God in whom they still believe.
5. Some parents develop entirely new worldviews after a long time of trying to deal with their grief in worldviews that do not work for

them. They change their beliefs about themselves and their world and find new ways of being themselves in a universe which they see as working quite differently from the way they used to see it. As they change, their continuing bonds with their dead children change too. The old beliefs that once brought the shame or guilt that prevented the parents from feeling in touch with their children in a way that brought solace now give way to more positive relationships to the spirit of the dead children.

Some Worldviews Stand the Test

The question is, Can the child's death be assimilated into the parent's worldview? Can the parent's worldview adequately include death in the radically new way the parent knows death, and can the worldview provide the parent with adequate models for living without the child? If the worldview can, then it can be maintained. The test is not the test of a particular belief. It seems to make little difference whether a person is Christian or Buddhist, or what kind of Christian or Buddhist. What is tested is the worldview as that parent holds it. Both conservative and liberal worldviews can pass the test, and both can flunk.

One group of parents in our study maintains the worldviews they held before their children's deaths, sometimes with little difficulty, sometimes after some effort. Nevertheless, they "keep their faith." One example of a person whose worldview withstood the test would be someone who holds a relatively modern worldview that sees the events of the world happening in a random fashion. If the universe functions randomly, the place and power humans can have in the universe is to be competent. If, in this worldview, parents can maintain a sense competence similar to what they felt before their children died, they can assimilate the reality of their children's deaths into the preexisting worldview. Among these parents, their continuing bonds with their children support their sense of competence and helps them maintain a sense of continuity. This sense of personal competence is especially important in traumatic deaths, because parents are often troubled by questions of the preventability of their children's deaths.

We interviewed a mother of two children. Her younger child has learning disabilities, and, at the time we interviewed her, the child was having many behavioral problems. Her older child had been bright and normal. She experienced a sense of competence as she learned to be a mother with the surviving child. The older child was killed as a toddler when a heavily sedated mental patient hit the car she drove. The mother's sense of competence was not threatened by the accident. She was, she said, just at the wrong place at the wrong time. There was nothing she could have done to prevent the accident. There is, in her worldview, no God or magic power in her world that intervenes with natural laws. She wanted to testify at the trial because it was something she could still do for her child.

> I agreed with the idea that I'd lost the right of protection for my child. One of our roles as a parent is to protect our child, and that right was taken away from me. So, I felt I needed to follow through as far as I could in the criminal resolution of what had happened. . . . I just thought we had to get him off the streets.

They lost the trial because the driver pleaded insanity. So the mother arranged to have information on the driver's medication given to the Bureau of Motor Vehicles, and his driver's license was revoked.

Problems with her surviving child often threaten this mother's sense of competence as a parent. When she is going through hard times parenting her surviving child, the memory of her dead child

> reassures me of my abilities as a parent. I can remember that I've had success as a parent. As much as relationships are reciprocal and people feed off each other, I still know that what's going on is somehow beyond him (the surviving child) or me.

We can see how this mother asserts the place and power of the self within a nonpredictable universe. For her, the universe may function randomly, but the individual can be competent and so maintain mastery in the random world. There is no Holy Other in this worldview, so the power must reside within herself. Testifying at the trial was a continuation of the competent motherhood she had always practiced. This competence gives meaning to her life. The memory of her former time with the dead child can sustain her through the challenges to her competence that she feels as she parents a troubled living child.

Worldviews that are very different theologically from each other can be retained when they continue to support a sense of selfhood that worked for the parent before the child died. The mother who found she could maintain her sense of competence has what theologians would call a rather liberal worldview. The following example is of a person who has what theologians would call a very conservative one. A woman referred for counseling by a social service agency had grown up in a dysfunctional family where she was labeled "ugly and stupid." One of the few comfortable places she found during her childhood was in church where the nuns taught her that she could pray to God who was a good father. She married, then had three children who died at intervals of two years from a genetic disorder resulting from a mismatch with her husband who left her when the third died. After the divorce, she was reestablishing life when she was hit by a drunk driver and was paralyzed below the waist. When I met her, she was an active participant in several Catholic prayer groups for spiritual healing. Led by a nun, one group on "healing the inner child" was especially important to her. She attended Catholic charismatic services often, and felt close to a small group of people whose main connection was to pray with and for each other. She told me that Jesus, Mary, and the saints are her real family and friends. In her prayer she maintained close interaction with her Holy Family and felt that she was under their protection and love.

Midway through our counseling, she told me that earlier in the week she had attended the funeral of a child because someone thought she could help the mother. She cried and left the church when she saw the little white casket up front, because "it brought it all back—all three." The evening after the funeral she collapsed on the floor of her apartment. She called a friend to come and pray with her. As she and her friend prayed, she felt the presence of Brian, the last child to die. She was most bonded to Brian because she lived in with him at the hospital. The other children had just stayed at the hospital until they died, while she cared for the children at home. After Brian died, she held his body and said goodbye. As she and the friend continued to pray, she saw Brian as a young man now standing near her and saying, "Mom, you will be OK. The baby who died is with Jesus." She reported this to her friend and the friend asked, "Can you see Jesus?" She could, and then she saw Brian and Jesus walking off together. She told me, "Now every day when I pray for the help and presence of God and the saints, it feels kind of special. I really do know one of them." To make sure I understood what she was saying, I asked, "So, it is like Brian is one with Jesus and the saints in heaven?" "Yes," she said, "he is one of them, and I am cared for by all of them. He is part of that."

As a child, this mother found solace in the sense of the presence of God the Father. Only in church and in prayer could she remember feeling good and protected. In turn, she accepted the whole Catholic worldview. Although her family was dysfunctional, she still belonged to the Holy Family. We might wonder what would have happened had her marriage worked out and the children lived, but that was not to be. In her grief, she returned to the Holy Mother Church, where she could find her place and power in the universe by working on healing her inner child. What is left of her children, the sense of their presence, has been adopted, like her, into the Holy Family. Her son is now an angel with Jesus, who cares for her just as the baby who died is cared for by Jesus. Her worldview has proven adequate to the test.

As we looked at parents whose worldviews hold in the face of their children's deaths, we first met a liberal, then a conservative. A third example is a man whose philosophical and theological search in his late adolescence paid off. Thomas Wyatt had developed a worldview that could include the child's death within an intelligent order. He wrote a poem, published in the newsletter, in which he asked traditional theological questions that come to almost everyone in bad times.

> I just want to raise my fists and
> scream to the sky;
> I demand to know the reason God, please
> tell me why?
> But that's not being fair to you,
> you didn't take my son;
> It wasn't payment for my sins, it
> wasn't something that I've done.
> It was an accident, just one of those things;
> But I'm drowning in the wake that this
> tragedy brings.
> I know that I can survive with you by
> my side, my heart is in your hands;
> Please forgive me Lord for my unanswerable
> demands. (by Thomas Wyatt)

He reaffirms the idea of a personal God who operates within a universe that includes natural laws. His faith in a personal God does not include God's violating scientific principles. If a one-ton car runs over a 30-pound child, the child will die, because that is a result of the laws of physics. Although a less mature faith in a personal God might include the concept of punishment for sins, the father's study of philosophy and theology had given him a less punitive God. God remains for him like a parent whose presence can provide solace in his grief, but he knows that even the Divine Father's power is limited. His worldview can comfort him in his grief, even if it cannot provide the just world for which he yearns.

As a way of maintaining their worldviews, many parents reinterpreted their children's deaths in ways that make some good come out of them. The perceptions of the deaths are modified, so that they can be assimilated into their previous religious symbols and affiliations with little accommodation. Virtually all the parents in the group forcefully reject the simple interpretation that their children's deaths were God's will. All parents in the group also reject the idea that the children's deaths happened so that something good could happen. At the same time, they accept that good may come from a bad thing. A mother struggling with the question "Why?" said,

> I just cannot accept that there is no reason for this. There has got to be some purpose. Rose was a beautiful girl. She didn't deserve to die. I am a good mother. I cannot accept that God just lets things happen. I feel these changes in me. I see good things happening, like the way the kids at the school responded and the pages in the year book. There is a reason for this, and good will come out of it.

We can see the continuing bond the mother has with her child: The good which came from the death is the expression of shared love for her child. The bond she still feels with her daughter is validated in the bond still felt by her daughter's classmates who put the pages in the yearbook. She feels changes in herself that are part of her growth within her identification with her dead daughter. She feels that in her relationships with other people, she is beginning to exemplify some of her daughter's admirable traits. A few years later, I talked with the mother during the social hour after a Candlelight Service. She spoke at length about the growth her husband had undergone in his grief and about the improvement in their marriage. She said, "You know, it's sad, but this wouldn't have happened if Rose hadn't died." With this interpretation of her new way of living in the world and of her daughter's continuing influence on herself and others, the mother can maintain her belief in a personal, just God.

In meetings, the issue of how to interpret the child's death is put as the simple question: "Do you really wish your child had never been born?" The question enlarges the frame. It puts the pain of grief in a balance with the joys of the child's life. Except in rare cases, parents conclude that the joys outweigh the pain, and so, while the death is bad, it is within a larger good. To support that interpretation, parents often refer to the present bonds with their children. While they miss their children, they still have their children. One mother found meaning in a letter her child's friend read at the funeral. The letter was written as if it were from the dead child.

> Would it have been better if I had never been? The pain of losing the presence of one you've loved so much is still better than never having that life at all. . . . I'll always be a part of you; your pain is mine and your joy is mine.

The letter continues by reminding the mother that she will be reunited with the child in heaven, and the child asks the mother to store up every moment of life as memory that she can share with the child when they meet again.

Some People Discover a New Worldview
in the Crisis of Dying and Grief

The crisis of caring for a dying child or the crisis of early grief provides some parents with experience of an authentic community on which they can base a new worldview that is adequate to the long term resolution of their grief. The new community includes their child. We find in these parents that, after the child is dead, the continuing bonds with their children provide them with a model for how they should live their life now.

When they learn that their children have serious diagnoses, parents are filled with strong new feelings and thrust into unfamiliar surroundings. They are asked to make decisions based on information they are just learning. They interact with professionals with an intensity they have not known before. Communities are tested severely in the crisis of a child's dying and death. When a child is dying, what is important and what is not becomes very clear. Communications between parents and family as well as communications between parents and professionals and between the parents themselves can become clear. Some communities show themselves at their finest in those weeks and months. Other communities marginalize the parents, because the reality is more than the community can handle. When parents no longer fit into their old social networks, they can find new and better ways of being in the world.

Some parents find a new worldview in their time of crisis that will endure for the rest of their lives. The world can become an authentic and meaningful place during and right after the death of their children. Some parents find religious faith during their children's illnesses, a faith that is nurtured in intense networks of interpersonal relationships. As their children go through many months of treatment, the parents find a supportive peer and professional group in the hospital. In those months of facing death, these parents experience a more authentic way of communicating and living than they have ever known in their lives. That is, the experience of their children's illnesses and impending deaths occasions a major accommodation in the parents' worldview. They change their understanding of how the universe works and of the place and power of both them and their children in that universe. Now all experience can be assimilated into the new worldview.

After her teenage son's death, a woman we interviewed returned often to the hospital to help parents whose children were dying. She had found what seemed to her to be an authentic community among the parents and staff in the hospital. During her son's illness she found meaning in her own life by helping other parents. After her son died, she felt strongly that she still wanted to participate in the community there. She did not want to return to what now seemed the superficial social circles she had maintained before the illness. She said that her son provided the model for her and her husband's present worldview by the way he faced his death. Her son's example supported her better self when he was sick and continues to support her better self now as she tries to be the kind of person he was.

> I think about the times when Gary was so worried about me. His concern was for me. He was strong, a wonderful example for me. He just loved us, and we could feel it. Gary brought us the example of showing love, and now we continue that with our other children. The kids all recognize it too. It is a beautiful experience. We believe in heaven and that Gary is where he should be. We feel that his purpose has been fulfilled; and for us, we are still working on it.

She now experiences her dead son as a saint who can grant favors. She said,

> I'll be on the highway in a traffic jam, and I'll say, 'OK, Gary, get me out of this.' I'll go by the cemetery and talk to him, or I'll be thinking about something, and I'll talk to Gary.

She and her husband are active in a Catholic prayer and support group. They say they have found the same authentic community there as they had in the hospital. Their Christian worldview is a very personal theology. The parts of their church's theology that are not useful in their grief are simply not brought to bear. Her husband talked about his brother who cannot understand why the couple can still believe in God after their son died so unfairly. "But, you know, my brother is still mad about the Spanish Inquisition," he said. He explained the wide sense of community in which he and his wife participate, and he explained the place his dead child plays in that community:

> I talk about what I call a big circle theory. Someone says, "I'm going to pay you back." "A" helps "B," and "B" helps "C," and they go all around the world. But it will come back. I really believe it.

If some parts of their Catholic theology are not useful, a new understanding of the doctrine of the communion of saints is. I asked, "Is Gary still a part of that?" The father said,

> He's there to help, and I call on him every once in a while. He's like a saint, like Joseph or Christopher. One of the letters of Corinthians talks about the body of Christ. . . . The dead are still part of that body. I don't hesitate to ask someone to pray for something. And I think that in talking to Gary. I figure, if you are going to get a favor, you might as well get it from someone who has an "in" somewhere.

These parents feel a direct bond with the transcendent which seems, to them, indistinguishable from the bond with their dead children. The parents' lives have taken on new meanings, meanings which are tied to the meaning they find in the child's death. The inner representations of their children are part of the religious symbols by which they live, and part of the supportive community in which the symbols were maintained.

Some communities, on the other hand, flunk the test of a child's diagnosis and death. Parents must find new communities, and within the new community they find a new worldview. We interviewed a mother who had become very active in Bereaved Parents. She reported that when her child had been diagnosed with an inoperable brain tumor, she found that her former support system failed her. None of her large family came to help when she needed it.

> I found total strangers to be more supportive than the family. In fact, most of the friends we had before Pamela died are no longer our friends. They disappeared through the illness, and did not come when she died.

She now sees herself as quite different from her family and former friends. She models herself now on the support group she joined during the time the child was ill and on Bereaved Parents which that she joined shortly after her child died.

> I don't think I could ever hear somebody say they felt alone and not feel, "Well, you're not alone, because I'm here." I can't walk away from someone who needs me.

Her transcendent reality is what theologians call immanent, that is, she now finds goodness in her relationship with others. Her continuing bond with the dead child is central to her new sense of relationship to others, because the life she now lives is the life that she first saw in her now-dead child.

> I value little things that happen with other people; maybe I wouldn't have noticed them before. Pamela made me aware of the nice things that people can offer. Maybe I pay more attention to those kinds of things than I would have otherwise.

The connection with others is a gift the child gave her and is experienced within a sense of connectedness with her child. As she talked about Pamela and how her sense of Pamela's presence validates her new worldview, her language was tentative. "It is almost like maybe," she says, and "almost somehow," because she seems to know that everyday speech will not hold the profound reality on which she now bases her life. But her worldview can remain poetic in her mind, because it is real in her soul, and more importantly, it is real in the way she is in her world. She knows that she is now something better because Pamela lived and died.

> I'm very aware of her presence; in a sense, she's almost with me more now than when she was ill. I think that she was like a gift, and it was almost like maybe she wasn't supposed to be there, that maybe she was just a spirit or something that I was supposed to get, and could have not gotten another way. . . . In my mind, almost somehow, Pamela and God are almost the same. . . . Even as an infant, there was something different about her, something unusual that I never could quite put my finger on. I knew that it was something that I had never quite seen, and, I think, in my mind it was like God and Pamela were inseparable. I feel that I was to be something better because she was here.

This sense of the meaning in the child's life expressed in the parent's personal growth and in significant bonds with others is important in the self-help process. Affiliation with the group and becoming a helper within the group play important roles in making the continuing bond with the child an important part of the self. The child lives on, not simply as a memory or in heaven. The child lives on in the virtues and character of the child that the parent now takes on as his or her own and that the parent expresses by helping other bereaved parents.

Some People Reinterpret the Symbols of Their Prior Worldview

Many parents do not find the strength they need from the worldviews they held before their children died, but they can still use these worldviews after they have revised them. The symbols and myths of religious traditions are deep and rich. People can discover meanings that they did not understand before. For example, the central symbol of Christianity is God's son suffering and dying. When bereaved parents make the connection between their experience and God's, they say, "God is a bereaved parent, too." The symbol takes on a meaning for them that changes their worldviews enough so that they can assimilate the experience of their children's deaths into it. Over the years, many bereaved parents have found Harold Kushner's book, *When Bad Things Happen to Good People* (1981) helpful, because it allows them to keep the symbol of a theistic God, albeit with limited omnipotence.

We can see the development within a religious symbol in one mother who had been taught in Catholic school that, if she were good, God would not let anything bad happen. In a counseling session she said:

A lot of people come up and tell me it was God's will. I just stop them and say, "Look, maybe you think that, but I don't believe that any more. So just don't say that to me." I mean terrible things happen all the time. Before, I protected myself because I thought I was safe. I feel the pain now, like what I see in the news. I talked to the priest that married us. He said my faith was maturing. I mean, Jesus suffered. That was God.

Over the years we have found several women who connected their grief and their mothering to the symbol of Mary, the mother of Jesus. Especially at Christmas, thoughts in the newsletter are sometimes about a mother's identification with Mary, and in that identification the dead child becomes the Christ child. Although such a relationship with Mary is not shared by the majority of those in their community or family, it relieves others of the strain of comforting the mother, so it does not bring conflict with fellow believers. One woman whose retarded child died wrote:

> Since it was God's will for me to have a retarded child, the greatest thing I can say about it is that I thank God He chose me to be Bonnie's mother. I feel almost as privileged as Mary must have felt to be chosen as the mother of God.

The parent-child bond is at the core of the central Christian symbol. Usually, believers see themselves as the child of the father God. But a few parents change and see God in terms of their own parental role. Their present reality can be assimilated into this paradigmatic symbol. One mother wrote:

> Last year, in preparing a Christmas memorial service for our group, I had another "faith experience." I always believed God sent His only son to die for us. Last year it hit me that if this is true, this makes God a bereaved parent too! I felt even closer to Him, because I realized He knew how I felt (at least sometimes). Whenever I can see human qualities in God, it makes Him more real to me.

Were the mother of a more mystical nature, she might have developed the symbol further. She might have found that she and her child had become one as the Heavenly Father and Son are one. The symbol has that potential. But for this mother, the symbol remains more concrete to her. So, as she prepares for the holiday, she feels a bond both with God and with her child, and, at the same time, she feels a distance from the child and from God. She concludes her newsletter article, "I go on, trying to keep Christmas special for our family, because I know my 'little drummer boy' in heaven wants me to."

The question of miracles is a common theological problem for bereaved parents. After all, Jesus cured the sick and raised people from the dead. If their faith were only strong enough or if their God were only caring enough, could not their lives be touched by a miracle and their children resurrected? On her fifth Christmas after her child died, one woman found herself reflecting back on how her understanding of miracles had changed. She remembered that during her first year, even though she thought of herself as a someone who had accepted the reality of her child's death, as the holiday approached, she found herself watching "those sappy TV programs" and reading articles about holiday miracles. "They give me a crazy kind of hope. Something wonderful would happen to me! The Miracle Maker wouldn't forget me—not if I believed hard enough." Maybe her son would be returned to her. But it didn't happen, and after that Christmas. "I never again asked for a miracle, because I stopped believing they existed." For the next few years when the holiday television programs came on, she felt only anger, "'That's such bull,' I'd say to the TV family. 'Let me introduce you to the real world, where children die, even on a holiday!'" Then, for her birthday, her sister had given her an embroidered wall hanging that said "Some of God's miracles are small." As she redecorated a room, she hung it under a picture of her dead child. As she put the embroidery on the wall, she had a moment in which she reinterpreted the meaning of miracle.

> I stared at it and tried to grasp its meaning. I shed a tear that I didn't get the miracle I asked for—or did I? I realized that most miracles are probably little ones—ones we may go a lifetime without recognizing.
>
> The miracle is that my son lived, that I received gifts that only he could give. And I discovered that I like the "new" me—better than the old one. I can now say without guilt that I'm a better person; now—not because my son died, but because he lived! Maybe it's not such a small miracle after all.

The miracle became the change in her that her son and her grief has brought. Her son's life, as now expressed in her life, is a miracle.

A case from the counseling practice can help us see how deeply religious symbols reach into the personal and cultural history, and the complexity of the process that underlies reinterpreting symbols. Sonya, a 43-year-old mother of two young children, was referred by a psychologist, who thought there was a link between her present anxiety attacks and the death of her infant daughter, Emma, nine years earlier. She had been breast feeding the child in the car on the way to a family Christmas dinner when the accident happened. She had seen a psychologist a few months after the crash. She reported the counseling had helped, because she was able cry "at the funeral I missed."

Sonya had a very successful business career, but that was not what she wanted. After several years of trying to have children, all her children were born using a fertility clinic. The children seem very fragile to her because it was so difficult to conceive them. The anxiety attacks began when her oldest child had a bout of severe stomach cramps for which the pediatrician had no diagnosis. "I need to be in control," Sonya said. "I don't do well when I am not in control." It seemed she did not recognize her feelings of fear until they reached a high threshold, and then the fear was out of control. We worked out a behavioral and cognitive program of managing the anxiety.

In the third session, Sonya worked up to the anxious feeling in the office. As we talked of Emma's death, she got a lump in her chest and became hazy in her thinking. She moved from talking about Emma's death to her son's recent illness and noticed, seemingly for the first time, that the feeling was similar.

In the fourth session she reported the good news that her son's stomach problem had been diagnosed as parasites, probably from drinking stream water on a camping trip. She was able to evoke her fear of the unpredictable world and to label the feeling. She felt more in control as she found our program of anxiety management was working. She said that, as she let herself recognize her feelings of fear, she realized that she had been avoiding everything associated with the accident, but now she needed to let the feelings and memories in.

As Sonya became more comfortable accepting her fears, she began talking about her relationship with God. She said, when Emma was born she trusted God that the baby would be okay. She had accepted the "dehumanizing" way the child was conceived in the fertility clinic, because, in the end, God had answered her prayers and given her the child. But now, it seemed, God had let her down. She was Catholic but had not been to confession since the accident. As a child, she was taught that if she were good, God would take care of her. She said that she had always trusted God. So she just controlled her moral behavior, an easy task in the small ethnic community in which she grew up, and she controlled her school and work life. She studied hard, got good grades, got a good job, worked hard, and was promoted rapidly within the company. After the accident, she now saw in retrospect, she needed to take over complete responsibility, because, it seemed, God was no longer trustworthy. I recommended Kushner's *Why Bad Things Happen To Good People* . She had read it by the next session. She began to free associate to memories of Emma. She recalled her birth and some events in Emma's short life. The inner representation seemed very clear to her, and she said that she would remember Emma always, because she decided being a bereaved parent would always be a part of who she is and who she would always be.

Given her fragile view of little children, we looked for other models of children, and she remembered participating in and then coaching junior high sports. Children of that age seemed safely established in life, so she decided that she could be on guard for the next few years, knowing that she needed to manage her watchfulness and fear. When her children reached junior high age, she would know that they would be fine, for then children are not fragile.

With the anxiety somewhat under control and the inner representation of Emma available to her as memory, Sonya turned in earnest to Catholic theological issues. The question took on some urgency, because her son was to have his first communion and the parents were supposed to go to confession in preparation for the ritual. She saw a movie at church about forgiveness in which the story was about the mother of a little girl hit by a drunk driver. Sonya saw that her panic attacks had a philosophical and theological dimension. "This is deeper than panic attacks," she said, pointing first to her chest and then to her stomach, when she raised the issue of going to confession again. Then she broke into quiet sobbing and seemed to collapse on the sofa.

For the next few weeks she sought out several priests for conversation. None of their answers seemed to satisfy her, but, she said, her relationship to God changed. God was, she said, no longer the "big watchman in the sky" for her. She would ask God to give her strength to deal with the bad things that happened in her life, rather than asking God to solve all the problems. She said that, as she made the decision to rely on God in a different way, she felt a freedom within herself that she had not felt since before the accident. Although, she said, she did not have adequate words to describe the inner change further. She was able to talk about Emma with sadness. Mixed with the sadness, she found some pleasure in remembering her.

Our counseling sessions were brought to an end when Sonya's husband's company changed managed care plans, but the drama had already played itself out. In the second to last session, she reported she had talked to a priest whom she met through a friend. It turned out that he was leaving the priesthood. They had a series of long person-to-person, not person-to-priest talks. On the priest's recommendation, she read a book on adult faith and one on how it is possible to hate God. As her God was becoming less an external authority and more an internal reality, the man who was giving up his priestly authority was probably a good person with whom to talk. The problem of having to go to confession was solved with the idea that confession was more like a therapy session in which God listened while she worked through her thoughts.

Sonya was still as much a Catholic as she had been when Emma died. But she was a different kind of Catholic now. She could reinterpret the symbols and hold them in a new way. There was still a God in heaven who could be known in the sacraments of the church, including confession. When she related to God in an adult way rather than her former childish way, she could use the sacrament of confession to make sense of a world that includes the death of her baby.

Some Parents Live in a Divided World

Some parents cannot maintain the symbols which support their world, but neither can they abandon their old worldviews and move on to new ones. They live in a divided world. That is, they seem neither able to assimilate fully nor to accommodate. In those cases, the parents divide the world of their lostness from the parts of their selves which still maintain a trustworthy world. For most of these parents in our study, the continuing bonds with their children connect them with a benevolent world, even as they feel cut off in other parts of their psyche. We have less data on these parents, because they are less likely to write about their doubts in the newsletter than parents who want to write about their faith. But in interviews, in meetings, and in counseling sessions their questions come out.

In a meeting, one father talked about how he feels after the months of praying during his daughter's illness for her recovery.

> Some of the children would get better, and some would not. One night, as she was going to sleep, Jessica asked me, "Daddy, how does God decide who gets the miracles?" I didn't know what to answer her. I still don't. I guess I still believe in miracles. How else do you account for the kids I saw get better with no explanation. But we didn't get one. So where am I now?

He believes that he and his daughter did not get a miracle, although he believes that others did. The Bible says, "The Lord giveth and the Lord taketh away. Blessed be the name of the Lord." In this father's heart, he is one from whom the Lord has taken. He sees no reasonable explanation for how God decided who got the miracles and who didn't, so he is unable to bless the name of the Lord. He "called unto the Lord," and the Lord didn't answer. In one part of his spiritual life he lives as one of God's nonchosen people. Although he might wish he could, he no longer feels a sure bond with transcendent reality.

Still, if he and his child were passed over in the distribution miracles, he does not believe that his child was passed over for heaven. He believes strongly that his daughter is in heaven with God, and he often thinks that she is in a better place than he is. He looks forward to the time when he will rejoin her when he dies. He also senses his daughter's presence sometimes, and her presence connects him with his better self. Once as he was making a difficult business decision which had ethical implications, he felt a strong bond with her and he acted, he said, for the good, not knowing whether he would pay a price for his ethical stand or not. To do otherwise, he said, would be to disgrace her memory. So he lives in a spiritually divided world. In one part of himself, he is one of God's unchosen; in another part of himself, he is intensely bonded to a child in heaven, and he looks forward to joining her. Until then, he lives a life he hopes is worthy of the child.

A counseling case can show the depth and complexity of a divided world. Anna's son, Noah, died in his early 20s, three years before we began our sessions. He fell five stories from a roof on which he was working and lay unconscious for a month in the hospital with massive head trauma. Anna was divorced from Noah's father, who had abused both Anna and Noah. She often feel guilty about the violence Noah suffered. She said Noah always carried the scars of the early violence. He was quiet and had a sadness at his center. His core sadness also made the mother and son soul mates. Theirs was a spiritual connection. He used to say, "Life sucks and then you die." In her frequent pessimistic moods, she often felt the same.

Anna thought there was no afterlife. As a teenager, she was in a coma after an accident. She remembered coming in and out of consciousness. "I didn't have a near death experience. There was consciousness, and there was nothing. It scared me, and I asked, is this what death is like? I decided the answer is yes." That made it hard, she said, because all that is left of her son seems to be the body rotting in the ground. When her father died after Noah:

> I believed what people said, that Noah and his grandfather are together like they were when they went fishing. But in my heart I didn't really believe that. It was just a way of fooling myself and not making other people uncomfortable.

When I asked, "Where is his spirit?" She answered:

> Easy answer: in my memory, and you create what you will of that. But the real spirit—what made him what he was—is gone. You have to make a distinction between spirit and memory. I have memory—but that doesn't mean enough. I still wonder, why go on. I was at a transition point in my life when he died, asking myself questions of what the rest of life means. So I still ask that. His memory is something I will always carry. But I am still a child of the sixties and don't know what it is all about like my parents did.

Sometimes Noah's memory supports a side of Anna she really enjoys. She told me about a customer on the phone who had called her a "fat ass." "Well, you can't find yours unless somebody's kissing it," she replied. "I got that off the Internet," she laughed. "I knew when I saw it that it was a line I would use someday, and I finally got to do it. I was so proud of myself." The customer called back a few moments later and apologized. I asked how Noah would have responded if he heard the story. She said he would have loved it. She told the story of the school principal calling to say that Noah was to be expelled for two days. She asked why. The answer was that he had a drawn a cartoon of questionable taste and hung it on his locker. When the principal asked him to remove it, Noah invoked his freedoms under the United States Constitution. When he got home, she knew she was supposed to be mad, but she just broke out laughing, "Why do you do these things?"

I asked, "What did he say?"

"What was to say?" she said, "We just looked at each other, and we knew. I never shared that way with anyone. That was just him."

"What does it feel like to be remembering him to me now?" I asked. "Strange," she said.

> I miss him so when I tell the stories, but it feels wonderful to tell them. There are few places I can do that now. People just don't take it well when you say 'let me tell you about my funny, adorable dead son.' But as I talk to you it seems real and good. It feels bad, and it feels good. One thing I am afraid of is that, as the years go by, no one will remember his story, fewer people will know the reality of him. I have an uncle that died at forty two. I loved him. His grave is in the family plot. I visit it when I go to Noah's grave. I often think that Irving (her husband) and he would have gotten along famously, but they will never meet. Will it be that way with Noah?

When Noah was in the hospital, Anna felt deep communion and spiritual intensity, but her son's death ended her bond with transcendent reality. In the hospital, she knew when the cranial pressure was too high. She felt it in her body. She would stand by his bed and will the pressure down. It was a battle of the spirit for which she summoned whatever powers might be in the universe to be her allies. Then one day, she came to the hospital and was kept out of the Intensive Care Unit because there was a problem. She could see through the crack in the door that a lot of people were around Noah's area. His heart had stopped, and they were restarting it. She tried to get in touch with him, but could not. "I lost him at that moment," she said. "I have never been in touch with him again except to feel the pain." His body lived a week more, but she never felt connected with him again. Now, almost four years after his death, she still did not feel in control of her life nor in touch with transcendent reality.

So Anna lives in a divided spiritual world. On the one hand she has memories of a deep spiritual connection with her son in an existential melancholia as deep and profound as Sartre's or Camus's. "Life sucks and then you die." In that "no exit" world, individuals can briefly triumph in seemingly absurd acts. They can claim constitutional rights to a school principal, and they can shout, "you can't find yours unless somebody's kissing it." Anna feels good when she remembers Noah acting that way, and she feels good as she sees herself learning to express the part of herself that is so like what he was. On the other hand, there is no life after this one, and she knows, when she fantasizes that her son is with her father, that she is only fooling herself. She has learned all too well the reality that she realized after her own teenage coma, that death is nothingness. She lost the spiritual battle for her son's life, and she knows better than ever to engage in such a delusion again.

Some Find a New Worldview, Even Years Later

Worldviews are remarkably resilient, even in the face of overwhelming pain. But for some parents, the symbols of their old lives do not serve well in the new world of parental bereavement. The old beliefs only bring shame or guilt which prevents the parents from feeling the bonds with their children in a way that brings solace. The experience of the child's death, and other experiences central to the self, cannot be assimilated comfortably into the old worldview. Some bereaved parents, often several years after the deaths, change their beliefs about themselves and about their world. They accommodate, that is, they transform (Wilber, 1980, pp. 40–44; 1995, pp. 59–61) into a new way of being themselves in a universe that they see as working quite differently from what they used to see. As they change, their bond with their children changes too.

One woman had a miscarriage 16 years before I interviewed her. Thirteen years before the interview, her two-year-old daughter, Glenda, died in an accident which she thought she should have been able to prevent. She described herself as very religious after a Protestant conversion experience when she was 17 years old. She was in this religious phase when she miscarried. Then she got cancer, and, while she was recovering, the toddler died. After the death and cancer, she asked "what else can happen? Well, I felt like God was saying, 'This is what else can happen and I can do a lot more.'" She continued to feel inadequate and punished by God for several years. After the miscarriage, she had a vision or dream of her grandmother standing at the foot of the bed "and this pair of hands just handing the baby to her. It was like protective." When Glenda died she used that vision and believed the child was in heaven, so "I can always be sure where she is." But in her feeling of being a failure she would "wonder in the back of my religious beliefs, if she can see all that we do. If she is ashamed of me as her mother. Would she want me to be her mother again." So the inner representation of the child brought some comfort, but it also played a role in her strong sense of inadequacy.

About five years before I interviewed her, this mother slowly began to change her worldview. She developed a mentor relationship with a superior at work who encouraged her to take on new responsibilities. She had never had a positive father figure before. She went back to school for her undergraduate degree and was given a job with many sensitive responsibilities. In this new self, she began to feel that she was worthwhile. In that new sense, she spoke of her hopes for her living daughters.

> I've grown to accept maybe it will be, and maybe it won't be. But I've tried, and I've finally come to the realization that I've done and tried as much as I can. I'm not going to blame myself any more for the mistakes they make"

I asked, "In answer to the question that you asked Glenda, 'Would you still want me for a mother?' you're saying?"

She said, "I think I'm not saying 'Would you want.' I'm saying, 'Well, regardless, I am. I was and I am.' I have to answer for whatever I am."

The child remains in heaven, and the mother no longer feels ashamed as the child looks down on her. She is the child's mother. She accepts her own shortcomings, and the child and God will have to accept her shortcomings too. The inner representation of the child who died long ago sometimes does not feel as close as it once did, but when she is in touch with the child, she feels only comfort.

Occasionally, life offers a second chance, so as they develop a new worldview, people can play out their life's story differently. I want, now, to tell about Barbara and Fred, the couple we met in the chapter on community. Their daughter, Abby, had been born with a congenital defect and responded to her fate by deciding to defy death and social convention.

The religion Barbara and Fred experienced in the small southern towns where they grew up was fundamentalist Protestantism. Religious people seemed, especially to Barbara, like "a bunch of hypocrites." As a child, she had prayed to God to protect her from her abusing father. But if there was a God, He didn't help. So, the universe functioned randomly for Barbara. She had no power to affect any change. Little wonder that she had been diagnosed as depressed when she visited a psychiatrist in connection with Abby's juvenile court hearing. She could secretly admire the power that Abby took in the world, but she usually felt incompetent as a parent and as a person. Fred asked no help from God, but at least he knew that he could take care of himself and his family. The stoic philosophers would have recognized him as one of their own. He was a good worker, often holding down two jobs. At home, especially when Abby was acting like the "white trash" his father so despised, Fred retreated to his work bench or to the garage where tools and car engines had a rationality his home life lacked.

Our sessions had become less frequent when their 17-year-old son, Chet, reported that he had impregnated Trina, his 16-year-old girlfriend, and decided to marry her. Trina's family was extremely dysfunctional. Trina had been in several foster homes, being taken from and returned to her mother several times. For both Barbara and Fred, memories of Abby became intertwined with their relationship with Trina, their new daughter-in-law, and with the baby. At first, Barbara did not want anything to do with either Trina or the baby. She identified the baby with herself. She felt a strong sense of impending doom as the birth grew nearer. She had a dream of sitting in a chair with the baby on the ground in front of her fussing. She picked up the baby to care for it, but she wandered away and became separated from the baby, so both were lost. Trina's family was like hers when she was young, she said, and so the baby would have a bad life like hers.

Trina reminded Fred so much of Abby that he kept himself isolated from her as much as he could. He said he feared his anger had driven away one child, and, if he let his anger out on his daughter-in-law, he might lose his son. Fred was also afraid that Barbara would be hurt again if she bonded to the child, and that he might lose Barbara too.

Both Barbara and Fred overcame their fears of getting attached to Trina and the baby. Just before the baby's birth, they invited Trina to join them at their celebration of Abby's death anniversary. They went into a park to a tree planted in her memory and released balloons with messages. Fred and Barbara's messages to Abby were about how much they had grown in the previous year. They said Chet's message to his sister was that he missed her. Trina wrote a message, but they did not know what it was.

As we talked about the pathology of Trina's family, Barbara developed a good objective understanding of Trina's relationship with her family and spent a great deal of energy setting boundaries around her relationship with Trina. She would make no demands of her daughter-in-law, but would provide what nurturing she could. She would give the baby a secure environment when he was in her home, but would take no responsibility for caregiving in Trina's parents' home. Her plan worked slowly. Trina began to see that the baby was happier in Barbara's care than in her mother's care. When Chet and Trina could not pay their rent and moved in with Fred and Barbara, they worked hard to set limits. Fred was very conscious that:

> I failed with one child. I am doing my best not to fail with this one. Trina is like Abby sometimes, but I can feel differently. I am just not used to the way she shoots off her mouth to me. Sometimes I just stand back and shake my head. Boy, it wasn't like that when I was growing up. It's kind of funny really.

When Trina and Chet were having an argument, they decided to come and see me for a few sessions. Trina told me that she felt very close to both Fred and Barbara. She said that her bond with Fred was the first healthy bond with an adult male she had ever had. A few weeks later I confirmed to Barbara and Fred that they had won the game with Trina. She was their daughter and a full member of their family. Barbara responded with a blush. Fred was pleased when he saw that it was safe for Trina and him to throw barbs at each other in fun.

Fred and Barbara live in a world where humans do not have ultimate control, indeed in a world where there may be no control. But they have learned to be competent. As they have learned that, they have been given second chances with Abby. She has come to them again, now in the person of Trina and in the person of the baby. They are very much aware of their memories of Abby and of the way they felt about Abby because they feel similarly about Trina. As they act competently in this second chance, they work hard at communicating feelings to each other, not without many relapses into old relationship patterns. Abby's memory is soothing to Barbara within her competency, because she has internalized some of Abby's strengths. Fred has learned to respect Trina, just as he has learned to respect his deceased daughter. Their battles can now be fun and safe for both of them.

☐ Conclusion

Summary

Worldviews answer two questions: How does the universe function? and What is my place and power in the universe? We have found many ways in which parents make sense of their children's deaths. In all of these journeys, we have found, at least among the parents who affiliated with Bereaved Parents, that the continuing bond with a dead child is central to maintaining or remolding a worldview. The patterns include:

1. Some parents, both liberal and conservative, retain the worldview they held before their children died. Retaining their prior worldview depends on parents being able to reinterpret the deaths of their children in ways consistent with their worldviews.
2. Some parents find new and compelling worldviews during the children's terminal illnesses. All their experience fit into that worldview. The crisis of caring for dying children provides these parents with experience of authentic community which includes their bonds with their children, and from which they can develop new worldviews adequate to their grief.
3. Some parents interpret symbols and myths within their worldviews in a new and profounder way. As people find meanings in the symbols and myths that they did not understand before, their worldviews change in a way that allows them to assimilate the experience of their children's deaths into them.
4. Some parents live with a divided self. They maintain bonds with the transcendent that are linked to the children, while in other parts of their lives they feel cut off from any transcendent meaning.
5. Some parents develop entirely new worldviews even after a long time of trying to deal with their grief in worldviews that do not work for them. They change their beliefs about themselves and about their world, and they find a new way of being themselves in a universe that they see as working quite differently from what they used to see.

What Might We Learn from Bereaved Parents?

If, as we listen to these accounts, we try to find beliefs that will be helpful to other bereaved parents or beliefs that are true because they have been tested in the crucible of a child's death, we will be disappointed. We find nothing but diversity. There is not one answer, or even a series of answers, to the meaning of life that works for every one. If we would like to learn something of the spiritual discoveries of parental bereavement, we cannot simply ask what they now believe.

Within Bereaved Parents, the relationship between the worldview one person holds and the worldviews other people might find has been worked out in a complex and sophisticated way. There is no doubt in the group that the solace and worldview each person finds are meaningful for each individual. But the members also recognize that the meaning they find in the presence of their dead children is only for them, and that others must find meaning for themselves. Members know that the underlying order each of them finds may be different from the underlying order another finds. The statement of principles by which the group is governed says, "We have learned that different people find different answers to the personal, family, and spiritual issues raised by the deaths of our children," it adds "We respect different answers members may find as we explore the dilemmas and discoveries our grief has brought to our religious beliefs." Thus, we find in Bereaved Parents that these vitally important realities have meaning for each, but not for all. At the same time, the reality each person finds is an important element in the bond that holds the community together. The meaning the members of Bereaved Parents find is, at the same time, individualistic, pluralistic, and existentially compelling; and it is a socially-shared reality around which the community is formed.

If the spiritual lives of bereaved parents have anything to teach us about finding meaning in the modern world, we need as complex and sophisticated an understanding of the nature of shared spirituality as do the bereaved parents whose lives we have examined. In a pluralistic world, perhaps spirituality needs to be split from religion. In the closed tribal worlds in which we developed the psyche that we now are trying to adjust to the global village, meaning could be a shared ontological reality. That is, it could seem as if it had a truth outside the self. The worldview could work for all the community members. The death of a child could be an occasion for reinforcing the community's myths and symbols. Certainly in other circumstances, many experiences we have described in this book would be the stuff from which myth, symbol, and theological dogma would be created.

In modernity, however, our shared reality is no longer a monolithic interpretation of experience. Rather, in modernity, the shared reality is the human quest for meaning. Members of Bereaved Parents have been forced by the deaths of their children to undertake that quest in a focused and inescapable way. We have tried to understand how bereaved parents transcend the human limitations they find in the deaths of their children. We have seen them do, in what Tillich called the "extreme situation" (1957, p. 12), what we all must do, albeit in less extremity. We have seen that finding meaning does not depend on the content. We have seen liberal and conservative, sophisticated and simple worldviews that are useful to bereaved parents. *Transcend* is a verb. It is not what people believe. Transcend is what people do. The common element within the diversity is not one design or a universal core of archetypical themes. Rather, the common element we have seen is that, within the continuing bond with their dead children, and in a community that shares their grief, members of Bereaved Parents find worldviews that are useful to them as they rebuild their worlds and their lives.

In looking at Bereaved Parents, perhaps we have seen a model for a community and worldview in the global village. It is not a community of the like-minded. It is a community of fellow transcenders, of fellow sojourners. In a speech at a Candlelight service, one of the leaders summed up her five years in the group, "This is how it works, it is one person stepping back into the darkness to walk the next one through." This community is not joined in the light of a shared faith. They have found each other, and they have bonded in the darkness through which they stumble. Perhaps what we need to learn in modernity is to help each other find meaning, rather than just to focus on the transcendent reality or worldview that we find for ourselves.

6

Implications for Professionals Who Want to Help

☐ **Billy**

Billy sat across the table from me in his orange jail uniform crying. We were in the conference room of a rural county jail in a state five hours' drive from my home. In a few weeks, I would be called as an expert witness in his trial. Three weeks after he found the body of his eight-month-old son, he had seriously injured another man in a fight and was being tried for aggravated assault. The child had suffocated when he rolled over onto his stomach while napping on the water bed. Both parents were in the kitchen, thinking the child was asleep. Billy told me that when he picked up the baby, the face had already turned blue. After the baby died, Billy started drinking heavily and returned to using some drugs that he had abandoned a few years earlier. Outside a bar, the other man was threatening Billy. Both had weapons in their hands. As he advanced, the other man said, "It's a good thing your kid died, so there's one less of you around." Billy pulled the trigger. The other man was severely wounded.

Billy had not lived an exemplary life. He was put in prison immediately after the shooting because he had violated his probation. Five years earlier he had been convicted for robbery and for passing bad checks. He should not have had the hunting rifle in his possession, and he should not have become involved in a violent confrontation. His wife tried to care for their surviving daughter but sank into a deep depression. The child protection agency had removed the girl from the home, and she was now in the custody of Billy's mother and step-father.

Billy told me that when he had learned that his wife was pregnant with a son "it was like somebody just handed you a couple hundred thousand dollars." The baby had been named after him—Billy Junior. During our two and a half hour conversation, I was struck that he never referred to the child except as Billy. When he told me about finding the baby and about the physician shaking his head when he came out of the examining room, it was as if he were describing events that happened yesterday, not two years earlier.

"It was just like I was hypnotized," he told me. "It felt like I had this big hole in my chest." He said that, in the weeks after little Billy died, his mind was full of ideas that were frightening to him. "I had a spiritual problem," he said. A week before the baby died, his cousin had called his mother to report a troubling dream. She had seen the angel of death standing over baby Billy. Did the dream mean that God had come to take little Billy back because Billy senior was a bad person who deserved to be punished? In one sense, he told me, it was a relief to be sent to prison, because he thought he was such a bad person that he deserved to be punished. Drugs and alcohol, he said, were the only ways he knew to dull the pain and stop the thoughts.

The baby's body had been cremated because he could not stand the idea of little Billy being in the ground. The town had offered a free grave, but Billy and his wife turned it down. He often carried the urn containing the baby's ashes with him.

> I wanted him to be with me just like before. I used to take Billy every-where. I'd go fishing and take him along and talk to him. "This is the way you tie the line." Or "Look at this nice one." He didn't understand, but I just wanted him to be part of everything I did.

Sometimes, he would just sit for hours at a time holding the urn and staring at it. He was holding it for a long time before he left it at his mother's house to go to the bar where the fight happened. "That was the last time I held him," he said. I asked if he ever felt little Billy is still near him. He said that, starting about a year ago, he had dreamed a few times of little Billy smiling and waving at him. "I think that he's telling me that he's okay," he said.

The first months in jail were hard. He was no longer protected by the drugs. The pain never stopped, and the thoughts were relentless. The visual image of the dead baby haunted him. Six weeks after the fight, he tried to hang himself, but another inmate saw him and called the guards. He was transferred to the corrections department psychiatric facility. I asked if he had gotten help there. "No, the psychiatrist didn't want to talk about Billy. All he would say is that I had to take the pills, and, if I didn't keep taking them, I would never get better." But the medication "made me feel like a zombie," he said, as he showed me by holding his body rigid. So, Billy refused to continue the medication and was transferred back to the general population with a note on his chart that he was noncompliant.

He had begun to find his way though grief when I talked to him. "I turned the spiritual thing around," he said. "I believe in God. God must have a reason. He didn't kill little Billy. That just happened. The baby was learning to roll over, and, when he got his face in the water bed, he couldn't turn his head to the side. We were in the next room and thought he was sleeping."

As the trial approached no one knew where Billy's wife was. He said he still needed to be a father to his surviving child. "If Billy is in heaven, I don't want him to see me like I was." He had enrolled in an auto body repair course and had completed his GED in prison. He said he had three more months in the auto body course. "I like to do that work," he said, and the program had a good history of graduates getting jobs after release.

This young family, which already was very fragile, had disintegrated when the baby died. A few days before the fight, Billy said, his father had told him to "pull myself together." He said he knew his father was right, but he hadn't a ghost of an idea how to go about doing it. His father admitted that neither did he. The minister who did the baby's funeral dropped by and told Billy that he needed to help his wife because she was suffering so badly. "What could I say to her?" Billy mused. "We were both lost. I couldn't help her. I couldn't help myself." Then there was the fight. The other person yelled that he was glad the baby had died. And another act of the drama began to play itself out.

Toward the end of the conversation I said that I had what I needed to testify on his behalf, said that I knew a lot about parental bereavement, and asked if there was anything he thought I might tell him. He did not hesitate, "Does it ever stop hurting?" It was the exact same question put in the same words that a vice president of a large corporation had asked me a few months earlier. I gave as best I could the answer I had been taught by other bereaved parents. No, but the pain doesn't stay the same. For the pain to go away, he would have to forget little Billy and he would not want to do that. Besides the pain is true. Little Billy really did live and love, and he really did die. The pain is real because the sadness is real. The question, I said, is how to live a life worthy of little Billy, even in prison.

At the end of our two and a half hour conversation, we stood at the door waiting for the guard to unlock it. We shook hands and looked each other in the eye, man-to-man. In the jail parking lot, I saw Billy's mother and stepfather sitting in a van with his little daughter in a car seat in the back. We talked for a few moments, and then they took the child in to visit with her father.

As I drove away, I felt angry. Billy was finding resolution to the spiritual crisis presented to him by the death of his child. He had established a bond with transcendent reality. He believes in God, and at the same time he has dreams of little Billy smiling and waving at him. He believes life has a purpose. But he has had to do that alone. In my mind's eye, I saw Billy sitting alone holding the urn, and then alone in the cell thinking through the problem of God, little Billy's death, and his life with only himself to talk to.

I was passing a small Jehovah's Witness kingdom hall, as I went over in my mind what I knew about the spiritual life of bereaved parents. Billy had a renewed bond with transcendent reality, and he had found a worldview by means of which he could make sense of his life and of the death of his child. But where was the community? Then I realized why I had traveled several hours to this remote town to talk to him and why I would later testify on his behalf. Several months earlier, the attorney assigned to defend him had called me. Could he and his legal assistant drop by my university office to talk? They had been given my name by a leader of a Bereaved Parents chapter in their state. A lawyer on a pro bono case willing to drive all that way to see me—that was someone I had to meet.

The lawyer had been assigned the case when his own child was near the age at which little Billy died. Something about Billy's case struck a chord with him, he said. Motioning to the legal assistant, the lawyer said that she was the "human" side of the team and that she had "encouraged me to learn more about grief and make Billy's grief part of the defense." They had come to me, they said, to ask me about what happens right after a child dies. We talked about anger and about how people might try to dull the pain. The lawyer and his assistant had become very personally involved in the case. They had decided that, as a team, they would provide the best defense they could though they knew it meant some very late nights and weekends of extra work. The legal assistant smiled as she said that the "men in Billy's family are pretty nonverbal. They don't talk much and especially not to out- siders." It had taken the legal assistant several visits to earn Billy's trust, so that he would open up to them. I remembered her describing

Billy as nonverbal when I sat in the jail conference room, while for more than two hours he spoke with simple eloquence about little Billy, about his spiritual problem, and about how he was finding his way though. In the process of winning Billy's confidence, the legal team became his allies. When he tried to answer their questions about how his grief affected his mind the night of the fight, Billy could give his sorrow words. As he told them his story, he learned to say aloud what was in his heart and mind. The lawyer and legal assistant had also worked hard to win the confidence of Billy's family. The legal assistant talked about how hard it was for Billy's brother to come to terms with the death of his nephew, and she said she wished she could locate some resources to help the little girl. Several weeks later, I would stand nearby as the legal assistant sat on the bench outside the courtroom, hugged, and tenderly consoled Billy's aunt as she cried for little Billy and for her own teenage son who had died four years earlier. The conversation in my office went on for about an hour and a half. At the end, the attorney asked if I would help by being an expert witness. I could see that they cared, and, over the years, I have found it to be a good policy to help people who care, so I said I would.

My thoughts continued as I pulled into the Dairy Queen for my dinner, I realized that I had joined the community that was instrumental in helping a man in jail toward a positive resolution of his grief over the death of the son named after him. It was not the facts in the case that caught me. I agreed to be part of the defense because I sensed that, in the lawyer and legal assistant, Billy had gained a caring community that bereaved parents need in order to resolve their grief. Billy was not just a case; he was a person. As I listened to Billy tell me his story in the jail conference room, I realized how few people outside his family seem to have reached out to care for him. Whatever had happened in school, he dropped out as soon as he could. As I listened to him tell me how he had let go of his idea that God was punishing him and begun to believe that God cared for him and for little Billy, I had the very strong sense that he could care for himself and believe God cares for him because his legal team cared for him. Once again, I felt pleased to be a part of something good, but I have to admit that I was still angry at the psychiatrist who would not talk about the dead baby, and at the pastor who said Billy should help his wife who needed him. And I wondered how many other professionals and paraprofessionals had missed opportunities to help.

I was not called to the witness stand until late in the second day of the trial. In the witness box I tried to describe how parents are the first few months after a child dies, but the prosecution objected, and I was told to just answer the question. I said to the judge that I was confused because I was trying to answer the question. The judge said that I should "stop trying to teach." I said I was sorry, but I am a teacher and it's hard not to. The defense attorney had apparently been told that he could not ask me about what I thought of Billy's growth since the baby died.

The legal assistant called a few days later to report that Billy was convicted on a lesser charge as the defense had hoped. He was sentenced to four additional years and should be paroled in two. We laughed about the hard time I had been given in my testimony. I said I had worked hard to get through to the jury, and she said I probably did, but there is no way to know.

As I write this, a bereaved father is in prison, a bereaved mother is somewhere that is probably not good for her, and their surviving child lives with her grandparents who take her each month to visit her father. As I recall the days I spent talking to the lawyer and legal assistant, talking to Billy, and testifying, I find two very strong positive feelings remain in my heart. First, I still feel the sense of human dignity that came from Billy as we shook hands while we waited for the jailer to open the door. Second, I remember the sense of closeness and friendship I immediately felt when I was with the lawyer and legal assistant as they briefed me before my talking to Billy and before the trial. Those two feelings merge into each other in my memory because they are both aspects of the healing community that I joined when I decided to be an expert witness at Billy's trial.

☐ Helping Bereaved Parents in Their Spiritual Journey

In this chapter we change our focus. I have been describing the spiritual life of bereaved parents. We now turn to asking how professionals can help them along their way. As I speak to my fellow professionals, I hope readers who are bereaved parents and their friends will stay with us. Reading what one professional has to say to others might help bereaved parents to know how to use professional help better, as well as to understand the special problems bereaved parents present to the professionals to whom they turn. In my mind, however, the audience for this chapter is professionals. The discussion of how professionals can help will roughly follow the description of bereaved parents' spiritual lives in the earlier chapters of the book. We will first discuss the implications of our definition of spirituality for professional practice, then move to professional relationships in the healing community, and finally to some issues connected with the worldviews professionals hold and the bonds in which they participate as they too come to terms with the deaths of children.

Everyone Can Be a Spiritual Helper

If, as we discovered in the more highly developed understandings of the world's religious traditions, there is no separate realm called "spiritual" outside of the everyday reality in which we live, then everyone can be a spiritual helper. Spirituality is woven into the fabric of our world. The question is not whether spirituality is present; the question is whether we see it. The color-blind and the color-sighted look at the same world; the difference is in the seer not the seen. That means that spirituality cannot be the exclusive province of any one profession or a specialization within any profession.

Everyone can help, no matter their profession, but that does not mean we all do the same thing. If spirituality is woven into every aspect of living, then spirituality forms a dimension of interactions between any kind of professional and bereaved parents. There is no special formula for defining or healing spiritual problems. If spirituality is as we have found it in the world's religious traditions, then helping parents along their spiritual path cannot be reduced to four or five tasks, six or seven stages, or a cluster of techniques. We give the best spiritual help to bereaved parents when we practice our professions in the best way we can, because spirituality is woven into what we do when we are living out our professional roles.

We bring different backgrounds to helping bereaved parents—different in the issues our educations and predilections help us to recognize, different in the expectations parents and the larger society have of us, different in how much we must stay within professional constraints, and different in the degree to which we can be explicitly religious in our interactions. The psychiatrist who tried to treat Billy in the psychiatric facility would have remained a psychiatrist even if he had reached out and come to terms with Billy's reality. If the prison chaplain had been able to minister to Billy, he would have remained a chaplain. The probation officer, the social worker, the nurse, the psychologist, and the hospice bereavement coordinator would all be operating within their particular professional roles if they were to choose to walk with Billy through his valley of the shadow of death, because the spiritual life is part of all other life. One of the answers Jesus gave to the question, "Lord, when did we see thee?" was "I was in prison and you came to me" (Matt 25:36 RSV). As we learned from the Buddhists, the world of suffering and the world of liberation are interconnected and codependent.

So we are different and see differently, yet we share common ground. Spirituality is an aspect of all our lives, and it is also the unifying element within our diversity. All professionals can help bereaved parents in their spiritual lives, but different professions help in different ways. In all the world's spiritual traditions, we find the concept of the *Many* and the *One*. God is in all things, yet God is One. In our case, God can be in all professional relationships, yet God is One. We are very different in what we do, yet we share common ground. As I turn, then, from talking about bereaved parents to talking about how we can help them, I do not want to gloss over the strengths and tools different professions can bring. If I explore the common ground, I hope readers can understand for themselves how it is manifest in their discipline. If my plan works, I may have taught readers something new, but more importantly, I will have taught readers how to use better what they already know.

I understand, of course, that there is no common ground that can be discussed apart from the many particulars. If, as I write this chapter, I try to find the common ground apart from the particular, I will end up mouthing meaningless cliches. On the other hand, were I to try to talk about the possibilities in every profession, readers would rightly object. No one can know the many. I cannot know the literature of all the professions to whom bereaved parents might turn for help. I would be presumptuously foolish were I to say I could tell a Christian pastor, a psychoanalyst, a yoga instructor, a hospice nurse, a school counselor, or a family physician how to best do their job with bereaved parents.

The teaching technique that I am using, therefore, is as old as the spiritual life itself. The only particular expression of the one that I know is my own. I can only tell what I have learned from my teachers, from my practice, and from my reflecting on my own practice. I think I have some intense and broadly based experience as a professional helping bereaved parents. If my descriptions of bereaved parents' spiritual lives made sense to the reader, perhaps my experience helping bereaved parents will make sense in the reader's own work. So, I will use what I have learned in my own work and what I have observed in the work of others that has informed my own. The level of abstraction of this chapter is a report from the field. There is a Sufi story about how a seeker can know God. It is, they say, like a meal in a restaurant. I can know the restaurant exists. I can hear from someone who has eaten there. I can locate the restaurant in the city where it is found. I can read the menu and perhaps learn the cook's recipes. All those are certain ways of knowing. But if I would really know, I must eat there myself. I think I can give a rather full account as someone who has eaten there often. If my reflecting on my own experience gives readers some concepts that help them to reflect on and improve their own practice, or if my report of my work encourages readers to try their own, then I think the chapter will have achieved its goal. I do not think I can tell readers how to help in the spiritual lives of bereaved parents any more than I can tell them how to experience a meal in a resturant. I think, however, that I can prepare them to discover for themselves how to help.

☐ A Web of Bonds and Meanings

As a way to focus our thinking, we can return to the diagram with which we ended Chapter Two. In attempting to define spirituality in a way that is adequate to the world's religious traditions and in a way that can describe the real inner and social lives of bereaved parents, we found ourselves pointing to a web of bonds and meanings. It seems that the spiritual lives of bereaved parents are played out within this complex of bonds and meanings. We made the following list as an abstraction of what we had discovered in our search for a definition:

> How the universe works
> Place and power of the self
> Bond with the child
> Bond with transcendent reality
> Meaning of parent's life
> Meaning of the child's death
> Community/family membership

Each item on our list is a personal narrative made up of myths, symbols, and personal and social history and maintained by habits and rituals. We can visualize the interactions by making a diagram with set lines connecting each set of bonds and meanings with every other. By laying out the diagram this way, I am trying to show that the impact on a parent of a child's birth, life, and death is manifested within the web. If one set of bonds and meanings change, all the others change too. Each person develops the different interactions in a unique way with each child.

I will illustrate how the interactions work out in the lives of one bereaved couple. Then, in the next section, I will draw some implications for professional practice. When a child is born, the meaning of the parent's life changes. Each child has a different meaning for each parent. Bereaved parents often say how much they resent people telling them to take comfort in the fact that they still have other children, because,

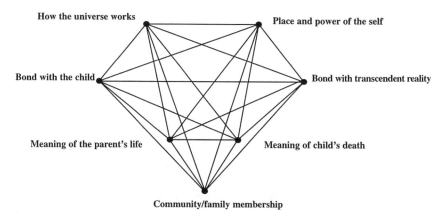

How the universe works — Place and power of the self

Bond with the child — Bond with transcendent reality

Meaning of the parent's life — Meaning of child's death

Community/family membership

FIGURE 6.1. A child's death impacts each bond and meaning in the web of spiritual life. Help we give bereaved parents at any point on the web will ripple through all the others.

as one mother put it, "Each of my kids is special to me. My love is not interchangeable." Billy told me the news that he would have a son was like someone handing him a couple hundred thousand dollars. In his world, daughters have different meanings than sons, so this child played a different role in his life than did his daughter. Parents often say how each of their children gives different meanings to their lives. It is common for couples to identify one child, as one mother described it, as "closer to her dad, but Connie, she was mine."

We can see the interactions more clearly by listening for a moment to one couple who were referred to me for counseling a few weeks after the death of their four-year-old daughter. They said this child was their "blessing child." They had three teenagers when the mother got pregnant. They said they loved the older children, but they had raised the older children while both parents were working hard on their careers and, at the same time, caring for aged parents. Parenting the older children had not been as much fun. In retrospect, the father thought he had been too strict with the older children, and he was now in the process of trying to be more personal and less "parental" with their older children. The child who died was born after the grandparents had died and after both parents were more secure in their careers. The mother was now a relocation specialist with a large corporation, and the father's retail franchise was thriving. Both parents, but especially the father, could love and enjoy this child in a way that was new to them. As the father remembered the hours he spent with the child and the love he lavished on her, I wondered if the father's intense attachment to the little girl occasioned any jealousy in the mother, but she answered my question before I asked. She said as her husband allowed himself to enjoy his attachment to the daughter, he became more emotionally available to the mother. Probably outsiders would have seen the child as a spoiled little princess, but when she died, it was the father's princess that died, not a spoiled child.

These parents' bonds with transcendent reality and their assumptions about how the universe functions and the place and power of the self in the universe were intertwined with their bonds with the child. The four-year-old girl was the blessed child. It felt to this couple, who grew up in a closed ethnic community, that the child was a special gift from God. She was a symbol of God's presence among them. The bond with the child reinforced their bond with transcendent reality. The child gave a deeper meaning to their individual lives and to their marriage. It was not a different worldview but rather the same understanding of the place and power of the self in which they had grown up, but it was deeper. The presence of the child proved and solidified their membership in their traditional Catholic community.

Then their princess died, and the meaning of the blessing became problematic. When they first sat in my office, God was still a big, powerful, person in the sky in their minds. They could not understand why God would give them the child only to have the child die when a elderly neighbor, on his way to get medicine for his sick wife, could not hear people shouting as he backed over the little girl playing in his driveway. The death made no sense to them. There was no one to blame, no reason that seemed to explain what happened. It had always seemed to the parents that the universe functioned in an orderly way. If a person was good and worked hard, good things would happen for them. The blessed child had seemed a reward to them. Nothing in how she died pointed the way for the blessed little girl to become their saint in heaven. So now, the meaning of the child's death called into question the way they assumed that the universe works. Their bond with the transcendent was dependent on their being obedient and maintaining a childlike faith in the father God. He had blessed them, and He would watch over the child. Somehow, God had let them down, but then to turn and blame God would have threatened every other construct in their lives. Was the child not blessed? Were they not good people in a good community?

The Interplay of Meanings

If the spiritual lives of bereaved parents are lived out within this interactive web, we can immediately see implications for professional practice. Anything we do to help bereaved parents in one set of bonds and meanings ripples through into all the others. Everything we do can affect the parent's spiritual life. Thus any issue or problem posed in one part of the web may be processed by beginning in any of the parts. In practice, this means first that professionals can use the skills they have on the areas that seem most familiar to them. Second, parents can use their coping styles and competencies that have worked for them in the past. Third, when parents seem to have hit a dead end in one place, professionals can help by redirecting them to other clusters of meaning. We can think through the interplay by looking at some possible scenarios in a case with which I have only passing acquaintance.

I once sat in a case conference in which a very experienced psychologist, who used family systems theory extensively, reported that, during a counseling session, a bereaved father had raised, what was for the father, the thorny problem of whether he could trust that his dead son was safely in heaven. The psychologist had said the father should talk to his pastor about the problem. The father replied that would be problematic, because he was still angry that, in the funeral sermon, the pastor had spent several minutes talking about alcohol abuse and referred often to the fact that the boy died while driving under the influence. "It was like that was the only part of my son's life that she seemed to know about," the father said. So, the psychologist suggested that the father find another minister to whom he could direct his question. In the case conference, the psychologist said he was trying hard to get the man to focus on the troubled communication within his marriage, because, in the psychologist's judgment, the marriage was in critical condition. For this psychologist, questions about heaven were out of his area of expertise, and, since the client had cast his problem in theological form (Was his child safely in heaven?), a professional who was an expert on heaven should be consulted. The psychologist knew about marital communication. He thought he could help with that. But the husband's problem with heaven seemed to be in the way.

The psychologist was rejecting our definition of spirituality when he referred the client to someone the psychologist thought might be an expert on heaven. The psychologist saw no connection between the man's concern about where his dead son is and the difficulties he was having in communicating with his wife and his inability to accept that the pastor's sermon expressed the proper meaning of his son's life. The psychologist was from a very different religious tradition than the client. In referring the client to his pastor, it probably seemed to the psychologist that he was respecting the client's membership in a religious tradition. Although other members of the psychologist's religious tradition do, I think the psychologist does not believe there might be such a place as heaven. From another conversation, I inferred that he believed that we only live on in memory.

The question of heaven was hard for the psychologist. It came from a worldview very different from the one in which he grounded his own personal and professional life. What he did know about heaven was that, in his mind, those who do believe in heaven say it is a place where the dead go. That is, he had heard heaven described in concrete operational terms and had given no further thought to the matter. Other people were entitled to their belief, but the concept had no place in his professional theory or in his personal faith. He did not see what we have seen, that, for bereaved parents well along in their grief, children safely in heaven are often children to whom the parents feel in close proximity. The question, "Do you feel out of touch with your son?" seemed silly to this psychologist. The son was dead, of course the father felt out of touch with him. In the psychologist's professional theory, the task the father faced was letting go of his son and reestablishing his life with the attachments he still had, and, clearly, he was doing poorly in the attachment with his wife.

In one respect, the psychologist was probably right. He did not think the question of whether the dead boy was safely in heaven would be a good one to pursue. It is a question within the father's bond with transcendent reality, and not one that can be solved within any "talk cure." In all likelihood, if the father sought out a minister with whom to discuss the issue, the minister also would not think the question was a good one to pursue. Theological questions seldom get answered in the form in which they are asked. If the minister stayed within the limits of the question, the minister's options were limited. She could say yes, the child is in heaven, citing the authority of holy texts or of her theological tradition, but she could cite no data other than external authority or her own opinion to support her statement. The father would be left with the options of accepting religious authority or not. The minister could say that she didn't know either. If she did, the minister's options would expand considerably, because now she could talk about faith as hope for things not seen and about how all of us need to be humble in the face of mystery. The minister would know that she was not really answering the father's question, and she would know that people's questions about God and heaven are usually not answered directly. In her first class in the philosophy of religion, she would have learned that all the logical proofs for the existence of God are interesting, but the arguments don't change anyone's mind. Unless the minister found a way to restate the question or to move the question to a different part of our diagram, the bereaved father would have hit a dead end in his spiritual journey.

If the spiritual life is lived out in an interactive web, the father's question touches every point on the web. When a person is unable to develop in one cluster of meaning, changes in any of the other parts of the web will affect the cluster of meanings in which they have dead-ended. Any change in one place ripples into the others. The minister or the psychologist could ask, for example, about the meaning of the father's bond with his son, and ask what does it mean to the father that his son died while driving drunk and that, during the funeral sermon, drinking seemed to be the only aspect of the boy's life that counted. The minister might think she was working toward confession and forgiveness while the psychologist might think he was working toward catharsis. Both would have shifted to working within another part of the web, each using the knowledge and skills their education had given them. If the psychologist were to understand how the question of heaven is an issue within the father's continuing bond with his son, then, when the couple came in to work on marital issues, he might ask how the bond with the child is part of the bond between the father and his wife. The psychologist's skills might be very useful in coming at the problem from that direction. If the minister were to engage the father in deep reflection on the place and power individuals have in the world, a question about which the minister has spent many years of study, it is very likely that the the father would need to reflect on how much power he had over his son's behavior when the son was living. The father's question about his son in heaven might then reframe itself in a way that would lead to a closer bond with his dead son and some forgiveness of his son's actions while alive. Both the minister and the psychologist have skills and insights from their education that can be brought to bear to help this bereaved father, but neither of them will find their skills and insights of much use if they remain in the cluster of meanings in which the father has dead-ended.

The interplay within the web also allows us to appreciate that individual coping styles predispose a bereaved parent to be more competent in resolving some sets of meaning more than others. All the bonds and meanings are equally valid, but that does not mean that for particular individuals they are equally useful. If professionals understand that every cluster is potentially the one in which a bereaved parent can find a solution to problems posed in another, then professionals can learn to walk with bereaved parent along the many paths parents find through their grief.

We might think, for example, about the common report that men are less likely than women to find talking in a group about their children's death and their grief useful. Grief support or self-help groups commonly have far more women attending than men. A bereaved father once said to me, "I don't say much in the meetings. Maybe if we went out for some beers, that might be a better way to do it." It seems to me that he is saying that a group process based less on expressing emotion and more on sharing ideas would feel more comfortable to him. Although he might mean that the alcohol might help him overcome his inhibition, it is more likely that he is saying that over beers or in a bull session men hash out the issues in the medium of ideas, albeit unsystematically. Those interactions typically focus on how the universe works and especially on how much power humans have in the world.

Men must define themselves within the hierarchy rather early in their lives, so they must learn to make very realistic assessments of the possibilities they have of control in their lives. "You just have to keep going." "There is nothing you can do about that." Or "Just hang in there." These are contemporary ways of talking about duty and dignity in the face of nothingness. The meaning of a child's life and death is set within the wider limitations of human agency. If the reality of human existence is, as Camus said, pushing a rock up the hill every day like Sisyphus, only to have it roll down again, then the transcendent moment is knowing that I can do it again tomorrow. Sharing my feelings does little good, because the rock will be there tomorrow, no matter how I feel about it. On the other hand, because the transcendent moment is consciously accepting my fate and knowing that I can do it again, then the community that helps is the one in which I know that others also have their rock, and that tomorrow they, too, must push it up that hill once more. Professionals can appreciate the value of ruminating—literally chewing things over. Sometimes ruminating with the client may include the professional's self disclosure. Professionals who ruminate with clients are connecting the client's ideas to larger philosophical systems, or giving the client a critical framework by which to examine and reflect upon his or her ideas. To have a bull session with clients does not mean that we tell them how to think about their life. Rather it means that, as equals, we bounce our ideas off each other. The way of understanding the place and power of the self and the way the world works that is worked out in the rumination will ripple though the whole web.

As a way of summing up the way we understand professional work within the idea that spirituality is an interplay of bonds and meanings, it seems to me, that we can draw three implications:

1. The skills professionals bring to work with parental bereavement can be applied in some clusters of meanings better than others. That

means that professionals can use their strengths as they work with bereaved parents. Professionals' work with bereaved parents is continuous with their education and work they do with other populations.

2. Parents bring a history of being more competent in some parts of the web than others. Since parents can work toward resolution in any of the cluster of bonds and meanings, professionals can identify the areas that have been most useful to the parent in the past and help the parents meet grief with their strengths.

3. If a parent hits a dead end in one part of the web, professionals can help by shifting the focus to another. The interplay allows both professionals and parents to use their strengths in coming to terms with the deaths of children, and it allows both parents and professionals flexibility as they try to come to terms with the hard problems the deaths of a children bring to the lives of their parents.

☐ Healing is within Community

As the parents have taught us, we grieve in our aloneness, however, the resolution of grief is an interpersonal process. Healing happens in community. Professionals, it seems, have two options that are not mutually exclusive in how they understand their practice in terms of the healing community. First, professionals can focus on the community and help the community. Second, they can join the healing community. We will discuss each separately to help professionals think about how they are applying their skills.

The first option is to help the community. Available to most professionals is the opportunity to apply their skills to help the communities in which parents grieve, so that those communities can be adequate to the reality of the death of a child. Clinicians who do couple or family therapy are really coaching the couple or family toward the kind of interaction patterns that will facilitate healing for all the members of the family. Pastors and other professionals who work within parishes and congregations equip the congregation members to be the kind of community in which bereaved parents can find their way. Social workers in some agencies are in the business of community development. At the most human level, community development means helping communities to function in fuller ways for their members in crisis. The most effective hospice bereavement coordinators I have observed think of their job as supporting the volunteers who are themselves usually people a little further along in their grief. In my role as professional advisor, my task has been mostly to help the group function smoothly so the parents can help each other. Most self-help groups look for professionals to serve on advisory boards, and many are willing to have professionals take a more active role if the professionals stay mindful of their place as outsiders. So, the first option is to help the community.

The second option professionals have is to become part of the community. Many professionals, whatever their expertise, help bereaved parents best by understanding that what they are really doing in their practice is joining the community in which parents are trying to find their way through their grief. When I become part of the community in which the healing takes place, questions and issues in every part of the web may come into the therapeutic alliance in their due time. All those issues that are so hard to articulate, and that can present such enormous spiritual complexity to bereaved parents, are connected to the bond between parent and child, and all will be expressed within the community of those who care.

We enter the healing community by accepting the burden of the parent's pain and by bonding to their child. We noted in Chapter Three that, for bereaved parents, the healing community is one that shares the pain of the children's death and shares their bond with their dead children. In some cases, when for a variety of reasons the larger community cannot integrate the parent's experience or the parent's continuing bond with the child, the community may just be a dyad— the professional and the client. I have had a few cases where the community remained just the parent and me. I remember, for example, a woman who miscarried twice and then, shortly after she and her husband divorced, had moved to a city in which she had few acquaintances. The grief and the healing never went outside my office door. Even after several years, as I think about her now, I still feel the intensity of those sessions because she saved everything for her one hour a week with me. In most cases, however, when I have done my job well, even if the community might have begun as just the client and me, the community expands as the parent learns to include the pain and the child within the other communities to which she or he belongs, or within new communities, parents joined. We have seen that a parent might find that early in the grief the child has social reality only in the self-help group, but later the parent transfers what has been learned in the self-help group to other communities. The process is similar in intense counseling with bereaved parents. If the counseling is successful, the parent learns to do in the wider community what he or she first learned to do in the counseling sessions.

The point on our diagram that provides professionals with the most direct entrance into being part of the healing community is the parent's bond with the child. Tony Walter (1994, pp. 18–22, 34–36) notes that one of the differences between the contemporary world and more traditional societies is that we live and work among people who are not attached to the same people as we are. Although we may keep pictures of our children in our cubicles, our colleagues only know *about* the children. They do not know the children. If a child dies, then, many people around us, including the professionals to whom we turn, feel badly for us, but they do not feel bad with us.

As I reported in the first chapter, the night I may have been first admitted into the circle of Bereaved Parents was the night I did not know what to say after they had passed around pictures of their dead children. I had seen their suffering, but now I knew their children, at least a little. For a few years after that night, veterans in the group repeated back to me the words onto which I had stumbled, "There are a lot of good looking kids in heaven." We have learned a lot about heaven by listening to bereaved parents. Where is heaven? Well, it is where parents hope to rejoin the child someday, and it is wherever balloon messages go. But heaven is also where the children of bereaved parents still live, in their parents' hearts and minds. For many bereaved parents, there is an easy intercourse between heaven and earth, because their child is still available to them, and, if others wish, the child is available to others. Each of us can relate to the child in heaven and use our differing professional knowledge to do so.

For bereaved parents well along in their grief, dead children speak in unsounded voices that encourage the parent's best self and always give solace. Before the continuing bond is established in the parent's inner world, however, the bond with the child is a painful empty hole in the middle of their being. Parental bereavement is like amputation. A piece is missing. Professionals who would share the bond with the child in order to be part of the transformation, must first accept the burden of very deep pain. When we join the community in which the bond with the child will be transformed, we move from feeling badly for the bereaved parents to feeling bad with them, because feeling bad with them is the first step in getting to know the child who died.

In my counseling practice, I have adapted an exercise from the Bereaved Parents group that helps me bond with the child, especially if only one parent is coming. After the initial session, if it seems to me that there were no issues that simply cannot wait, I tell the parent that it would help if I get to know the child as well as I can. I ask him or her to bring to the next session photographs and whatever might help me. The parents usually bring many, sometimes arranged in an album, but more often in a pile that they had been meaning for some years to sort and arrange in a book. Sometimes the child's art work or favorite things help me, but I find I rely on the photographs. I give the photographs the same attention that I give to great art on a museum wall. I try to let the photographs speak to me. I sit beside the parent on the sofa slowly going through the photographs. I note the developmental changes, note the similarity in build, facial features, or expression to other people in the photos. I look intently at photographs that show the child in the family group or with a group of peers, because I often find that I get a sense of the child from the body postures and the physical relationships of the people in the picture. As thoughts occur to me, I make comments, and the parent confirms or clarifies what I see. Sometimes the parent introduces a photo with the child's reaction to it. "She hated this picture," a parent might say "because she thought it made her look too fat." Sometimes no one photograph captures a child, and so I slowly construct the child's image in my mind. I take the task at hand very seriously. I want to get to know that child. By the end of one or two sessions I usually have.

Sometimes one photo jumps out, for example one of an eight-year-old girl sitting alone leaning against the textured bark of a tree. I asked, "Is this the real her?" The mother said, "Yes, that is who she was. I don't know if I ever really touched that core, but it was beautiful when she let it show." I knew we were at the place we needed to be. Several years later, I was visiting a center that worked with autistic children and ran into the mother of the child leaning against the tree in the photo. We stepped into a quiet place where she told me that, after our sessions were over, she had gone back to school to learn to work with these autistic children. She said, "I don't think I ever really touch their core, but it is beautiful when I come close." We both had tears in our eyes for a moment. For the two years we spent in weekly sessions, she and I had been the whole community that mourned her child. Now she had found a community where the pain and the bond with her dead daughter could be expressed, though I doubt that many people at that center understood what her work meant to this bereaved mother.

I find it very difficult to look too long at some of the photographs. Children who die have often gone through hard times. Photographs of children who died of cancer include a few from trips they took between treatments. A group shot of teenagers, most with the bald heads caused by chemotherapy, happily mugging for the camera on a Florida beach, or one of a boy who looks very emaciated, standing next to his favorite player on the Cardinals baseball team, leave me with strong and sometimes very mixed feelings. It is hard, too, when children have died deaths from causes society disapproves of. When we know the end of the story, it is hard to watch as the photographs of the grinning boy in the scout uniform give way to the smirking young punk or when the skinny preadolescent girl roughhousing with her dog begins posing in heavy make up and holding her now adolescent body seductively.

I have asked parents to help me get to know their children. By spending a session or two looking at photographs of the child, I am trying to know the child in a way that I might know children of acquaintances. Sometimes, along with the photographs, a parent will bring items that conclude the child's life story: an autopsy report, a program from the funeral, the newspaper article of a child's last confrontation with police, a portrait of the body in the casket. I try to open myself to both the child and the parent whose child has died. Once I have bonded both the child, I become a member of the community in which the parent can begin to move toward resolution.

One of the first decisions we make as professionals is whether our task is to care for the community or to become part of the community that cares for the parent. I find that, when I help the community to function well, surprises pop out, because people's creativity can flourish within it. I worry about where the next group facilitator will come from, or about how the group will handle a difficult person who has started to attend. But, it turns out, I usually worry for no reason. Healthy groups find solutions. Other times I understand that the therapeutic alliance is part of the community. In therapeutic alliance, when I give my full attention to the parent before me and to a child who has died, I can enter the parent's spiritual life in a way that allows me, with a little luck or a touch of grace, to help.

"What should I do to begin the process of enlightenment," asked the young Buddhist monk in our example earlier. "Have you had your breakfast?" asked the master. "Yes," said the young monk. "Then," said the master, "wash your bowl." Both helping the community and joining the community are tasks that come naturally within our practice. Both deserve the best skills we have to offer. But they are different tasks calling for different skills. If we know which task we are doing, we will do it better.

☐ Professionals' Worldviews

The death of a child presents the same threat to professionals' assumptions about how the world works and about our place and power in the universe that it does to parents whose children die. The difference is that professionals can avoid the questions. Parents cannot. Yet, even when professionals avoid them, the questions remain lurking in the background, and, like other unconscious or semi-conscious threats to our psychic equilibrium, they influence our thoughts and actions. To work closely with parents whose children have died, we will be more effective if we are very aware of how we ourselves make sense in a world where children die. Our discussion of professionals' worldviews will take us in two directions. First, we will look at how professionals respond to and understand bereaved parents' pain. Second, we will look at one cultural narrative that American parents and professionals are likely to bring to the deaths of children. In asking about the adequacy of that narrative, we can explore the professional relationship to the cultural meaning systems available to parents as they seek to make sense of their children's deaths, and to make sense of their own and their children's lives.

Pain for Professionals

The Reality of Pain

The defining feature of parental grief is pain. Parents describe it in graphic terms. It is like a piece of them has been ripped out. It is as if their arm or leg has been amputated. Each part of the web of their spiritual life holds its own kind of pain for bereaved parents: guilt for real or imagined sins of commission and omission, emptiness in the face of the Why questions, rage at the cause or causer of the death, estrangement from the world that does not share their loss. As I look back over what I have written in this book, it seems to me that what is missing is an adequate description of the pain. But parents describe it as indescribable, and they are right. I do not know that I can comprehend, much less, communicate the excruciating, mind-numbing pain that parents feel when a child dies. After bereaved mother Ann Finkbeiner reviewed the professional literature in preparation for her book of interviews with parents, she concluded, "Grief researchers have a mild obsession with how people recover" (1996, p. xi). She seems to be saying that the professional literature focuses away from the pain, or defines the issues in a way that implies that the pain is not permanent. Bereaved parents have told us that the pain does not go away, that they never get over it. If we are to become part of the healing community, therefore, we must share the pain as best we can. It might help if we spend a few moments thinking about our relationship to pain as we try to help bereaved parents.

Pain in the Modern World

Pain has lost much of its meaning in the modern world. When we use the phrase, "bite the bullet," we are recalling a time when people were given a lead bullet to hold between their teeth while their arm or leg was being amputated without anesthesia. Hospice physicians now claim that they can medically manage the physical pain of dying, so that the patient can focus on interpersonal relationships and on finding a final meaning of life and death. We are creating today, says Lyn H. Lofland (1978, pp. 74ff.), a "Happy Death Movement." Death is not a bad thing, members of the movement say, because it happens to old people. With the physical pain managed, death itself—both the moment of death and that which follows—may be blissful, serene, and pleasurable, perhaps even "orgastic." In the happy death movement, she says, all that those dying or those grieving need do is express emotions. Grief is understood to be is a universal human emotion or set of emotions generally accompanying any loss the person finds significant. Grief after a death, say members of the movement, is like the grief after a divorce. Loss is loss. Grief, says the happy death movement, has an internally generated "normal course" (called the grief process) that, for the health of the survivor, must be "worked through" (p. 79). So, we find a kind of plumbing model of grief in the culture. Grief is an emotion that is only harmful if it backs up into the psyche. The bereaved person only needs to get it out, to let it flow. Professional help is often aimed at facilitating the expression of emotion because, professionals believe that expression of emotion moves the person through successive states that ends in acceptance.

The contemporary view has reduced anger and guilt to primarily psychological dilemmas. Even works published by churches or written for pastoral counselors see the question of God's role in the death of a child as only one question among many that can occur to those who have lost a child. In this psychological framework, the questions are manifestations of feelings. The questions are not legitimate in themselves. By making grief the problem and not looking at the real problems grief presents, we do a disservice to the reality of parental bereavement. When we reduce the existential pain of bereaved parents to a predictable psychological process, we are distancing ourselves from the reality parents are experiencing. Saying, "Well, of course you feel bad. You are in grief," is like saying, "You are sick because you have a disease." Grieving people feel bad because something bad has happened. If we are to help them, we need to come to terms with what has happened.

In Wendy Simonds and Barbara Rothman's (1992) study of literature written for and by bereaved mothers in America from colonial times to the present, they say the contemporary way of conceptualizing the grieving process marginalizes and trivializes the experience of grieving people. In a great deal of current writing, they say, it is as if the emotions could be sorted out, and as if time guarantees a safe and easy passage from one stage to another (p. 163). "Rather than focusing on essential religious truths and experiences, current writers report on scientific or pseudoscientific research about grief, legitimating and validating the grief itself" (p. 158). The pain parents feel at the deaths of their children is reduced to stages or a series of temporary feelings. "Anger, and to a lesser extent, guilt, are dealt with not in substantive ways but only as transient feeling states—to be experienced and then surpassed" (p. 161). They say:

> Reality-based questions about grief (Could I indeed be responsible? Might I have done things differently?) are transposed to psychologically based questions (Should I be feeling this way? Are my feelings normal?) (pp. 174–175).

They note that, in the nineteenth century, anger and blame were treated as a crisis of faith, so it was an intellectual as well as a psychological problem, because, "theologies, after all, are an intellectual exercise within the boundaries of belief" (p. 166).

The pain is real and parents tell us that it never goes away. The anger and guilt, and all the other emotions are real because something real has happened. The death of a child is an irreparable loss. Parents well along in their grief tell us that the pain may change over time. Parents may habituate to the pain much as an amputee may habituate to a wheelchair, but that does not take it away. Parents may learn to hide their pain from people who pull back from them because of the pain. As years pass, the pain may transmute to a more tender sense of the world's fragility or to deep pessimism. Yet, whatever turns the pain may make, it remains part of the bereaved parent's world because something beautiful is gone and will never come back. If there is a positive emotional resolution in parental grief, it is in the sense of solace. Solace, as we noted in Chapter Five, does not replace pain, but rather occurs in the midst of pain. Solace is the paradoxical feeling of pleasure within devastation.

So if, as professionals, we want to help bereaved parents, we must find ways of accepting parents' pain and not be overwhelmed by it. As in other areas of our professional lives, we find ways both to protect ourselves and to give ourselves. Effective professionals have already spent time, often under supervision, examining the kinds of strategies they use to give their selves with clients and yet to maintain selves apart from them. Especially in the counseling practice, I find that I often understand as much about parents' pain by observing the ways I defend myself against it, as I do from listening to parents describe it. The irreparable loss of a child's death presents special challenges to professionals. My sons were in grade school when I began meeting with bereaved parents. I found that I needed to draw a circle around my house so that when I was home, I did not think about what I was learning. Home could be my safe place. In my clinical practice, I had to learn the trick of giving my full attention to one client for 50 minutes, showing that client out, answering messages for five minutes, and then meeting the next client in the waiting room. So, I learned to draw lines in my psyche between the pain of parental bereavement and my own parenting and to draw lines between my intense experiences inside the counseling office. I also learned that I needed areas of my professional life that did not directly include thinking about the deaths of children. Shortly after I started intensive work with bereaved parents, I also started teaching business ethics in my university's management program. I would make a joke that both corporate economic power and death inescapably impinge on our lives, but that was the only connection I could find. It was good to have a teaching area separate from parental grief.

Each of us has our tolerance level for the pain of parental grief. One of our tasks as professionals is to balance our practices and to manage our inner lives so that we can be in touch with the pain but not overwhelmed by it. We do not need to absorb the pain of all the world's dead children. Quaker mystic Thomas Kelly once said that we do not have to be crucified on every cross. Some of the parents who come to us need only a little advice or validation. Some need only a hand over some rough spot in their life; they do not need us to walk all the way down their road with them. As professionals, we can learn to know when we are holding the pain at a distance and when we are letting it in. The difference between lay people and professionals in the human services is disciplined self-awareness. Obviously, if we find that we are keeping everyone at a distance, it is time to get out of the business. On the other hand, if we find that we are unable to hold anyone out, we probably need to get some supervision to find what is happening inside us, or what personal needs we are getting met by immersing ourselves in the parents' pain.

One of the good ways to regulate how much we share the parents' pain and bond to their children is to maintain a balance between helping the community and being part of the community as we discussed in the previous section. When our focus is on helping the community, we absorb less pain than when we join the healing community. Probably, we help more bereaved parents when we help the communities of which they are members—families, congregations, neighborhoods, or self-help organizations—than when we take on the task of joining individual parents in their grief. I have found that I cannot choose to stay on one side of the balance only. If I am to be useful in helping the community, I find that I need to bring my experience of sharing the grief. On the other hand, if I am to be useful to individual parents as a professional, I need to keep in touch with my professional models, especially of family functioning, even if I find myself deeply bonded to the dead child.

A question that a parent asked me at a business meeting following the candlelight memorial service helped me reflect on how I balance joining the community and helping the community, and how I manage the pain I feel from the parents around me. I attend the candlelight service alone and use it as a time to get in touch with the baseline reality of the Bereaved Parents process. At the end of the service as their children's names are read, parents, often accompanied by their families, rise and light a candle. I am very aware, at that part of the service, that I am not a member, only an advisor. I wait until the end, and then rise and light a candle. At the meeting, one of the leaders of the infants and toddlers group looked across the table and said, "Dr. Klass, I was sitting behind you, and I was wondering. Who did you light a candle for?" Maybe we professionals who claim to be helping bereaved parents should ask ourselves that question once a week.

I answered what had been true that year, "I lit it for all your children." As I stood holding my candle that year, I felt an incredible solidarity with the group, although I am not a member. The group had found its way to some creative solutions to problems that year. I had seen the leaders work hard to make every meeting the best possible experience for both old members and newcomers. I was proud to have been a part of the process, and, in lighting my candle, I was honoring their children who are the source of the group's energy. Over the next few days, I realized that I had done it differently other years. One year, I lit a candle for a dead little boy whom I had known, but whose parents never came to a meeting. Another year, I lit a candle for the dead child of a therapy client, who probably had no one but his mother and me lighting candles that year. So as the balance shifts I choose different options, both in the way I relate to parents and in the way I relate to the pain of children's deaths.

Bereaved parents find meaning and solace in a world in which they know, at the gut level, the awful truth that children, their children, died. They find a community in which interactions are based in that reality, and they learn to deal with communities in which the reality is not recognized. We have seen in this book, that the parents find meaning and solace using many different theologies and philosophies and experiencing many kinds of solace-bearing phenomena, and that they learn to live in a world that wants them to get over the deaths of their children.

The task of professionals who are not bereaved parents is similar to, but unlike that of bereaved parents. Professionals need not do it while their world has fallen apart. Professionals who want to help bereaved parents must come to terms with the world as bereaved parents find it. That world includes deep pain. When we know the world as bereaved parents know it, we live with a great deal less comfort and less complacency than we did before. Personally, I have found the task to have some benefit. It is, after all, an exercise in mental health. The pain that bereaved parents feel may be the basis for the most sane life anyone can live. Children do die and when we know that down deep, it helps us straighten out our values and priorities in life.

Finding Meaning in Pain

"If we know anything about humans," Lofland says, "we know that they do not confront meaningless situations for very long" (1978, p. 36). In the face of meaninglessness, parents construct for themselves new sets of beliefs, new orientations, new ways of looking and feeling which fill the void. Professionals have to make sense of their world too. I do not propose to tell readers how to do that. Library shelves and museum cases are full of what people before us have left of their constructions of ways to fill the void. But I would propose that professionals have a special problem. The ways in which they make sense of the pain may be different from the ways parents, whom they are trying to help, make sense of the pain. Therefore, professionals have an obligation that others do not have. A professional has the obligation to make sense of his or her world, and to be equipped to help people who are making sense in a way that is different from the way the professional does it.

The task professionals face is to find a way to ground themselves in the face of potential existential absurdity, and then to realize that the truths upon which they base their lives yield only one possibility among a wide range of choices. That task is very difficult because our worldview tells us how the world functions and what our place and power in the world is. That is, a worldview is a faith. Faith means trust. We trust that the world is as we think it is. We bet our lives on it, in the sense that we make the important choices in our lives based on the assumptions within our faith. To do that requires a great deal of certainty. We need to feel as if we are right, or at least that the community that shares our faith is right. It is very hard to maintain certainty in a world where children die, and yet to know that others may find the same sense of certainty in a worldview very different from ours.

Humans have a hard time living with a relative worldview. There are enough wars based on religious differences for us to realize that even the granting of religious equality is not an easy step for humankind. In the developed West, during comfortable political times, it may be easy to grant differences in worldview on the intellectual level. There are lots of religions, we can say, and it would be a good idea if we learned to get along. We might even have friends of different religious traditions with whom we can share our humanity and discuss philosophical questions. Interreligious dialogue today need not threaten our sense of certainty. Bereaved parents' questions of meaning, however, are at a deeper and much more human level than those at an interfaith prayer breakfast. Their pain threatens our sense of certainty. It could happen to us. Unless we can make sense of the pain for ourselves, we cannot stay close for very long or very often. At the same time, we come up against the fact that what seems so right to us may not be right for someone else.

Perhaps we can learn something from the members of Bereaved Parents about finding our own meaning and also helping others find theirs. The task of balancing our own answers to the big questions of life with respect for the answers that others may find is a recurring problem in the Bereaved Parents chapter. Theological or philosophical truths that seem so right are all some parents have to cling to during the first years after their children have died. As they grow in their grief, many parents find answers that give them a sense of peace with their pain. Yet, when they share their worldview too forcefully, they make others uncomfortable, because there are no one-size-fits-all worldviews. What *you* have discovered at the end of a long spiritual quest may be an answer that does not work for *me*. I have seen members of Bereaved Parents gently tell other members that it would be better if they would remember that some might feel and think differently. A woman who had just taken over the task of facilitating a meeting said, "You know, my faith is very strong. But I know that everyone must find answers for themselves, so I have had to learn not to jump in, but to let everyone help each other."

Professionals often do not get as good a level of feedback from their colleagues as we find among the leaders of Bereaved Parents. So professionals must often rely on their own critical self-appraisal. To do a good job, professionals need to be very self-aware of how they are making sense of the pain. They must do so in order to understand how their worldviews interface with other worldviews. That is, they need to know how the way they make sense of the pain is different from how other people might make sense of the pain.

The issue is more than simply respecting other view points. How we make sense of the pain bereaved parents bring to us affects how the parents themselves come to regard their pain. It would be easy if we simply said that professionals could put aside how they see the world and be client-centered enough to respect clients' worldviews. But, in parental bereavement, that is impossible. Parents have been thrown into a new world that often has little connection with the world they once knew. They have been thrust into the social role of bereaved parent, but it is not a role that they know how to play. They are trying to make sense out of their new world. We professionals give cues about what is important to us in both our verbal and nonverbal response to what they say. This is as true for mental health workers as it is for religious workers who operate out of an explicit theology. Indeed, mental health workers may have the harder task in understanding the implicit cues they are giving to clients, because many of them have very strong, but unarticulated, worldviews. Implicit in a great deal of counseling and therapy theory are cultural values that are so pervasive they are seldom explicit enough to question. As professionals, we will point the way for some of the bereaved parents whose lives we touch, whether we want to or not. We owe it to them to point to ways of making sense of the world that are adequate to the profound questions raised by a child's death.

I hope that the reflecting about pain that I have done over the last few pages leads to one conclusion. As Kermit the Frog said, "It ain't easy being green." In my experience it is not easy being a professional working so close to the pain that comes when children die. As professionals who work well with bereaved parents, we are continually finding the balance between between three poles: first, making meaning for ourselves; second, knowing that others may make different meanings; and third, knowing from experience that some meanings work better than others. If we do not find our own grounding, we will be overwhelmed by the absurdity of the pain. If we believe too strongly in our own meanings, we will insist, however subtly, that the parent walk down our road. If we think all meanings are equal, we will be of little help when parents turn to us for help in making sense of their world. I know of no formulas for maintaining the balance, but self-awareness and self-criticism are probably the best friends we have in the task.

☐ Optimism, Pessimism, and the American Civil Religion

Optimism as a Cultural Value

Often the cultural narratives or cultural worldviews that parents bring to the deaths of their children are not held by any particular religious tradition but rather are part of the general cultural worldview. Religious studies scholars use the term "civil religion" to describe myth, symbol, and belief systems that bind people together as a nation but do not have the institutional trappings of religions such as ordained clergy, formal creeds, or authoritative scriptures. Because the group of spiritual guidelines within the American civil religion is now such a strong, but unexamined, set of beliefs among professionals as well as among bereaved parents, it will be helpful to explore this worldview.

The United States has sometimes been called the "nation with the soul of a church" (Mead, 1974). That is so in the sense that a set of values, symbols and myths, that transcends the many religions traditions that make up the American mosaic, organize the national consciousness, set the national social agenda, and encourage behaviors that undergird the economic system. The core values of North American culture are progress, optimism, and individual autonomy. From Emerson's essay on Self-Reliance, to the mind cure movement of the nineteenth century, to modern humanistic psychology, positive thinking rings out as a dominant theme in the American symphony. There are other themes—the blues play too—but still, one of the strong cultural messages is that if I believe that "every day, in every way I'm getting better and better," I will. The deaths of children do not fit easily into this optimistic worldview. During a conversation after a meeting, a woman, who before her child's death had made a living giving positive thinking seminars, told me, "I just can't positive think this away." We have seen that bereaved parents often do not fit well into a world that values success and happy endings.

Scholars in religious studies have largely confined their discussion of civil religion to its political implications. For example, they might show how Martin Luther King, Jr., used Jefferson's rhetoric in the Declaration of Independence to awaken the national conscience into rejecting segregation. Scholars have also pointed out that civil religion has a personal element. For example, in the late nineteenth century, the Protestant work ethic was extended in the Horatio Alger myth which taught that honest, hard-working poor boys could rise to riches and power (see Bellah, 1975, pp. 61–86). As the twentieth century progressed, the earlier drive for financial success became conflated with that for success in personal living. By the latter part of the twentieth century, the civil religion had developed to a worldview centered on personal autonomy and self-esteem and broadly applied to very private personal matters. It could even be used to make sense of a child's death. Sometimes this worldview is called popular psychology (or disparagingly, "psychobabble"). It is a standard message in popular entertainment and publishing. Many bookstores have whole sections devoted to this worldview. Afternoon talk shows feature authorities who tell viewers that this worldview will open the door to happiness and love.

Some bereaved parents are able, after a good deal of searching, to fit their child's death into this optimistic worldview. This worldview can be especially prominent in books by bereaved parents because, as part of making something good of their children's deaths, some parents publish the stories of their child. Kay Talbot (1996–7, 1997–8), a bereaved mother, divides bereaved parents into two groups, survivors and perpetual grievers. In the struggle to come to terms with the deaths of children, she says, there are winners and losers, those who are a success in their grieving and those who fail. In her mind, parents either survive or they grieve perpetually. Her division is not very scientific. She had 80 bereaved mothers complete one life attitude scale and then she identified people with the five highest scores as survivors and the five with the lowest scores as perpetual grievers. She then compared survivors and perpetual grievers, groups of five people, with each other. She did not consider the 70 people in the middle. Still, within her worldview, Talbot's claim is right. "The overriding commonality among mothers I studied who have survived the death of their only child, versus those who remained in a state of perpetual bereavement," she says, "is the survivors' ability to find meaning in life once again" (1997–8, p. 45). She finds no meaning or value in perpetual grief.

Talbot makes a strong statement for contemporary social values applied to bereavement—self-esteem, internal locus of control, taking care of the self, jettisoning relationships that don't help. Her narrative represents one very popular worldview that has grown within late twentieth century individualism. She finds that mothers who are survivors

> made a conscious decision to survive and to reinvest in life. All sought and accepted help from others and learned to use a wide variety of coping skills to deal with their grief and take care of themselves. Nonsupportive family and friends have been replaced with new, understanding others (1996–7, p. 185).

And "all have taken responsibility for their own healing" (1996–7, p. 185). Bereaved parent and grief scholar Catherine M. Sanders also bases her concept of the turning point in grief on similar American values. "Recognizing the alternatives in life, and the freedom to choose, opens amazing possibilities" (1989, p. 99).

Because this worldview is so deeply rooted in the American psyche, and because it is often incorporated into the talk show and psychotherapy culture, we often do not examine the assumptions in it. If every bereaved parent were able to work Talbot's program, professional work with bereaved parents would be considerably easier than it is. But, bereaved parents whom Talbot labels as perpetual grievers also make profound meaning of their children's deaths, and we as professionals can learn to appreciate the meanings they are making, even if we do not find our own spiritual home among them.

A Brief Stroll with William James

As a way of critically reflecting on the spiritual guidelines in the American civil religion, we will devote a few moments to William James, who was, perhaps, the last American person of letters who could move with complete facility between psychology and philosophy. James was one of our primary guides as we searched for an adequate definition of spirituality in Chapter Two. So it is appropriate that he guide us as we examine the implications of our definition. Readers who deserve a reward for being very good, and who have not already done so, might want to give themselves the pleasure of reading *The Varieties of Religious Experience* (1958; first pubished in 1902; see Barzun, 1983), for a warm and humane introduction to James.

At the beginning of the twentieth century, James was responding to the American religious character when, like Talbot, he looked at the extremes, not the average, and divided people into two spiritual types, the healthy minded and the sick souls. His descriptions are remarkably like Talbot's descriptions of the bereaved mothers whom she labels survivors and perpetual grievers. The critical difference between the two types, James said, is the threshold at which evil in the world and pain in the soul determine the individual's assumptions about how the world works and their place and power in the world. "The sanguine and healthy-minded live habitually on the sunny side of their misery-line, the depressed and melancholy live beyond it, in darkness and apprehension" (James, p. 117). The question for James is, does evil count? James himself was of the latter type, so sometimes his description of healthy-mindedness borders on caricature, as when he describes the healthy-minded as "your robust Philistine type of nervous system, forever offering its biceps to be felt" (p. 37). But still, his types are very useful for us as we try to understand how the American civil religion comes to terms with the death of children. What James called the sick soul includes what today we would call depression and certainly James would be willing to include "perpetual grievers" in that category. Healthy-mindedness is, James says:

> a religion in which good, even the good of this world's life, is regarded as the essential thing for a rational being to attend to. This religion directs him to settle his scores with the more evil aspects of the universe by systematically declining to lay them to heart or make much of them, by ignoring them in his reflective calculations, or even, on occasion, by denying outright that they exist. Evil is a disease; and worry over disease is itself an additional form of disease, which only adds to the original complaint (p. 112).

But healthy-mindedness, James says, only maintains itself by insisting, often against the evidence, that evil and death do not have the final innings. The core value of healthy-mindedness is a determined optimism that things will finally work out for the best. Setbacks may discourage us, but we can maintain a positive attitude so they do not devastate us. A positive thinking pastor once quoted scripture to me, "All things work well for those that love the Lord." I did not have the heart to tell him that, at that moment, I might not have been loving the Lord very much.

Sick souls habitually live on the opposite side of the pain threshold. Crossing over to their side of the pain threshold

> will bring the worm at the core of all our usual springs of delight into full view, and turn us into melancholy metaphysicians. The pride of life and glory of the world will shrivel. It is after all but the standing quarrel of hot youth and hoary eld. Old age has the last word; the purely naturalistic look at life, however enthusiastically it may begin, is sure to end in sadness. . . . Let sanguine healthy-mindedness do its best with its strange power of living in the moment and ignoring and forgetting, still the evil background is really there to be thought of, and the skull will grin in at the banquet (p. 121).

The question for James is not in which world it is the easiest to live. Anyone who has sounded the depths of depression whether from genetic predisposition or horrific life experience, however briefly, would agree that healthy-minded optimism is the more comfortable. The question, James says, is which of these ways of being in the world opens us to the fullest interpretation of life's experience. The question, James says, is which can account for the wider spectrum of human living and human consciousness. James finds that the denial of the essential evil and suffering that lies at the core of healthy-mindedness, makes it a religion founded on an illusion. Depression and perpetual mourning may after all, he thinks, open us to more profound aspects of the human experience than healthy-mindedness. The sick soul does not deny some reality as does the healthy-minded, and so the sick soul sees the world as it is, not as we wish it to be.

> There is no doubt that healthy-mindedness is inadequate as a philo-sophical doctrine, because the evil facts which it refused to positively account for are a genuine portion of reality; and they may after all be the best key to life's significance, and possibly the only openers of our eyes to the deepest levels of truth (pp. 137–138).

So, James concludes, "The completest religions would therefore seem to be those in which the pessimistic elements are best developed" (p. 139).

In introducing James's views as a critique of the spiritual guidelines in the contemporary version of the American civil religion, I am not casting my vote for either the healthy-minded or the sick soul. I am one of the majority who find themselves habitually between the ex-tremes. Sometimes I am healthy-minded, and other times I feel like a sick soul. At a national gathering of bereaved parents, a woman told me that the first time she heard me speak she knew I was not a be-reaved parent because, "We don't laugh as deeply as you do." Yet, at times when I watch the political pettiness both in national politics and at my university, I wonder why people do not just realize that they are going to die and stop scrapping over the small stuff. I suspect that most professionals who help bereaved parents are also in the middle majority, healthy-minded enough to think they can make a difference and sick souled enough so that the pain of bereaved parents stabs them deeply. Because we stand in the middle, I am suggesting that professionals who would like to help bereaved parents in their spiri-tual lives can learn a great deal from James' way of thinking about the message of the civil religious worldview that is so much a part of popular culture.

Implications of James' Critique

It seems to me that we can draw three implications from James's thinking that might help professionals who would walk with bereaved parents in their spiritual journey:

1. In the way we use the self in our professional work,
2. As a way of orienting ourselves in the particular worldview the bereaved parent brings to us, and
3. As an impetus to explore religious and philosophical systems in which "the pessimistic elements are best developed."

First, as we use the self for both diagnostics and therapy, we can use our own depressive moments to try to understand the world of bereaved parents. Even after 20 years, I do not think I can really know what it must be like to have a child die. But I have been depressed and have wondered in those times whether the sick souls are right. I have felt the overburdening sadness that perhaps life is a tale told by a fool, that my moments of joy and exaltation are merely brief respites on the way to nothingness, that life is more than I can bear, and that, perhaps, I should take the shortcut out. Those sick-soul parts of my self are not comfortable to me, but they do put me as close to the reality of parental bereavement as I think I can come. As I come into contact with parents whose children have died, I meet my own worst dreams. Only as I allow myself to be in touch with those parts of my self can I really stay in touch with bereaved parents, both to understand their experience and to help them through it.

Second, both healthy-minded spirituality and sick soul spirituality are found in all the world's religious traditions and in the philosophical literature that has grown up within those traditions. We can use James to orient ourselves to the particular worldview a bereaved parent brings to us. If we are to help parents come to terms with the awful reality that their children have died, one of our first tasks is to get into their stream. They have worldviews that they are testing against their new experience, or they have fragments of worldviews from which they will construct satisfactory answers to the questions about how the world functions, about what is their power in the universe, and about what are the meanings of their lives and their children's deaths. We can be of quicker help if we can understand their assumptive world more quickly.

I have found the healthy-minded/sick soul concept to be a useful one for beginning the process of listening to individual bereaved parents because it helps me look a little way down their road early in our relationship. If theirs is a healthy-minded spirituality that seems reasonably full and deeply seated whatever their religious tradition, then I can proceed as if their worldview will hold, albeit in a modified form. My initial assessment might be wrong, and I may need to think again about how their grief is interfacing with the cultural narrative, but even in that reassessment, James' ideas about healthy-minded and sick soul spirituality are helpful. If I find the parent using a sick-soul spirituality, then I can ask what kinds of deliverance are available within their religious tradition. When I am working with couples or families, James is also useful in my assessment. If I see, for example that a father and a mother habitually live on different sides of the "misery-line," I will do better marital counseling. I need more than James' types of religious experience in order to help bereaved parents in their spiritual life, but those types offer a good beginning place, especially as parents are testing to see whether the worldview they had before the child died will serve them in their new world.

Third, we can use James to help both the healthy-minded and the sick soul. I find that some, perhaps even the majority, of bereaved parents can use the healthy-minded spiritual directions in the contemporary American civil religion as Talbot does. The cognitive therapy view that depression is a "thought disorder" not a "mood disorder" (Beck, Rush, Shaw, & Emery, 1979) has been very helpful to me in work with both depression and bereavement. But depression is not grief. The sadness parents feel after the death of a child is not the same as the sadness depressives feel. If we understand healthy-mindedness, then we can join healthy-minded parents in their journey. They are engaged in a form of cognitive therapy because they are consciously willing themselves to think differently about themselves and the world as they find it after the deaths of their children. If they are finding the spirituality of the civil religion useful, we can help them follow its path. We do not have to subscribe to the civil religion's worldview in order to help parents use it, because it is so pervasive in our culture that we understand it, even if we do not wholeheartedly believe it. We can help parents identify their false thinking about themselves and others. We can support their self-esteem and striving for autonomy. We can help them identify and move away from those relationships that are impeding them from living what seems to them to be a more fully actualized life. If we take our own worldview from this aspect of the American civil religion, we can lead the way and even take some joy in the fact the bereaved parents are finding peace in the same beliefs that we do.

If, on the other hand, we find parents who are on a sick-souled path through their grief, we can help them if we ourselves have done some exploration in the ways religions and philosophies have navigated those routes. When we understand why James thinks healthy-mindedness is an inadequate philosophical system, we can explore various religious and philosophical systems in which "the pessimistic elements are best developed." Bereaved parents may not know about the many great minds and spirits before them who have explored and charted the territory into which they have been dropped. The deepest parts of all the world's religions begin here. For Christianity, the death of God's son and the redemptive quality of suffering are core themes. "Blessed are the poor in spirit," said Jesus, "for theirs is the kingdom of heaven" (Matt. 5:3 RSV). The First Noble Truth of Buddhism is that all life is suffering. Learning that truth sets one on the road to enlightenment. In Hinduism, the goddess Druga astride her lion comes to devotees in order to destroy their illusions and thereby set them free.

Philosophers, East and West, have blazed trails that bereaved parents might be following, but we will not be able to help them follow those trail markers if we have not explored them ourselves. Lao Tzu taught the way of nonresistance to both internal and external necessity. The ancient Stoics taught that noble spirits could do their duty with dignity in the face of unbearable reality. The modern existentialists teach that in the face of absurdity we can create our own meaning even as we know that it is meaningless.

All these and other religious and philosophical ideas were pioneered by people who took being-unto-death very seriously. These spiritual trails through the valley of the shadow of death are less traveled. Often they lead through frightening and uncomfortable terrain and end in territories that may be sparsely populated. These are, however, the spiritual paths that take those who follow them through, as James said, the deepest and most profound possibilities of the human experience. Although we ourselves might habitually stay on the sunny side of our misery-line, if we have walked ourselves a little way down the sick souls' paths, we will be more prepared to walk with bereaved parents as they follow them.

The spiritual teachings in the American civil religion will work for a great many bereaved parents, but if professionals do not, like James, examine the assumptions within that tradition, they will be unprepared to offer bereaved parents the help they might. If professionals themselves accept the spiritual teachings of the American civil religion uncritically, they will be unable to help parents who take the more difficult, yet more profound spiritual paths through their grief, because, by denying that evil and suffering are at the essential core of the human experience, they will be unable to help those who find differently. If, on the other hand, professionals have themselves taken one of the less traveled paths (for example, if they find that suffering is redemptive and can only be assimilated if we identify our suffering with God's when His son died), then they will be poor companions for bereaved parents who are finding a healthy-minded resolution for their grief. As professionals we must find our own meaning in a world where children die.

The parents who come to us for help may find meaning in the same worldview as we do, or they use different worldviews. William James provides the set of ideas by which we can begin to understand our own and others' worldviews so that we can understand where we have grounded ourselves and how our ground of being is situated relative to the worldviews others find useful. As with much else in our professional lives, critical self-awareness is the best tool we have.

☐ Conclusion

We began this chapter with the story of a bereaved father in jail and of how his legal team facilitated his beginning to resolve his spiritual difficulties. The lawyer and legal assistant did not change out of their pinstrips and into clerical collars or monk's robes when they offered their spiritual help. They remained a legal team doing the best job they could to present a defense that was adequate to the human drama that the case presented. In asking Billy about his child's death and about his grief, they entered into his life story in a way that gave him words to narrate the story to himself, and so helped him move the narrative forward. In showing him that they cared, they became part of the community in which he could work out his spiritual crisis. Billy's spiritual life was interwoven with his legal defense, just as it was with the psychiatric crisis that brought on his suicide attempt or with the needs of his surviving daughter. If the psychiatrist or the social worker in the child protection agency had practiced their profession well, they might have been as helpful in Billy's spiritual life as was his legal team.

If the lawyer and legal assistant could be helpful, then we can all help. There is no special realm of life called "spiritual" that is divorced from the rest of life. Helping parents in their spiritual journeys is a part of all our practices, whether we recognize it or not. Spiritual helping is within what each professional already does, no matter our profession. I have no special techniques or tasks to be accomplished that I label "spiritual" as opposed to the techniques that I use in the mundane, everyday world. Every relationship I enter has the possibility of becoming an I-Thou that will reveal, to me and to the other, the Eternal Thou. The world of suffering and the world of liberation are the same.

We have seen that the spiritual life of bereaved parents plays out in an interactive web of bonds and meanings. Any change in one part of the web ripples through all the other parts. The skills we professionals bring may be applied in some meanings and bonds better than others, but the effect of our help will reverberate in all the meanings and bonds. Parents bring a history of being more competent to operate within some meanings and bonds than others, but no matter what meanings and bonds parents work in, all the others are affected. So, as professionals we can facilitate parents using their strengths, rather than pulling the parents to some sets of meanings and bonds that are less familiar to them. If parents hit a dead end in one set of meanings and bonds, we can assist by helping the parent shift their attentions to other meanings and bonds.

A theme throughout our description of bereaved parents' spiritual lives is that healing happens in community. The resolution of grief is an interpersonal process. As professionals we can relate to the healing community in two ways. We can help the community develop and maintain interaction patterns that facilitate the healing of bereaved parents who are members of the community. And we can become a member of the community by accepting the burden of the parent's pain and by bonding with the child. Both ways are good; but it is useful to be aware of which task we have chosen. We can apply our skills best when we know for what ends we are using them.

If we are to stay close to parental bereavement, we must somehow come to terms with the pain the death of the child has brought. The pain occurs in every part of human life. Whatever the issues in our professional interaction with bereaved parents, the pain is present. Even if we choose to ignore the pain, it still influences our thoughts, feelings, and behaviors. The pain is more than a temporary psychological feeling. The pain is real because the child really died. As professionals, our task is to find ways of accepting the pain but not being overwhelmed by it. The best way of finding and maintaining the balance of opening ourselves to parents' pain and protecting ourselves from their pain is disciplined self-awareness.

The worldviews of both bereaved parents and professionals are made up of assumptions about how the world works and what place or power we have in the world. The deaths of children challenge parents' assumptions, and challenge our assumptions, although we professionals can, if we want, avoid the challenge. Professionals have a difficulty that parents do not. As professionals who would try to help parents with issues within the parents' worldviews, we need to hold our own worldviews in a more relative way. We are in a difficult situation. We must make sense for ourselves in a world that includes the deaths of children, yet the answers we find may not be the ones that are useful to the parents with whom we interact.

We have looked at the difference between the healthy-minded worldviews adopted by the majority of people in contemporary culture and the sick-souled worldviews that set the paths of a minority. The healthy-minded and the sick soul travel different paths on their spiritual journeys. I have suggested that, as professionals, we will offer more skillful practice if we are familiar with the many paths available for bereaved parents' spiritual journeys, not as philosophical theory or as theological doctrine, but as the lived experience of real human beings. As in so much else in our life as professionals, disciplined self-awareness is the best tool we have in knowing how the routes though the valley of the shadow of death that the parents in our practice are taking are the same as, or different from our own.

The spiritual lives of bereaved parents reaches the depths of human suffering and their resolution points to the furthest possiblities of human living. Such spiritual reality does not admit to reduction to a set of tasks, stages, or symptom relief. Helping the spiritual lives of bereaved parents is just part of everything we do. The best way to help bereaved parents in their spiritual lives is to practice our professions well. If we do that, the help we offer will be useful to them.

Research Method: How Can an Outsider Understand?

Bereaved parents say that no one can really understand having a child die except another bereaved parent. One of the premises on which a Bereaved Parents self-help group functions is that only those who have "been there" know what it means to have a child die. I have never "been there," and I hope I never will. How, then, was I as an outsider to grasp the reality and to put words to it in a way that could communicate with the parents in the group and to other outsiders?

Personally and philosophically, I have often found the questions "What do you know?" and "How do you know what you know?" compelling and problematic. The basic insight that helps me to understand is this: All knowledge is contextual. That is, we can see only from where we look. I have been a professional advisor to a self-help group for 20 years, and I have been a psychologist to whom bereaved parents came for counseling. Those two roles provided the context for my understanding. Mine would be a different context for understanding than a quantitative researcher peering through the knothole of statistical correlations between items on a questionnaire, or the janitor who cleans the room after the meeting. The empiricist and the janitor could also form concepts that might be as valid as mine, but the context would create different concepts (see Wilber, 1995, pp. 144–149).

☐ On Being an Advisor

Two approaches to understanding seemed available to me in the advisor role the group had given me. First, be with them as they try to understand themselves and to rebuild their lives. Second, help them use their self-knowledge to design the activities, rituals, programs, and governance structure for a self-help group. In each of these approaches, I realized I would have to conduct my scholarly work in a way that harmonized with my participation in the group.

The first activity was to be with them as they tried to understand themselves and to rebuild their lives. Just as their world was foreign to me, it was foreign to them too. They were in a world that was new to them. They had difficulty understanding how their world had changed and how they responded to their changed world. Thomas Attig says, "When we are bereaved, we suffer loss of wholeness in three interconnected ways: Loss shatters the patterns of our present lives, disrupts the narrative flow of our autobiographies, and leaves us feeling disconnected from larger wholes of which we have thought ourselves a part." We find our way though grief, he says, when "we reestablish coherence in our present living; we reestablish continuity in the ongoing stories in our lives; and we recover old meanings and find new ones in the larger wholes in which we are, or become, parts" (1996, p. 144).

At one of the early meetings, a woman said that since her child had died it was like moving to a new town. "You can't go back, and even if you did, it wouldn't be the same." So bereaved parents must learn to live in a changed world with a changed self. They must rebuild their lives in a world that is forever poorer. If as an outsider, I do not understand, they as insiders do not understand at first either. In many ways, the resolution of grief is finding their way around their new world and then learning to live fully in it.

Working closely with the self-help group, I could listen to them, and be in conversation with them as they learned to understand themselves, as they rebuilt their lives to include their new reality. I could know many bereaved parents well over a long time as they renegotiated the bond with their children and as they found ways to include their children in their ongoing lives. Occasions for conversation included monthly meetings, business meetings, advisory committee meetings, workshops, and national and regional conventions. The monthly meetings lasted an hour and a half, and after the meetings, people stayed for coffee and cookies for nearly another hour talking in small clusters. During the after-meeting time, new members would find others whose stories were similar to theirs. Members further along in their grief would make contact with a new person who reminded them of themselves. Or people who had formed friendships in the group could check up on each other's progress. People did not mind if I listened in on their conversations and, if it were not too intrusive, I could ask questions. If his wife were still engaged, a man might come to chat with me while he waited. At national and regional meetings, everyone from the chapter went out to dinner together, and we often found each other at the end of a long day to chat over drinks. Over the months and then years, I felt that I knew many members well. I had wondered at their first meeting how they could make it through a day. Then I appreciated how they responded to another person's pain. Later, I marveled at how some became meeting facilitators and ran a meeting with a competence many professionals would envy. I knew their stories, and I could observe over time how the story of their grief integrated into the larger story of their life. I met their surviving kids and relatives, and sometimes we just talked baseball.

I am not a bereaved parent. Group leaders and members have been unwavering in maintaining the distinction. But neither could I be a passive participant. I had to earn my right to stay by contributing to the group. When they asked me to talk and write, it was an opportunity for me, as an outsider, to engage in conversation with the insiders about my understandings of their grief and of the ways they were resolving their grief. It has been an ongoing conversation that has taken many forms. For the first year or so, I was asked to say a few words to sum up the meeting. It was partly, I think, that they did not trust themselves yet, and it helped to have Doctor Klass lend legitimacy to their interactions. After the meetings, some people would let me know if I had gotten it right. I was also asked to write a regular column in the newsletter, which I did for about five years. I called my column "Reflections," partly because it was my occasion to reflect, but more importantly, I wanted to mirror back to the members what I was hearing them say. I tried to just let the reflections write themselves. I would think a few days and then sit down (it was at a typewriter in those days) and see what came out. The reflections were published in our local chapter's newsletter, and some were copied in chapter newsletters around the country. Occasionally, I still see one reprinted in a newsletter. The feedback was invaluable. Group members would talk to me about what I had written. At national and regional meetings, people knew who I was. Some people from other chapters told me that, when they read my reflections, they thought I must be a bereaved parent, and they were surprised to learn I was not. I was on the right track, because the people I was writing about said so. They were, after all, the experts, so when they said I understood, then I did.

And when they said I didn't understand, then I knew I needed to think about it some more.

I was also asked to be a speaker for monthly meetings and to give workshops at national or regional conventions. I tried to use those times to reflect back to the members how I understood what was going on in their lives and in the processes within the group. I tried to engage the bereaved parents in conversations about themselves. The rule I set for myself was that if I could not clearly say what I knew about bereaved parents to bereaved parents, then I really did not understand. As I began writing about bereaved parents in the scholarly literature, many bereaved parents read what I had written and responded. A gratifying measure of the collaboration we have achieved is that, over the years, some of the things I have said or written have been incorporated into the group's self understanding. I feel a sense of satisfaction when I read the literature of the group that I am studying, and find that members of the group use words that I have written about them to describe themselves.

☐ Understanding Bereaved Parents in a Counseling Practice

Eight years after the group was founded, I began a small clinical psychology practice in which many of the clients were bereaved parents. Most of the early referrals came from traditional places: employee assistance programs, hospitals, hospices, physicians, and later from managed care groups. Although some referrals came from meeting facilitators, I urged virtually all the bereaved parents who come to me to try the group. Because I was no longer regularly attending monthly meetings, it was easy to remain professional with the newly bereaved who were clients. If leaders in the group came for counseling, the group was firmly established in their lives, so we had a shared fund of experience and acquaintances we could bring into in our sessions.

The intensive interaction and broad scope of material in the therapy room provided both a wider and a deeper context in which to understand parental bereavement. For example, "Grief and Marriage" and "Father's Grief–Mother's Grief" are regular topics for monthly meetings and members talk honestly about their relationships. What holds the conversation together are the common experiences they share. There is little time to explore the complex family and individual histories each couple has brought to the meeting. Couple or family therapy provides parents with a forum where they can think through their individual stories and the stories of their marriages, and sometimes of their divorces, in depth and detail. Children die in functional and in dysfunctional families. The death of a child changes all family systems. Therapy after a child dies can provide a time to look at previous functioning honestly, and a time to ask how the changes grief brings can be changes toward mutually supportive and health-promoting relationships. The self-help group meetings are largely about the here and now; but therapy is also about history. People in therapy recall their history, reframe their history, and self-consciously plan for the future of their history. Therapy also provides a place in which parents can explore the connections between the death of a child and other parts of life. People with depression or other mental illnesses can have children die. The interactions between their normal symptoms and the symptoms of grief can be complex, as can the changes that the resolution of grief bring to the state of their mental health. A skilled therapist can help the parent see how the parent's usual symptoms are being expressed within the grief, and how the resolution of the grief might provide changes in the parent's worldview that will impact how the parent understands the world.

☐ The Study of Parental Bereavement

The first way I have tried to understand parental bereavement, then, is to listen in the many opportunities provided in the self-help group and in therapy sessions, as parents go through the difficult process of understanding their new world and as they rebuild meaningful lives after the deaths of their children. While listening has been my major activity, I have been more than an active listener. I also have been engaged in many kinds of active dialogue with those whom I study. I have sought to understand parental bereavement, and I have been in many kinds of significant, extended conversations with bereaved parents as they have sought to understand themselves.

The second way I have tried to understand is to participate in their lives. Beyond listening and engaging in dialogue, my roles have also made me a participant in the process. I have been a full participant with the parents as they organize and manage the group that helps them and helps them help other bereaved parents. At first, we did not know how to do that. The process of solving the problems that come with organizing and maintaining a self-help group provides clear insights into the nature of parental bereavement. What kind of programs would be most helpful for meetings? How could the group's housekeeping tasks be accomplished when one of the characteristics of severe grief is the inability to concentrate? What kinds of social activities would express the bond members felt for each other and yet not create a clique from which the newly bereaved would feel excluded? How does the group decide who will move into leadership positions and how (and this is one of the hardest) do we keep a flow of leadership? We discovered early on that the secret of the group was that helping others was one of the best ways for parents to help themselves. But how were we to operationalize that? Sometimes people volunteer, but others need to be asked. When we asked too early, people felt we were asking what they could not yet do. When we asked too late, they felt left out. How do we help people move out of leadership roles when the group needs the help, but the activity no longer serves as healing for the individual's grief? I could be a full participant in those discussions. Indeed, after 10 or 12 years I was an important participant because only three or four of us had been around for that long. We were the repository of the group's memory.

I could participate somewhat less fully with counseling clients as they made changes in the ways that they managed their lives. Yet, over time as clients would plan strategies for change and then evaluate their successes or need for revision, I helped them put their particular coping styles in the service of growth. I needed to be in touch with myself the whole time, both in terms of what I was learning from the counter transference, and how my skills in various therapeutic techniques could be best applied to a specific client in a specific situation.

Knowledge gained in building a self-help organization and in psychotherapy is something like a craftsman's knowledge. At Mesa Verde National Park, we can still see the remains of garden terraces built down a ravine to make the most efficient use of the little rain that falls there. The terraces demonstrate a more intimate knowledge of land and water than does modern farming in the West where wells deep into the aquifer bring up water to be sprayed over chemically-managed fields. Modern irrigation makes beautiful green circles that passengers can see from an airplane window 35,000 feet above the ground, but the pattern cannot be seen when we stand next to the field. As a participant, my relationship to the landscape of parental bereavement is more like that of the ancient farmers of Mesa Verde to their landscape. Like them, in self-help and in therapy, we work on immediate problems with the materials we have on hand. Occasionally, especially when I write, I pull myself back and let myself think that I comprehend the whole pattern, though my viewpoint is never so distant that I cannot see the details, and I never have that detached sense of being above it all.

As I sit in the evening meetings of steering and advisory committees,

Saturday morning business meetings, or the Saturday morning Meeting Effectiveness Workshops, and when I listen, week after week, in the counseling office, my viewpoint is up close. A client lost a job because, after her child died, she no longer had the stomach to play hardball company politics. Acting that way now seemed to her to be dishonoring her child's memory. For a few weeks, our sessions turned to career counseling, because she was still a single mother with two surviving children. She may have seemed weak and helpless to me when she talked about her child's death, but there was no denying her shrewd insights and creative problem-solving as she sought out and won a position managing a program in quality assurance for nursing homes. The view from up close is complex and multifaceted. At that range, people do not fit easily into preconceived data categories.

The holiday Candlelight memorial service is a big event. "It has as many details as the wedding I planned for my living daughter," said one chairperson. The advisory committee chooses the speaker who should be a bereaved parent whose grief is largely resolved. This is a way for the group to honor people for their contributions. The committee discussions regarding this service are polite, but frank, and provide a very personalized consensus on the nature of resolution. Discussion at a business meeting about what songs could be sung provides a close view of what music gives voice to the parents' feelings. Then, three weeks before Christmas, I attend the service in the sanctuary of a Jewish synagogue with 900 parents and family, many of whose deceased children I know. I stand holding a burning candle while a children's choir sings "Rainbow Connection," and the spiritual bond that parents maintain with their children is hard to miss. The bond I feel with the group and with individual members of the group is also very clear to me at that moment. When we were having problems finding a chair for Candlelight, as we sometimes do, I suggested that we not have a big service, but that each of the meetings have a small one. My idea was rejected out of hand. It was a good way to learn what is important to group members. As we experimented with how to be the kind of group we wanted to be, the group did not always get it right the first time. It took three major reorganizations before we found a governance structure that worked. But as in most of life, it is the mistakes that taught us, because we asked ourselves what we had done wrong. We understood the processes of parental bereavement better as we learned how those processes could be harnessed in the service of a healing group.

In each of these approaches, I functioned as a professional working with a self-help group or a clinical psychologist in practice. Being the advisor of a self-help group and being a clinician, gives me access to data which is as reliable and valid as any empirical social scientist would find, but my role also put severe constraints on the kinds of research I could do. Had I brought in a battery of surveys or psychological instruments to either the group or to the practice, I would have irrevocably damaged my usefulness. I would be the researcher and they would be the subjects. The distance between us would make further work impossible. Were I to claim to have a way to understand them that was somehow construed to be superior to the way they were understanding themselves, I would have undermined the self-help nature of the group and violated the basic principles of counseling.

One of the early tasks the group assigned to me was to act as a gatekeeper for other professionals and researchers who wanted access to the group. After a psychotherapist came to a meeting and passed out her cards, many members were very angry. They did not want to keep professionals out of the meetings, because they thought one of the group's functions should be to educate professionals. Yet, they would not have the group used as a place for professionals to market their services. I was asked to write the ground rules for professionals attending meetings. Researchers, from psychiatrists with medical school tenure to psychology graduate students, asked for the group members to be data sources. Some wanted a whole meeting for members to fill out their questionnaires, and one wanted to draw blood to learn about the physiology of grief. Group leaders wanted scholars to learn more about bereaved parents, but the purpose of the group was to help other parents. The research requests were a distraction they did not need. So, research requests were routinely sent to me, and I would report to the researcher how "the committee" had decided to help or not help them. The basis on which I decided was simply this: Would the interaction between the group and this research project help the group move forward in its self-understanding and in its development? When David Balk (1981, 1990, 1991) reported his work on bereaved siblings back to the group, the leaders were able to find better ways of integrating members' surviving children into the group's process. But most of the researchers saw the group as an easy way to get data on bereaved parents, and made no provision in their research to ask how the group functioned, or to ask how these members were different from those who did not participate in a self-help group. Those requests were politely refused. Over the years, a number of requests have come from bereaved parents whose experience had led them back to school for graduate work in the helping professions. The research was part of the healing, and in many ways part of the self-help process. Those requests were approved.

There were research tools I could use. I could make notes after meetings, though I was too tired at eleven o'clock or midnight, when I got home, to do the notes immediately. My remembered accounts of the meeting, however, never captured the complexity of a room full of people sharing their stories and the intense interactions between them. I found that I could slow the process down for myself by asking individual parents or couples to sit with me and tape record an interview. I also interviewed some bereaved parents who were not members of the group, and a few people who learned of my project asked if I would interview them. The interviews were extremely helpful at the many times when I was confused. Within the first few months after the chapter was founded, a newsletter was published. It has continued bimonthly, and occasionally monthly. In it, the members write for each other and for themselves. They write poetry, advice, thoughts. I did not need to design instruments which would help them describe their inner life to me; they were in a process of self-reflection and exploration, and they wanted to share what they found. As I sit down to write, I consistently find that the newsletters are the best source of materials. Our chapter was one of more than 600 chapters around the country, many of which published newsletters. I was on several of those mailing lists and material passed easily between newsletters around the country.

After I had begun to formulate some theoretical understandings of parental bereavement and of the group's processes, my notes began to be more useful, because I could separate them into categories or topics which could be managed in computer files. From the beginning, I kept full notes on the therapy clients. Before I left the counseling office for the night, I would write from a paragraph to a page or more on each of the day's sessions. Near the end of their therapy, several parents, some at my request, have written up their own account of their healing and shared a copy with me. I reviewed the files on many of the clients after our work was done and wrote full case studies which are part of the computer files. In a few cases, clients returned years later to work on other matters, and I was able to revise the case study, because I could see the long-term effect of what had happened when I knew them so well earlier. As I was writing this book, I found myself thinking about some clients whose cases I had not written up, so I went back to the files and did so.

At the same time I was working at understanding bereaved parents, other scholars, using both qualitative and quantitative methods, were doing good work with bereaved populations that included bereaved parents. Over the years, I have been in extended conversations with many of them in the Association for Death Education and Counseling, in the International Work Group in Death, Dying, and Bereavement, and by mail (and later by e-mail). As I learned about how others were thinking and what they were finding, I could bring those things into my deep involvement with the bereaved parents. As I have integrated other scholars' work into my own, I have included it in talks and workshops and in case conferences. A few bereaved parents came to me as counseling clients after they had read an article or, in a few cases, a book I had written, and found the ideas useful enough to want to base their counseling on them. Thus, a great deal of the current scholarship on bereavement, especially on parental bereavement, has been integrated into and processed through the feedback loop of my dialogue with group members, clients, and colleagues.

☐ The Ethnographic Tradition

The ways I have chosen to understand parental bereavement are, of course, not original. My method of research has a well-developed scholarly lineage. What separates academics-at-their-best from others is self-awareness or self-reflection in the knowing process. In scholarly jargon, thinking about the way we know is called "methodology," because we are thinking about the research methods we use or about the methods by which we are applying conceptual frameworks. I found that, when I could use the methodological literature, I could function more effectively and could see better what and how I was understanding.

In the social sciences, my observing, listening, and engaging in dialogue with group members and with clients is called participant observation, or ethnography (Powdermaker, 1966; Whyte, 1973; Wax, 1971; Geertz, 1973; Hammersley and Atkinson, 1983; Hammersley; 1992). In the process, the researcher asks a question or formulates an idea about what is going on, and then refines the question or idea based on feedback in the interactions with those being studied. This process goes on until the question and the feedback reach a balance in the researcher's understanding, and it is hoped, in the interactions between researcher and subjects. Geertz (1973, pp. 2–3) calls it *thick* description. Just as we can reread a good poem for continually deeper meanings, when we look again and again at the same interaction, it reveals deeper and deeper levels of reality. The criteria by which such research is judged

> is not so much truth or truthfulness, but justness, appropriateness; not whether my thought corresponds to the world of *objects,* not whether I am being *subjectively* truthful, but whether I am *intersubjectively* in tune, appropriately meshed with the cultural worldspace that allows subjects and objects to arise in the first place. . . . In other words, the criterion

for validity . . . is not just the *truth* of my statement, nor the *truthfulness* with which I put it, but whether you and I can come to *mutual understanding* with each other (Wilber, 1995, p. 138, original emphasis).

Glaser and Strauss (1967) call the results of this interaction "grounded theory." As group members were expressing the pain of their grief and rebuilding their lives, they did so by telling, understanding, and reconstructing their life stories with a group of people whose stories are like theirs. "My story" became "our story." In the counseling office, clients reviewed their life stories to see how the deaths of their children could be integrated into them or how the stories would have to change to include these new realities. In sharing their stories, the parents construct meaning—the meaning of their children's lives, the meaning of their children's deaths, and the meaning of the children's lives and deaths in the parents' present worlds (Anderson, 1991; Epston & White, 1990; Brunner, 1990). As the group members began to develop a fund of answers to their practical questions like how to celebrate holidays and began to use their experience to help those newer in their grief, they were creating what Brunner (1990, pp. 33–65) calls "folk psychology," which is, he says, more holistic than academic psychology, but just as valid. I have listened and participated in the processes that have helped bereaved parents find meaning and construct new biographies of themselves and of their children. In this book, I have tried to share what I have learned in that process. The criterion on which this part of the task can be judged remains intersubjective. That is, it depends on whether nonbereaved parents who are reading the book are brought into the mutual understanding that the bereaved parents and I have been able to develop with each other.

As I worked to help bereaved parents use their own experience to design the activities, rituals, programs, and governance structure for a group to help themselves and other bereaved parents, we were in a sense doing what is called action research (Lewin , 1952; Corey ,1953; Elliot, 1991; Altrichter, Posch, & Somekh, 1993). Action research was developed to help professionals improve their practice. Good action research is self-conscious. We were just bereaved parents and a professor feeling our way along. The parents were in too much pain to muster the kind of self-awareness throughout the process that true action research involves. But, in retrospect, we can see that we engaged in all the components of the recursive cycle of action research: action—reflection—planning—action.

In psychotherapy, as in ethnography, the knowing process is always interpersonal—except in the treatment of severe psychosis—and the validity of what is known is intersubjective. Carl Jung once said that in psychoanalysis, the correct interpretation of a dream is one on which the patient and the analyst agree. Robert Neimeyer (1995) sums up ideas similar to Jung's in more contemporary psychotherapeutic theory. Therapy, he says is science, albeit, a personal science. In the therapeutic relationship, the client is a scientist, formulating, testing, revising, and elaborating personal hypotheses that will serve as the constructs that guide behavior and emotions after therapy. The client comes to therapy because the constructs that had been guiding the client's life do not seem to be working, possibly because they were developed in dysfunctional relations early in the client's life, possibly because the current relationships are dysfunctional so healthy patterns do not work, and possibly because traumatic life changes, such as the death of a child, have thrown previous constructs, or worldviews as we have called them, into question. The function of therapy, therefore is narrative reconstruction. The therapist attempts to help the client get free from a problematic life story or find better ways to resist demands the story makes on the client's life. The special alliance between therapist and client facilitate the scientific process, because the key dynamic in the alliance is the dialectical interplay between the therapist's and the client's experiences, self-observation, and critical self-reflection.

In both the ethnographic study of a self-help group of bereaved parents and in psychotherapy with bereaved parents, the question is not factual objectivity that can be reduced to a few statistics in quantitative descriptions that are designed to be used in prediction and control. In work with bereaved parents, the objectivity of the child's death is irreducible and undeniable. Rather, the question is the interpretation of all of life in the light of that very objective fact. The question is meaning: the meaning of the parent's life, the meaning of the child's life, the meaning of the child's death, the meaning of the communities to which the parent belongs, and the meaning of the world in which the parent finds himself or herself. In scholarly jargon, the process of interpretation is called "hermeneutics," after the Greek god Hermes, the messenger. Bereaved parents and those who would help them are in a hermeneutic process. Bereaved parents and those who would help them try to interpret life and the meanings of life in the same way the literary scholar tries to find the meaning in the text. A text is worthy of our attention when it interfaces with our life in a way that the text reveals something of our life to us and our life helps us to understand the text better. The story of a child's death and the parent's life after the child's death is a worthy text. We cannot understand, however, if we stand outside the text. As an advisor and as a clinician, I am never outside the hermeneutic circle. Who I am when I am with parents and who they are when they are with me are important aspects of the text we are trying to interpret.

The central question in hermeneutics, says M. J. Mahoney (1995), is the validity and objectivity of the interpretation. The vast majority of scholarly thought on hermeneutics relies on the idea that truth is in the interaction between the reader and the text, that the text has a context. That is, the text, like our life has a history. It was written under circumstances which may or may not be the same as the circumstances under which it is read. Bereaved parents developed the meaning with which they lived their lives in a different context than the one in which they now find themselves. For most contemporary thinkers, the reader is in the text, languaging it into the reader's world. Literary hermeneutics, ethnography, and narrative psychology work with stories and meanings that are personally interpreted. Literary hermeneutics, ethnography, and narrative psychology involve active, generative, and reflective processes, the validity of which is worked out in community, the community in the therapy office, the community of the self-help group, and, one hopes, in the communities in which the parents were members before their children died. The truth or validity of the interpretation, as Jung said so long ago, is that on which people who care agree.

When we study the spiritual lives of bereaved parents, we are part of some very long hermeneutic traditions that provide us with a large community in which to test the validity of our interpretation. In Paul Gilbert's (1992) work on the evolution of human instincts that we discussed in Chapter Two, we saw a good, indeed a spiritual, test of the rightness of the interpretation. An interpretation is good when the community formed around it facilitates the human instincts of cooperation, care, nurturing, and love, and facilitates controls on the primitive instincts within the individualistic competition for dominance. One of the mistakes we can make when we believe that truth of the interpretation in the interaction between the reader and the text is the conclusion that any interpretation is fine, that if it feels good, then we should believe it. Such simple-minded relativism ignores a teaching common to the world's religious traditions. Even though our examination of the world's religious traditions shows an amazing diversity, we also saw that the best parts of all the world's religious traditions favor cooperation and caregiving over the lower instincts of competition and dominance. It seems to me that the world's spiritual traditions have given us a "still more excellent way" (I Cor. 12:31) to judge the truth or validity of what we know.

We noted in Chapter Two that Gilbert found cooperation and caregiving to be instincts that developed later in human evolution and, in that sense, he found them to be the better parts of human nature.

> To learn that one is an agent of value and has something to contribute which is valued by others can be enormously beneficial in overcoming deep senses of alienation, hatred and envy. It may be that our genes are selfish; . . . and it may also be that the wish to leave some contribution after our death, to leave the world a better place than we found it is a defense against death anxiety. . . . Be this as it may, the fact is that humans are deeply committed to contribute to the welfare of others and to the development of human social culture. And it seems to me there is generally a great preference to do this co-operatively rather than individually. (Gilbert, 1992, p. 208)

In the study of the spiritual lives of parents whose children have died, a good test of whether what we know is true is to ask whether the way we understand helps develop communities based on the cooperation and caregiving that are at the core of parenting and at the core of the healthy resolution of parental grief.

Scholarly theories and models of human interactions have no more truth value than the meanings and bonds by which parents find resolution in their grief. Both the meanings the parents find and the theories we scholars build are attempts to make sense of a world that includes the deaths of children. If we scholars build our models and theories so we can predict and control, we have to ask: In whose service do we predict and toward whose ends do we seek to control? If, on the other hand, we put our scholarship in the service of the cooperative and caregiving part of human nature that is so evident in parenting-at-its-best, if the criterion of the truthfulness of our statements is mutual understanding between researchers and those they study, then our scholarly theories and models can be used within the communities where individuals and families can find healing. The parents' question in the face of their children's deaths, as we noted in our discussion of worldviews, is whether their God is useful. The same question should be the one we ask about the way we study parental grief and about the sense we, as outsiders, make of it. Are our models and theories useful—useful in enabling the community that includes bereaved parents' pain and includes the dead children, and are they useful to people who are not bereaved parents, including professionals, who would like to help? We can only see from where we look. If we stand among those trying to create a healthy community, then what we see is probably true.

REFERENCES

Alcoholics Anonymous. (1976). *The Big Book* (3rd ed.). New York: Alcoholics Anonymous World Service.

Altrichter, H., Posch, P., & Somekh, B. (1993). *Teachers investigate their work: An introduction to the methods of action research.* New York: Routledge.

Anderson, T. (1991). *The reflecting team: Dialogues and dialogues about the dialogues.* New York: Norton.

Anisfeld, E., & Lipper, E. (1983). Early contact, social support, and mother-infant bonding. *Pediatrics, 72*(1), 79–83.

Armstrong, K. (1993). *A history of God: The 4000-year quest of Judiasm, Christianity and Islam.* New York: Knopf.

Attig, T. (1996). *How we grieve: Relearning the world.* New York: Oxford University Press.

Averill, J. R. (1968). Grief: Its nature and significance. *Psychological Bulletin, 70,* 721–748.

Balk, D. E. (1981). Adolescents' grief reactions and self-concept perceptions following sibling death: A study of 33 teenagers. *Journal of Youth and Adolescence, 12,* 137–161.

Balk, D. E. (1990). The self-concepts of bereaved adolescents: Sibling death and its aftermath. *Journal of Adolescent Research, 5,* 112–132.

Balk, D. E. (1991). Sibling death, adolescent bereavement, and religion. *Death Studies, 15,* 1–20.

Barnard, G. W. (1997). *Exploring unseen worlds: William James and the philosophy of mysticism.* Albany: State University of New York Press.

Barzun, J. (1983). *A stroll with William James.* New York: Harper & Row.

Batson, C. D., Schoenrade, P., & Ventis, W. L. (1993). *Religion and the individual: A social–psychological perspective.* New York: Oxford.

Beck, A. T., Rush, J. A., Shaw, B. F., & Emery G. (1979). *Cognitive therapy of depression.* New York: Guilford.

Bellah, R. N. (1975). *The broken Covenant: American civil religion in time of trial.* New York: Seabury Press.

Bellah, R. N., Madsen, R., Sullivan, A. S., & Tipton, S. M. (1985). *Habits of the heart; Individualism and commitment in American life.* Berkeley: University of California Press.

Benedek, T. (1959). Parenthood as a developmental phase. *American Psychoanalytic Association Journal, 7,* 389–417.

Benedek, T. (1975). Discussion of parenthood as a developmental phase. *Journal of the American Psychoanalytic Association. 23,* 154–165.

Bloch-Smith, E. M. (1992). The cult of the dead in Judah: Interpreting the material remains. *Journal of Biblical Literature, 111*(2), 213–224.

219

Brunner, J. (1990). *Acts of meaning*. Cambridge, MA: Harvard University Press.

Buber, M. (1970). *I and thou*. (W. Kaufmann, Trans.). New York: Charles Scribner's Sons.

Chidester, D. (1990). *Patterns of transcendence: Religion, death, and dying*. Belmont, CA: Wadsworth.

Corey, S. M. (1953). *Action research to improve school practice*. New York: Columbia Teachers College.

Dawson, L. (1989). Otto and Freud on the uncanny and beyond. *Journal of the American Academy of Religion, 58*(2), 283–311.

Doi, T. (1973) *The anatomy of dependence*. (J. Bester, Trans.). Tokyo: Kodansha International.

Durkheim, E. (1915). *The elementary forms of the religious life*. (J. W. Swain, Trans.). New York: Free Press.

Durkheim, E. (1951). *Suicide: A study in Sociology*. (J. A. Spaulding and G. Simpson, Trans.). New York: Free Press.

Elliot, J. (1991). *Action research for educational change*. Philadelphia: Open University Press.

Elson, M. (1984). Parenthood and the transformations of narcissism. In R. S. Cohen, B. J. Cohler, & S. H. Weissman (Eds.), *Parenthood: A psychodynamic perspective* (pp. 297–314). New York: Guilford.

Epston, D., & White, M. (1990). *Narrative means to therapeutic ends*. New York: W.W. Norton.

Erikson, E. (1963). *Childhood and society* (2nd ed.). New York: W.W. Norton.

Finkbeiner, A. K. (1996). *After the death of a child: Living with loss through the years*. New York: Free Press.

Finucane, R. C. (1996). *Ghosts: Appearances of the dead and cultural transformation*. Amherst, NY: Prometheus Books.

Fowler, J. W. (1981). *Stages of faith*. San Franscisco: Harper and Row.

Freud, S. (1961). *Civilization and its discontents*. (J. J. Strachey, Trans.). New York: W.W. Norton.

Geary, P. J. (1994). *Living with the dead in the middle ages*. Ithaca, NY: Cornell University Press.

Geertz, C. (1973). *The interpretation of cultures*. New York: Basic Books.

Gilbert, P. (1992). *Human nature and suffering*. New York: Guilford.

Gilday, E. T. (1993). Dancing with the spirit(s): Another view of the other world in Japan. *History of Religions, 32*(3), 273–300.

Glaser, B. G., & Strauss, A. L. (1967). *The discovery of grounded theory: Strategies for qualitative research*. Chicago: Aldine.

Goodenough, E. R. (1986). *The psychology of religious experience*. New York: University Press of America.

Habermas, J. (1971). *Knowledge and human interests*. Boston: Beacon.

Hammersley, M. (1992). *What's wrong with ethnography? Methodological explorations*. London: Routledge.

Hammersley, M., & Atkinson, P. (1983). *Ethnography: Principles in practice*. New York: Tavistock Publications.

Harper, R. (1991). *On presence: Variations and reflections*. Philadelphia: Trinity Press International.

Hillman, J. (1986). *On paranoia*. Dallas, TX: Spring Publications.

Hood, R. (1977). Eliciting mystical states of consciousness in semistructured nature experiences. *Journal for the Scientific Study of Religion, 16*(2), 155–163.

Horowitz, M., Wilner, N., Marmor, C., & Krupnick, J. (1980). Pathological grief and the activation of latent self-images. *American Journal of Psychiatry, 137*(10), 1157–1162.

Horton, P. C. (1981). *Solace, the missing dimension in psychiatry*. Chicago: University of Chicago Press.

Jacobson, D. (1980). Golden handprints and red-painted feet: Hindu childbirth rituals in central India. In N. A. Falk & R. M. Gross (Eds.), *Unspoken worlds: Women's religious lives in non-western cultures* (pp. 73–93). San Francisco: Harper & Row.

Jacoby, S. (1983). *Wild justice, the evolution of revenge*. New York: Harper & Row.

James, W. (1958). *The varieties of religious experience: A study in human nature*. New York: Mentor.

Janoff-Bulman, R. (1985). The aftermath of victimization: Rebuilding shattered assumptions. In C. R. Figley (Ed.). *Trauma and its wake* (pp. 15–35). New York: Brunner/Mazel.

Janoff-Bulman, R. (1989). Assumptive worlds and the stress of traumatic events: Applications of the schema construct. *Social Cognition, 7*(2), 113–136.

Jones, E. (1957). *The life and work of Sigmund Freud*. New York: Basic Books.

Kallenberg, K. (1995). Suffering and death: Eternal questions in a new context. In J. Kauffman (Ed.), *Awareness of Mortality* (pp. 51–61). Amityville, NY: Baywood.

Kauffman, J. (1994). Dissociative functions in the normal mourning process. *Omega, Journal of Death and Dying, 28*(1), 31–38.

Kellehear, A. (1996). *Experiences near death: Beyond medicine and religion*. New York: Oxford University Press.

Klass, D. (1987). John Bowlby's model of grief and the problem of identification. *Omega, Journal of Death and Dying, 18*(1), 13–32.

Klass, D. (1988). *Parental grief: Resolution and solace*. New York: Springer.

Klass, D. (1996). Ancestor worship in Japan: Dependence and the resolution of grief. *Omega, Journal of Death and Dying, 33*(4), 279–302.

Klass, D., & Heath, A. O. (1996–97). Mizuko kuyo: The Japanese ritual resolution. *Omega, Journal of Death and Dying, 34* (1), 1–14.

Klass, D., Silverman, P. R., & Nickman, S. L. (1996). *Continuing bonds: New understandings of grief*. Washington, DC: Taylor & Francis.

Kübler-Ross, E. (1969). *On death and dying*. New York: Macmillan.

Kushner, H. (1981). *When bad things happen to good people*. New York: Schocken Books.

LaFleur, W. R. (1988). *Buddhism: A cultural perspective*. Englewood Cliffs, NJ: Prentice Hall.

Lewin, K. (1952). Group decision and social change. In G. E. Swanson, T. M. Newcomb, & F. E. Hartley, (Eds.), *Readings in Social Psychology* (pp. 459–473). New York: Holt, Reinhart, and Winston.

Lifton, R. J. (1974). On death and the continuity of life: A "new" paradigm. *History of Childhood Quarterly, 1*(4), 681–696.

Lofland, L. H. (1978). *The craft of dying: The modern face of death*. Beverly Hills, CA: Sage Publications.

Luckmann, T. (1967). *Invisible religion: The problem of religion in modern society*. London: Macmillan.

Mahoney, M. J. (1995). Continuing evolution of the cognitive sciences and psychotherapies, In R. A. Neimeyer & M. J. Mahoney (Eds.), *Constructivism in psychotherapy* (pp. 39–67). Washington, DC: American Psychological Association.

Mannheim, K. (1936). *Ideology and utopia: An introduction to the sociology of knowledge*. (L. Wirth & E. Shils, Trans.). New York: Harcourt, Brace & World.

Maslow, A. H. (1964). *Religions, values, and peak-experiences*. Columbus: Ohio State University Press.

Marty, M. E., & Appleby, R. S. (Eds.). (1991–1993). *The fundamentalism project: A study conducted by the American Academy of Arts and Sciences*. Chicago: University of Chicago Press.

McDannell, C., & Lang, B. (1990). *Heaven: A history.* New York: Vintage Books.

Mead, S. E. (1974). The 'nation with the soul of a church.' In R. E. Richey & D. G. Jones (Eds.). *American Civil Religion* (pp. 45–75). New York: Harper and Row.

Moller, D. W. (1996). *Confronting death: Values, institutions, and human mortality.* New York: Oxford University Press.

Morgan, K. W. (1990). *Reaching for the moon: On Asian religious paths.* Chambersburg, PA: Anima.

Niebuhr, H. R. (1962). *The meaning of revelation.* New York: Macmillan.

Neimeyer, R. A. (1995). Constructivist psychotherapies: Features, foundations, and future directions. In R. A. Neimeyer & M. J. Mahoney (Eds.), *Constructivism in psychotherapy* (pp. 11–38). Washington, DC: American Psychological Association.

Neimeyer, R. A. (1998). *Lessons of loss: A guide to coping.* New York: McGraw-Hill.

Neimeyer, R. A., and Stewart, A. E. (1996). Trauma, healing, and the narrative emplotment of loss. *Families in Society* (June), 360–375.

Neusner, J., Frerichs, E., & Flesher, P. V. M. (1989). *Religion, science, and magic: In concert and in conflict.* New York: Oxford University Press.

Nietzsche, F. (1967). *On the genealogy of morals.* (W. Kaufmann and R. J. Hollingdale, Trans.). New York: Vintage.

Offner, Clark B. (1979). Continuing concern for the departed. *Japanese Religions, 11*(1), 1–16.

Orbach, C. E. (1959). The multiple meanings of the loss of a child. *American Journal of Psychotherapy, 13,* 906–915.

Otto, R. (1923). *The idea of the holy.* (J. W. Harvey, Trans.). New York: Oxford University Press.

Pagels, E. (1995). *The origin of Satan.* New York: Random House.

Pals, D. L. (1996). *Seven theories of religion.* New York: Oxford University Press.

Passman, R. H. (1976). Arousal reducing properties of attachment objects: Testing the functional limits of the security blanket relative to the mother. *Developmental Psychology, 12,* 468–469.

Passman, R. H., & Weisberg, P. (1975). Mothers and blankets as agents for promoting play and exploration by young children in a novel environment: The effects of social and nonsocial attachment objects. *Developmental Psychology, 11,* 170–177.

Piaget, J. (1965). *The moral judgment of the child.* (M. Gabain, Trans.). New York: Free Press.

Plath, D. W. (1964). Where the family of god is the family: the role of the dead in Japanese households. *American Anthropologist, 66*(2), 300–317.

Pollock, G. H. (1975). On mourning, immortality, and utopia. *Journal of the American Psychoanaltyic Association, 23*(2), 334–362.

Powdermaker, H. (1966). *Stranger and friend: The way of an anthropologist.* New York: Norton.

Prest, L. A., & Keller, J. E. (1993). Spirituality and family therapy: Spiritual beliefs, myths, and metaphors. *Journal of Marital and Family Therapy, 19,* 137–148.

Reps, P. (Ed.). (1961). *Zen flesh, Zen bones: A collection of Zen and pre-Zen writings.* Garden City, NY: Doubleday.

Riches, G., & Dawson, P. (1996). Communities of feeling: The culture of bereaved parents. *Mortality, 1*(2), 143–161.

Rizzuto, A. M. (1982). The father and the child's representation of God: A developmental approach. In S. H. Cath, A. R. Gurwitt, & J. M. Ross (Eds.), *Father and child: Developmental and clinical perspectives* (pp. 357–607). Boston: Little, Brown, and Company.

Roberts, K. A. (1992). A sociological overview: Mental health implications of religio-cultural megatrends in the United States. In K. I. Pargament, K. I. Maton & R. E. Hess (Eds.), *Religion and prevention in mental health: Research, vision, and action* (pp. 37–56). New York: Haworth.

Rynearson, E. K. (1987). Psychotherapy of pathologic grief: Revisions and limitations. *Psychiatric Clinics of North America, 10*(3), 487–499.

Sachs, O. (1995). *An anthropologist on Mars: Seven paradoxical tales.* New York: Alfred A. Knopf.

St. Anselm (1962). *Basic Writings* (2nd ed.). (C. N. Deane, Trans.) Lasalle, IL: Open Court.

Sanders, C. M. (1989). *Grief: The mourning after.* New York: John Wiley & Sons.

Shibayama, Z. (1974). *Zen comments on the Mumonkan.* (S. Kudo, Trans.). New York: New American Library.

Shore, B. (1996). *Culture in mind: Cognition, culture, and the problem of meaning.* New York: Oxford University Press.

Simonds, W., & Rothman, B. K. (1992). *Centuries of Solace: Expressions of Maternal Grief in Popular Literature.* Philadelphia: Temple University Press.

Smart, N. (1996). *Worldviews: Crosscultural exploration of human beliefs* (2nd ed.). Englewood Cliffs, NJ: Prentice Hall.

Smith, R. J. (1974). *Ancestor worship in contemporary Japan.* Stanford, CA: Stanford University Press.

Stroebe, M., Gergen, M. M., Gergen, K. J., & Stroebe, W. (1992). Broken hearts or broken bonds: Love and death in historical perspective. *American Psychologist, 47*(10), 1205–1212.

Sullivan, L. E. (1987). Death, afterlife, and the soul. *Selections from the encyclopedia of religion,* M. Eliade, (Ed. in Chief). New York: Macmillan.

Suzuki, D. T. (1963). *Outlines of Mahayna Buddhism.* New York: Schocken Books.

Tahka, V. (1984). Dealing with object loss. *Scandinavian Psychoanalytic Review, 7,* 13–33.

Talbot, K. (1996–7). Mothers now childless: Survival after the death of an only child. *Omega, Journal of Death and Dying, 34*(3), 177–189.

Talbot, K. (1997–8). Mothers now childless: Structures of the life-world. *Omega, Journal of Death and Dying, 36*(1), 45–62.

Thoreau, H. D. (1951). *Cape Cod.* Arranged with Notes by D. C. Lunt. New Haven, CT: College & University Press.

Thoreau, H. D. (1960). *Walden or, Life in the Woods.* New York: New American Library.

Tillich, P. (1951, 1957, 1963). *Systematic theology,* Vol. I–III. New York: Harper and Row.

Tillich, P. (1952). *The courage to be.* New Haven: Yale University Press.

Turner, V. (1969). *The ritual process. Structure and anti-structure.* Ithaca, NY: Cornell University Press.

The Upanishads. (1965). (Juan Mascaro, Trans.). Baltimore: Penguin.

Volkan, V. (1981). *Linking objects and linking phenomena: A study of the forms, symptoms, metapsychology, and therapy of complicated mourning.* New York: International Universities Press.

Walter, T. (1994). *The revival of death.* London: Routledge.

Walter, T. (1996). A new model of grief: Bereavement and biography. *Mortality, 1*(1), 7–25.

Warren, B. (1995). The idea of "the glorious dead": The conversion of a uniquely personal experience. In J. Kauffman (Ed.), *Awareness of mortality* (pp. 39–50). Amityville, NY: Baywood.

Wax, R. (1971). *Doing fieldwork: Warnings and advice.* Chicago: University of Chicago Press.

Weber, M. (1958). *The Protestant ethic and the spirit of capitalism.* (T. Parsons, Trans.). New York: Scribner.

Webster New International Dictionary of the English Language. (1913). Springfield, MA: Merriam-Webster.

White, M., & Epston, D. (1990). *Narrative means to therapeutic ends.* New York: Norton.

Whyte, W. F. (1973). *Street corner society: The structure of an Italian slum.* Chicago: University of Chicago Press.

Wilber, K. (1980). *The atman project.* Wheaton, IL: Theosophical Publishing House.

Wilber, K. (1981). *Up from eden.* Boulder: Shambhala.

Wilber, K. (1995). *Sex, ecology, spirituality: The spirit of evolution.* Boston: Shambhala.

Winnicott, D. W. (1953). Transitional objects and transitional phenomena. *International Journal of Psychoanalysis. 34,* 89–97.

Winnicott, D. W. (1971). *Playing and reality.* New York: Basic Books.

Wyatt, T. *Demands.* Unpublished manuscript.

Yamasaki, T. (1988). *Shingon: Japanese esoteric Buddhism.* (Richard & Cynthia Peterson, Trans. and adapters, Y. Morimoto & D. Kidd, Eds. Boston: Shambhala.

Zaleski, C. (1987). *Otherworld journeys: Accounts of near-death experiences in medieval and modern times.* New York: Oxford University Press.

INDEX

advisor, approaches to Bereaved Parents, 206–208
Alger, Horatio, 194
al-Ghazzali, 22
altruism, parenting as, 36
ambivalence, parent/child bond, 75–76
American civil religion, 194. *See also* James, William
angels, 37–38. *See also* Bodhisattvas
solace and, 100
anger, 66
anxiety attacks, 154–155
Association for Death Education and Counseling, 213
Attig, Thomas, 206
autonomy, child, 18
Averill, J. R., 52–53

Balk, David, 212
bereaved parent
change in worldview of, 141–143
continuing bond with dead child, 5–6, 8, 77
divided spiritual world, 156–159
lessons learned from, 163–165
permanent condition of, 8
Bereaved Parents of the USA, xiv
author as advisor to, 206–208
author's association with, 6–8
as a community, 27, 60
dynamics of grief resolution, 87–88
memories's sharing at, 111–112
parents of murdered children and, 70
parents' own death and, 49
professionals's research and, 212
psychoanalytic theory of spirituality and, 33

social bonds within, 53
bereavement, study of parental, 209–214
Bhakti Hinduism, *Dar'san*, 22
birthday, 48
Bodhisattvas, 37, 124. *See also* angels
bond
ambivalence in parent-child, 64–67
with the child and parent's healing, 75–76
with child and transcendent reality, 34, 43, 176
dead child and bereaved parent continuing, 5–6, 8, 50–52
with the deceased and spirituality, 39–42
expression of continuing, 79–80
grief resolution and continuing, 82–83
newly-bereaved parent's anticipation of continuing, 57–58
parenting as a spiritual, 32–34
parent's psychic and social world and continuing, 52
solace within continuing, 100–118
stabilization of continuing, 77
transformation after child's death, 61, 63, 74
web and meanings of spirituality, 43–44, 174–175
Western culture parental, 37
Brunner, J., 215
Buber, Martin, 18–19, 21, 98
Buddhism. *See also* Mahayana Buddhism
grief and, 50
transcendent reality in, 98–99
bystander, acceptance of powerlessness, 11–12